AMC'S BEST DAY HIKES IN
THE BERKSHIRES

Four-Season Guide to 50 of the Best Trails in Western Massachusetts

Fourth Edition // René Laubach and John S. Burk

Appalachian Mountain Club Books // Boston, Massachusetts

AMC is a 501(c)3 nonprofit, and sales of AMC Books fund our mission to foster the protection, enjoyment, and understanding of the outdoors. If you appreciate our efforts and would like to become a member or make a donation to AMC, visit outdoors.org, call 603-466-2727, or contact us at Appalachian Mountain Club, 10 City Square, Suite 2, Boston, MA 02129-3740.

outdoors.org/resources/books-and-maps

Copyright © 2025 René Laubach and John S. Burk. All rights reserved.

Distributed by National Book Network.

Front cover photograph of a hiker at Bash Bish Falls © Kristen Valenti
Back cover photograph of hikers on South Taconic Trail © TheTurducken, Creative Commons on Flickr
Title page photograph of a view from West Stockbridge Mountain's Charcoal Trail © John S. Burk
Interior photographs by René Laubach and John S. Burk
Maps by Ken Dumas © Appalachian Mountain Club
Interior design by Abigail Coyle
Cover design by Marissa Wandrey

Published by the Appalachian Mountain Club. No part of this publication may be reproduced or transmitted in any form or by any means, electronic or mechanical, including photocopying and recording, or by any information storage or retrieval system, except as may be expressly permitted by the 1976 Copyright Act or in writing from the publisher.

Library of Congress Cataloging-in-Publication Data

Names: Laubach, René, author. | Burk, John S., author.
Title: AMC's best day hikes in the Berkshires : four-season guide to 50 of the best trails in western Massachusetts / René Laubach and John S. Burk.
Description: Fourth edition. | Boston, Massachusetts : Appalachian Mountain Club Books, [2025] | Includes index. | Summary: "Whether you're looking for a rugged Appalachian Trail trek or a quiet stroll through scenes from Colonial history, you can find it in the Berkshires. With an at-a-glance trip planner and handy icons, you can easily pinpoint the ideal hike for you, whether you're looking for a hike that is universally accessible; great for kids; provides opportunity for fishing, swimming, or snowshoeing; and more"-- Provided by publisher.
Identifiers: LCCN 2025018438 | ISBN 9781628421880 (trade paperback)
Subjects: LCSH: Hiking--Massachusetts--Berkshire Hills--Guidebooks. | Walking--Massachusetts--Berkshire Hills--Guidebooks. | Trails--Massachusetts--Berkshire Hills--Guidebooks. | Berkshire Hills (Mass.)--Guidebooks.
Classification: LCC GV199.42.M42 B474 2025 | DDC 796.5109744/1--dc23/eng/20250607
LC record available at https://lccn.loc.gov/2025018438
The paper used in this publication meets the minimum requirements of the American National Standard for Information Sciences-Permanence of Paper for Printed Library Materials, ANSI Z39.48-1984. ∞

Outdoor recreation activities by their very nature are potentially hazardous. This book is not a substitute for good personal judgment and training in outdoor skills. Due to changes in conditions, use of the information in this book is at the sole risk of the user. The authors and the Appalachian Mountain Club assume no liability for accidents happening to, or injuries sustained by, readers who engage in the activities described in this book.

Interior pages and cover are printed on responsibly harvested paper stock certified by The Forest Stewardship Council®, an independent auditor of responsible forestry practices.
Printed in the United States of America, using vegetable-based inks.

5 4 3 2 1   25 26 27 28 29

Title page photo: Charcoal Trail leads to two lookouts with views to Monument Mountain's Peeskawo Peak and West Stockbridge.

MIX
Paper | Supporting responsible forestry
FSC® C005010

DEDICATION

*This book is dedicated to my late, good friend
Don Reid, who loved the outdoors.
—René Laubach*

*And to Esin Atil, who appreciated scenic places.
—John S. Burk*

LOCATOR MAP

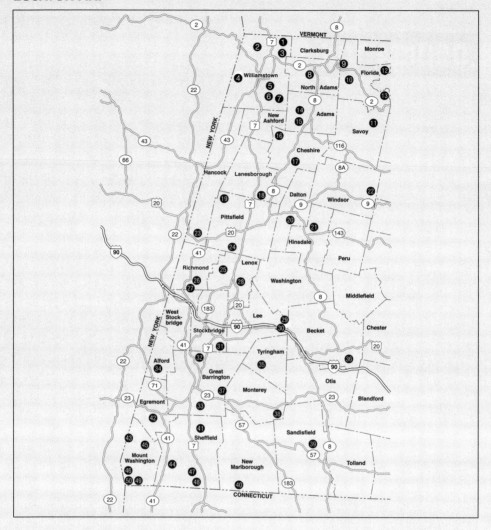

KEY TO ICONS

 Brook crossing

Exposed ledges (trail crosses an exposed ledge—a consideration in severe weather or in wet or icy conditions; hikes that end at a scenic ledge but do not cross an exposed ledge en route are not marked with this icon)

Steep

Good for kids

 Dog-friendly

 Accessible

Waterfall

Pond, stream, spring, or other water feature

Shelter or hut

 Scenic view

Designated tentsite

Swimming

Picnic area

Visitor center

Fee

Fishing

Fire or observation tower (although some are more stable than others, all towers should be considered climb-at-your-own-risk)

 Horse

CONTENTS

At-a-Glance Trip Planner	viii
Acknowledgments	xiv
Introduction	xv
How to Use This Book	xvii
Trip Planning and Safety	xix
Leave No Trace	xxii

1 // NORTHERN BERKSHIRES — 1

1.	Mountain Meadow Preserve	3
2.	Hopkins Memorial Forest and Taconic Crest Trail	8
3.	Pine Cobble and East Mountain	13
4.	Berlin Mountain	19
5.	Greylock Range Traverse	24
6.	Hopper Trail to Mount Greylock Summit	32
7.	Stony Ledge via Haley Farm Trail	39
8.	Mount Greylock and Ragged Mountain via Bellows Pipe Trail	43
9.	Hoosac Range Trail to Spruce Hill	49
10.	Spruce Hill via Busby Trail	54
11.	Tannery Falls and Parker Brook Falls	61
12.	Dunbar Brook	67
13.	Mohican–Mohawk Recreational Trail: Clark and Todd Mountains	73
14.	Saddle Ball Mountain	78
15.	Mount Greylock State Reservation: East Side	84
16.	Mount Greylock State Reservation: Jones Nose and Rounds Rock	90
17.	Cheshire Cobbles and Gore Pond	95

2 // CENTRAL BERKSHIRES — 101

18.	Ashuwillticook Rail Trail: Lanesborough to Cheshire	102
19.	Pittsfield State Forest: Lulu Cascade, Berry Pond, Tilden Swamp	107
20.	Warner Hill	112
21.	Old Mill Trail	118

v

22.	Windsor State Forest and Notchview	122
23.	Shaker Mountain	127
24.	Mahanna Cobble	132
25.	Pleasant Valley Wildlife Sanctuary: Lenox Mountain and Beaver Pond Loops	138
26.	Lenox Mountain: Burbank Trail	145
27.	West Stockbridge Mountain: Charcoal Trail	149
28.	Schermerhorn Gorge Trail	154
29.	October Mountain State Forest: Finerty Pond	159
30.	Upper Goose Pond	166

3 // SOUTHERN BERKSHIRES — 171

31.	Ice Glen and Laura's Tower	172
32.	Monument Mountain Reservation	177
33.	Riverfront Trail and Housatonic River Walk	183
34.	Alford Springs	188
35.	Tyringham Cobble Reservation	194
36.	Becket Quarry	199
37.	Benedict Pond and the Ledges	205
38.	Bob's Way	210
39.	Clam River Reserve	214
40.	Campbell Falls	219
41.	East Mountain and Ice Gulch	223
42.	Jug End State Reservation and Wildlife Management Area	227
43.	Bash Bish Falls	232
44.	Race Brook Falls and Mount Race	238
45.	Guilder Pond and Mount Everett	244
46.	Alander Mountain Trail	249
47.	Lime Kiln Farm Wildlife Sanctuary	254
48.	Bartholomew's Cobble Reservation	259
49.	Sages Ravine and Bear Mountain	264
50.	Round Mountain, Mount Frissell, and Brace Mountain	270

ESSAYS

Cat o' Tall Tales	18
An Immense and Amazing Grandeur: Mount Greylock's History	30
Old-Growth Champions	38
Pinecone Johnnies	48
Pathway to History: The Mohican–Mohawk Recreational Trail	59
A Bear in the Woods	94
Trail Tribulations	117
Taking the High Road	136
Bringing Back the Beaver	144
Alien Invaders	153
Ash under Siege	164
Written in Stone	182
Pool Party	204
Feeding the Fires of Industry	253

APPENDIX: INFORMATION AND RESOURCES — 275

Index	279
About the Authors	285
About AMC in Western Massachusetts	286
AMC Book Updates	287

AT-A-GLANCE TRIP PLANNER

Trip number	Trip name	Location	Difficulty	Distance	Elevation gain
SECTION 1 // NORTHERN BERKSHIRES					
1	Mountain Meadow Preserve	Williamstown, MA; Pownal, VT	Moderate	4 mi	690 ft
2	Hopkins Memorial Forest and Taconic Crest Trail	Williamstown, MA; Petersburg, NY; Pownal, VT	Strenuous	10.4 mi	1,650 ft
3	Pine Cobble and East Mountain	Williamstown and Clarksburg, MA	Moderate	4.8 mi	1,340 ft
4	Berlin Mountain	Williamstown, MA; Berlin, NY	Strenuous	4.7 mi	1,545 ft
5	Greylock Range Traverse	Williamstown, Adams, and North Adams, MA	Strenuous	12.1 mi	2,390 ft
6	Hopper Trail to Mount Greylock Summit	Williamstown and Adams, MA	Strenuous	9 mi	2,390 ft
7	Stony Ledge via Haley Farm Trail	Williamstown, MA	Moderate–Strenuous	5.1 mi	1,460 ft
8	Mount Greylock and Ragged Mountain via Bellows Pipe Trail	North Adams and Adams, MA	Strenuous	8.6 mi	2,140 ft
9	Hoosac Range Trail to Spruce Hill	North Adams, MA	Moderate	5.4 mi	540 ft
10	Spruce Hill via Busby Trail	Florida and North Adams, MA	Moderate	2.6 mi	670 ft
11	Tannery Falls and Parker Brook Falls	Savoy, MA	Easy–Moderate	0.6 mi (round trip) or 4.5 mi (loop)	200 ft (round trip) or 615 ft (loop)
12	Dunbar Brook	Florida and Monroe, MA	Moderate–Strenuous	6.8 mi	1,010 ft
13	Mohican–Mohawk Recreational Trail: Clark and Todd Mountains	Florida, Savoy, and Charlemont, MA	Moderate–Strenuous	8.2 mi	2,120 ft
14	Saddle Ball Mountain	Adams, Cheshire, New Ashford, and Williamstown, MA	Strenuous	9.6 mi	1,675 ft
15	Mount Greylock State Reservation: East Side	Adams, MA	Moderate–Strenuous	6.7 mi	1,930 ft

Estimated time	Trip highlights	Trip features
2.5 hrs	Wildflower meadow and panoramic views	
5.5 hrs	Research forest, Taconic ridgeline trail, Snow Hole	
3 hrs	Stunning views	
2.5–3.5 hrs	Highest Taconic peak, partial views from summit	
6.5–8 hrs	Four summits, outstanding vistas	
5–6 hrs	Boreal forest and Greylock summit	
2.5–3 hrs	Outstanding perspective of Greylock Range	
5 hrs	Magnificent view of Greylock's east face	
2.5–3.5 hrs	Stunning vistas at Sunset Rock and Spruce Hill	
1.5–2 hrs	Fabulous views, migrating hawks in fall	
30 minutes (round trip); 2.5 hrs (loop)	Ravine with twin waterfalls, cascading brook, fall foliage, wildflowers	
4 hrs	Old-growth trees and roaring brook	
5.25–6.25 hrs	Historical American Indian path on original Mohawk Trail, vista	
6–7 hrs	Flower-filled meadow with wonderful views, boggy wetlands	
4–4.5 hrs	State's highest summit, waterfall at shelter	

AT-A-GLANCE TRIP PLANNER   ix

Trip number	Trip name	Location	Difficulty	Distance	Elevation gain
16	Mount Greylock State Reservation: Jones Nose and Rounds Rock	Cheshire and New Ashford, MA	Easy–Moderate	2.9 mi	235 ft
17	Cheshire Cobbles and Gore Pond	Cheshire and Dalton, MA	Moderate	7.6 mi	1,250 ft

SECTION 2 // CENTRAL BERKSHIRES

Trip number	Trip name	Location	Difficulty	Distance	Elevation gain
18	Ashuwillticook Rail Trail: Lanesborough to Cheshire	Lanesborough and Cheshire, MA	Easy–Moderate	7.4 mi	20 ft
19	Pittsfield State Forest: Lulu Cascade, Berry Pond, Tilden Swamp	Pittsfield, Lanesborough, and Hancock MA	Moderate	5.8 mi	1,000 ft
20	Warner Hill	Dalton and Hinsdale, MA	Moderate	6.3 mi	430 ft
21	Old Mill Trail	Hinsdale and Dalton, MA	Easy	3 mi	155 ft
22	Windsor State Forest and Notchview	Windsor, MA	Moderate-Strenuous	4.7 mi	1,000 ft
23	Shaker Mountain	Hancock, MA	Moderate	5.7 mi	790 ft
24	Mahanna Cobble	Pittsfield and Lenox, MA	Moderate	3 mi	790 ft
25	Pleasant Valley Wildlife Sanctuary: Lenox Mountain and Beaver Pond Loops	Lenox, MA	Strenuous (Lenox Mountain); Easy (Beaver Pond)	3 mi (Lenox Mountain); 1.8 mi (Beaver Pond)	825 ft (Lenox Mountain); 115 ft (Beaver Pond)
26	Lenox Mountain: Burbank Trail	Richmond and Lenox, MA	Easy–Moderate	3.2 mi	540 ft
27	West Stockbridge Mountain: Charcoal Trail	Stockbridge, West Stockbridge, and Richmond, MA	Moderate	1.6 mi	530 ft
28	Schermerhorn Gorge Trail	Lenox, Lee, and Washington, MA	Moderate–Strenuous	3.7 mi	620 ft
29	October Mountain State Forest: Finerty Pond	Becket and Washington, MA	Moderate	6 mi	870 ft
30	Upper Goose Pond	Becket, Lee, and Tyringham, MA	Moderate	3.7 mi	385 ft

SECTION 3 // SOUTHERN BERKSHIRES

Trip number	Trip name	Location	Difficulty	Distance	Elevation gain
31	Ice Glen and Laura's Tower	Stockbridge, MA	Moderate	3.7 mi	610 ft
32	Monument Mountain Reservation	Great Barrington, MA	Moderate	2.7 mi	765 ft

Estimated time	Trip highlights	Trip features
1.5–2 hrs	Great vistas, prolific blueberries in season, wildflower meadow	
4 hrs	Fantastic vista point, scenic pond	
3 hrs	Wildlife-rich wetlands, mountain views, historic railroad	
3–3.5 hrs	Waterfall, high-elevation pond, vista, cascading brooks	
3–3.5 hrs	Attractive northern hardwoods, evergreen stands, Greylock view	
1.5–2 hrs	Industrial history, universally accessible segment	
3.75 hrs	Brook ravine, expansive hilltop meadows, riverside picnic area	
3–4 hrs	Shaker historical sites	
2 hrs	Views from rocky cobble	
2 hrs (Lenox Mountain); 1.25 hrs (Beaver Pond)	Views from Lenox Mountain, wildlife-rich beaver wetlands	
1.5–2 hrs	Attractive woodland, pleasing lookout	
1–1.5 hrs	Mature woodland, ridgetop vistas, Olivia's Overlook	
2–2.5 hrs	Cascading brook, massive trees, Woods Pond	
3.5 hrs	Serene pond ringed by mountain laurel	
2.5 hrs	Serene and scenic Upper Goose Pond	
2.25 hrs	Magical rocky cleft, ancient evergreens, views from tower	
2 hrs	Picturesque summit of quartzite boulders, Devil's Pulpit	

AT-A-GLANCE TRIP PLANNER

Trip number	Trip name	Location	Difficulty	Distance	Elevation gain
33	Riverfront Trail and Housatonic River Walk	Great Barrington, MA	Easy	2.3 mi	minimal
34	Alford Springs	Alford, MA	Moderate	5.1 mi	940 ft
35	Tyringham Cobble Reservation	Tyringham, MA	Easy–Moderate	2 mi	380 ft
36	Becket Quarry	Becket, MA	Easy–Moderate	3.9 mi	400 ft
37	Benedict Pond and the Ledges	Great Barrington and Monterey, MA	Easy–Moderate	3 mi	240 ft
38	Bob's Way	Monterey and Sandisfield, MA	Easy	2.9 mi	430 ft
39	Clam River Reserve	Sandisfield, MA	Moderate	5.5 mi	860 ft
40	Campbell Falls	New Marlborough, MA; Norfolk, CT; and North Canaan, CT	Easy	1.3 mi	175 ft
41	East Mountain and Ice Gulch	Sheffield and Great Barrington, MA	Moderate–Strenuous	7.2 mi	680 ft
42	Jug End State Reservation and Wildlife Management Area	Egremont, MA	Easy	2.9 mi	365 ft
43	Bash Bish Falls	Mount Washington, MA; Copake Falls, NY	Easy–Moderate or Moderate	2 mi or 3.8 mi	470 ft or 900 ft
44	Race Brook Falls and Mount Race	Sheffield and Mount Washington, MA	Strenuous	6.2 mi	1,625 ft
45	Guilder Pond and Mount Everett	Mount Washington, MA	Moderate	4 mi	825 ft
46	Alander Mountain Trail	Mount Washington, MA	Moderate	5.8 mi	790 ft
47	Lime Kiln Farm Wildlife Sanctuary	Sheffield, MA	Easy	1.8 mi	135 ft
48	Bartholomew's Cobble Reservation	Sheffield, MA	Moderate	3.5 mi	310 ft
49	Sages Ravine and Bear Mountain	Mount Washington, MA; Salisbury, CT	Strenuous	3.9 mi	915 ft
50	Round Mountain, Mount Frissell, and Brace Mountain	Mount Washington, MA; Salisbury, CT; Millertown, NY	Moderate–Strenuous	4.4 mi	1,425 ft

Estimated time	Trip highlights	Trip features
1.5 hrs	River views, interpretive signs, historical sites, birding	
2.5–3 hrs	Views, quiet ridge trails, great for skiing	
1.5 hrs	Bucolic pastures, lovely views	
1.5–2 hrs	Former granite quarry artifacts, woodland trails, vista	
1.5–2 hrs	Scenic pond and splendid long views	
1.75 hrs	Beaver pond, view from wooded hilltop, wildflowers	
3 hrs	Wild remote river valley, historical sites	
1.25 hrs	Picturesque waterfall, brook, great for families	
4–4.5 hrs	Splendid views, rocky cleft	
1.5 hrs	Meadows, views of mountain ridges	
1.5 or 2.5 hrs	Massachusetts's most spectacular waterfall, views of Taconics	
4 hrs	Wonderful series of waterfalls, fabulous ridgetop views	
2.5–3 hrs	Guilder Pond laurel bloom, picturesque summit with rare pitch pines	
3–4 hrs	Tri-state vistas, scenic ridge	
1.5 hrs	Rolling hay meadows, magnificent vistas	
2–2.5 hrs	Great biodiversity, panoramic view from hilltop meadow	
2.5–3 hrs	Charming chasm, roaring brook, views	
3.5 hrs	Three peaks in three states, great views, Connecticut's state high point	

ACKNOWLEDGMENTS

This book would not have been possible were it not for all the hardworking individuals and groups who protect open spaces and construct and maintain the wonderful system of trails that we are so fortunate to have in the Berkshires.

Many people and organizations provided helpful updates, feedback, and resources for this fourth edition of *AMC's Best Day Hikes in the Berkshires*. Special thanks to Cosmo Catalano, AMC Western Massachusetts Chapter, for ongoing timely updates and information on the Appalachian Trail hikes. Thanks to Dale Abrams, Great Barrington Land Conservancy; Biodrawversity Ecological Consulting and Communications; Shannon Cahill, Pleasant Valley Wildlife Sanctuary; Copake Iron Works National Heritage Area; Anthony D'Amato, University of Vermont; Pat Flinn and Shelby Marshall, Laurel Hill Association; Mariah Fogg and Josh Hopmans, Berkshire Natural Resources Council; Dustin Griffin; Dan Gura, Williamstown Rural Lands; Hancock Shaker Village; Massachusetts Department of Conservation and Recreation state forest and parks staff; Mount Greylock State Reservation Visitor Center; David Orwig, Harvard Forest; James Pelletier, Massachusetts Appalachian Trail Management Committee; Ken Smith, Becket Land Trust; Cathy Talarico, Williamstown Rural Lands; The Trustees of Reservations; Martha Waldman, Taconic Hiking Club; Christine Ward, Housatonic River Walk; and Illyse Wolberg, Massachusetts Department of Conservation and Recreation.

John Burk would like to thank the AMC Books staff, including senior books editor Tim Mudie, map-maker Ken Dumas, copyeditor Lenore Howard, and proofreader Marisa Crumb.

INTRODUCTION

Home to a diverse array of natural features, abundant scenery, and varied flora and fauna, the Berkshire Hills have beckoned hikers, naturalists, tourists, artists, and writers since the nineteenth century. Within this compact but diversified region are iconic attractions such as Mount Greylock—Massachusetts's highest summit and first state park—the cascades of Bash Bish Falls, and the quartzite cliffs of Monument Mountain.

I've enjoyed exploring the region and reading René Laubach's well-written guides for many years, and it was a pleasure to revise this fourth edition of *AMC's Best Day Hikes in the Berkshires*. The new hikes added to this edition include a variety of natural features and trails suited to all abilities. A historically and ecologically significant section of the Mohican–Mohawk Recreational Trail traverses a former American Indian path on Clark and Todd Mountains (Trip 13). In the remote hills of Windsor, a less traveled hiking route in Windsor State Forest and Notchview (Trip 22) leads through a brook ravine and the expansive meadows of a former high-elevation hilltop farm. Mahanna Cobble (Trip 24), a rocky peak at the northern end of Lenox Mountain, offers views across the south-central Berkshires.

Riverfront Trail and Housatonic River Walk (Trip 33) traverse easy, universally accessible paths along the Housatonic River with interpretive signs, historical sites, and connections to downtown Great Barrington. Formerly owned by noted Berkshire conservationist Bob Thieriot, Bob's Way (Trip 38) offers a pleasant loop circuit featuring wooded hills, a beaver pond, and wildflowers. Campbell Falls (Trip 40), one of the Berkshires' most scenic waterfalls, lies within a reserve encompassing contiguous state parks in Massachusetts and Connecticut. New essays detail the long and rich history of Mount Greylock, one of New England's best-known natural landmarks, and the High Road, an exciting new initiative that links hiking trails, conservation areas, and communities.

All hikes from the previous edition have been fully revised and updated with feedback from land managers. The appendix includes listings and contact information for the region's campgrounds, state forests and parks, ski areas, and outfitters.

Whether you're looking for a rugged mountain trek, an easy and family-friendly outing, or a place to sample the area's diverse flora, fauna, and history, you'll find a wide choice of trails to explore. Fifteen of the hikes include portions of the Appalachian Trail, which runs through the heart of the region for 90 miles, linking well-known landmarks and hidden treasures. Other featured long-distance routes include Taconic Crest Trail, South Taconic Trail, the Mohican–Mohawk Recreational Trail, and the aforementioned High Road. Several destinations, including Ashuwillticook Rail Trail,

Old Mill Trail, Pleasant Valley Wildlife Sanctuary, and Riverfront Trail in Great Barrington, offer universally accessible sections suited for people of all abilities.

A wealth of interesting natural features, such as the botanically rich limestone knolls of Bartholomew's Cobble (Trip 48), giant old-growth trees sheltered in Ice Glen (Trip 31) and along Dunbar Brook (Trip 12), rare old pitch pines capping Mount Everett's summit (Trip 45), and colorful wild azalea fields on Berry Mountain (Trip 19), await your discovery. Many artifacts of the region's long and rich history also are here, including well-preserved Becket Quarry (Trip 36) and Copake Iron Works (Trip 43), former farm fields that provide crucial habitat diversity for wildlife, remains of old mill sites along the Housatonic River and other waterways, and former railroad and trolley lines that have been revitalized as recreational paths. And, of course, plenty of scenic views abound, overlooking mountains, rolling hills, and unbroken forests.

In addition to enjoying the attractions, please treat these areas with respect and support the region's many land protection and trail organizations.

—John S. Burk, October 2024

HOW TO USE THIS BOOK

With 50 hikes to choose from, you may wonder how to decide where to go. The locator map at the front of this book will help you narrow down the trips by location, and the at-a-glance trip planner that follows the table of contents will provide more information to guide you toward a decision. Once you settle on a destination and turn to a trip in this guide, you will find a series of icons that indicate whether fees are charged, whether the hike is good for kids, whether dogs are allowed, whether the trail is good for snowshoeing, and much more.

(For hikes with the "good for kids" icon, the authors have used the designation conservatively, basing suggestions on hikes we think are appropriate for children whose families hike together regularly. Some of the hikes designated for kids visit waterfalls or cliff lookouts; these can be great rewards for kids' efforts to get there but can also be hazardous. Ultimately, to determine whether a hike is appropriate for your family, gauge your child's level of interest, motivation, and ability.)

Information on the basics follows: location, rating, distance, elevation gain, estimated time, and maps. The ratings are based on the authors' perception and are estimates of what the average hiker will experience. You may find them to be easier or more difficult than stated. The distance and estimated hiking time shown are for the whole trip, whether it's an out-and-back hike (with distance noted as "round trip") or a loop. The estimated time is also based on the authors' perception. Consider your own pace when planning a trip. The elevation gain is calculated from measurements and information from U.S. Geological Survey (USGS) topographic maps, landowner maps, and Google Earth. Information is included about the relevant USGS maps, as well as where you can find trail maps.

The boldface summary that follows the list of basics provides an overview of what you will see on your hike. The directions explain how to reach the trailhead by car and include Global Positioning System (GPS) coordinates for parking lots. In the trail description, you will find instructions on where to hike, the trails on which to hike, and where to turn. You will also learn about the natural and human history along your route, as well as about flora, fauna, and any landmarks or objects you will encounter. The trail maps that accompany each trip will help guide you along your hike, but it would be wise to take an official trail map with you as well, which will show additional details of side paths and other information for the area. Official maps are often—but not always—available for download or purchase online, at the trailhead, or at the visitor center. Each hike description also lists the best available topographic map of the area. We highly recommend that hikers purchase these maps.

Each trip ends with an interesting fact related to the site's natural or cultural history, a "More Information" section that provides details about access times and fees, the property's rules and regulations, and any other pertinent information about the location. The "Nearby" section offers suggestions for places to continue the experience when the hike is done and where to find the closest restaurants.

TRIP PLANNING AND SAFETY

Planning your trip well is the first step to having a safe hike. Some of the trips in this book ascend to higher elevations or summits where winds and lower temperatures necessitate extra clothing. Other hikes visit clifftops or waterfalls or have rocky stretches where you'll need to use extra caution with children and dogs. Learn about the terrain you will travel through so you can pack the right gear and prepare for the experience. Allow extra time in case you get lost. You will be more likely to have an enjoyable, safe hike if you plan ahead and take proper precautions. Before heading out, consider the following:

- Select a hike that everyone in your group is comfortable taking. Match the hike to the abilities of the least capable person in the group. If anyone is uncomfortable with the weather or is tired, turn around and complete the hike another day.
- Plan to be back at the trailhead before dark. Before beginning your hike, determine a turnaround time. Don't diverge from it, even if you have not reached your intended destination.
- Check the weather and assume it will be cooler and windier on the mountain than at the base. If you are planning a ridge or summit hike, start early so that you will be off the exposed area before the afternoon hours, when thunderstorms most often strike, especially in summer. Weather conditions can change quickly, and any changes are likely to be more severe the higher you are on the mountain.
- Bring a pack with the following items:
  - Water: Two quarts per person is usually adequate, depending on the weather and the length of the trip. On extended day hikes, consider carrying some method of water purification so you can refill your water bottles en route.
  - Food: Even if you are planning just an hour-long hike, bring some high-energy snacks such as nuts, dried fruit, or snack bars. Pack a lunch for longer trips.
  - Map and compass: Be sure you know how to use them. A handheld GPS device may also be helpful but is not always reliable.
  - Headlamp or flashlight, with spare batteries.
  - Extra clothing: Waterproof/breathable rain gear, synthetic fleece or wool jacket, hat, and mittens or gloves.
  - Sunscreen.

- First-aid kit, including adhesive bandages, gauze, nonprescription painkillers, moleskin, and any necessary prescription medication in case you are on the trail longer than expected.
- Pocketknife or multitool.
- Waterproof matches and a lighter.
- Trash bag.
- Toilet paper and double plastic bag to pack it out.
- Whistle.
- Insect repellent.
- Sunglasses.
- Cell phone: Be aware that cell phone service is unreliable in rural areas. If you are receiving a signal, use the phone only for emergencies to avoid disturbing the backcountry experience for other hikers.
- Trekking poles (optional).
- Binoculars (optional).
- Camera (optional).

Wear appropriate footwear and clothing. Wool or synthetic hiking socks will keep your feet dry and help prevent blisters. Comfortable waterproof hiking boots or shoes will provide support and good traction. Avoid wearing cotton clothing, which absorbs sweat and rain and contributes to an unpleasant hiking experience. A synthetic or wool base layer (T-shirt, or underwear tops and bottoms) will wick moisture away from your body and keep you warm in wet or cold conditions. Synthetic zip-off pants that convert to shorts are popular. To help avoid bug bites, you may want to wear synthetic pants and a long-sleeve shirt.

When you are ahead of the rest of your hiking group, wait at all trail junctions until the others catch up. This avoids confusion and keeps people from getting separated or lost.

If you see downed wood that appears to be purposely covering a trail, it probably means the trail is closed due to overuse or hazardous conditions. If a trail is muddy, walk through the mud or on rocks, never on tree roots or plants. Water-resistant boots or shoes will keep your feet comfortable. Staying in the center of the trail will keep it from eroding into a wide hiking highway.

Leave your itinerary and the time you expect to return with someone you trust. If you see a logbook at a trailhead, be sure to sign in when you arrive and sign out when you finish your hike.

After you complete your hike, check for deer ticks, which carry the dangerous bacteria that causes Lyme disease.

Poison ivy is always a threat when hiking. To identify the plant, look for clusters of three leaves that shine in the sun but are dull in the shade. If you do come into contact with poison ivy, wash the affected area with soap as soon as possible.

Wear blaze-orange items in hunting season. Hunting seasons vary. Check with state game commissions: mass.gov/hunting-in-the-parks.

Check on trail or road closures with land managers before heading out in any season, particularly in winter. Certain forest roads may also be closed in the winter months; check with the relevant park agency to get updated information on gaining access to certain trailheads.

Winter hiking can be an enjoyable way to experience the Berkshires, but it requires extra gear and planning. All winter hikers need to bring more food and warm layers than they would in summer, as well as exercising more caution; fewer daylight hours, colder temperatures, and slower travel times magnify any problems that may occur, such as getting lost or twisting an ankle. Frigid temperatures freeze hoses on hydration systems. Consider using insulated water bottles and packing them as close as possible to your body so body heat can help keep the water from freezing during the day. (*Note*: Small-mouthed water bottles tend to freeze faster.) Traction devices—such as Microspikes—can help you navigate icy stretches. Prudent winter travelers do not go out alone, and they make sure at least one person in the group has a sleeping bag and a small camp stove in case of emergency. When properly prepared, hikers can safely and comfortably experience the deep quiet and spectacular beauty of the Berkshires in winter.

When the weather warms up, the bugs start to come out. Mosquitoes can be a nuisance in some places, depending on seasonal and daily conditions. West Nile virus and eastern equine encephalitis (EEE) virus can be transmitted to humans by infected mosquitoes and cause rare but serious diseases. More prevalent, however, are deer ticks, which can transmit Lyme disease. Reduce your risk of being bitten by using insect repellent and wearing long sleeves and pants. Check yourself carefully for ticks when you finish your hike. A variety of options are available for dealing with bugs, ranging from sprays that include the active ingredient DEET, which can potentially cause skin or eye irritation, to more skin-friendly products. Head nets, which often can be purchased more cheaply than a can of repellent, are useful during especially buggy conditions.

LEAVE NO TRACE

TheAppalachian Mountain Club (AMC) is a community partner of Leave No Trace, a nonprofit organization dedicated to promoting and inspiring responsible outdoor recreation through education, research, and partnerships. The Leave No Trace program seeks to develop wildland ethics—ways in which people think and act in the outdoors to minimize their impact on the areas they visit and to protect our natural resources for future enjoyment. Leave No Trace unites four federal land management agencies—U.S. Forest Service, National Park Service, Bureau of Land Management, and U.S. Fish and Wildlife Service—with manufacturers, outdoor retailers, user groups, educators, organizations such as AMC, and individuals.

The Leave No Trace ethic is guided by the following seven principles:

1. **Plan Ahead and Prepare.** Know the terrain and any regulations applicable to the area you're planning to visit, and be prepared for extreme weather or other emergencies. This will enhance your enjoyment and ensure that you've chosen an appropriate destination. Small groups have less impact on resources and on the experiences of other backcountry visitors.

2. **Travel and Camp on Durable Surfaces.** Travel and camp on established trails and campsites, rock, gravel, dry grasses, or snow. Good campsites are found, not made. Camp at least 200 feet from lakes and streams, and focus activities on areas where vegetation is absent. In pristine areas, disperse use to prevent the creation of campsites and trails.

3. **Dispose of Waste Properly.** Pack it in, pack it out. Inspect your camp for trash or food scraps. Deposit solid human waste in cat holes dug 6 to 8 inches deep, at least 200 feet from water, camps, and trails. Pack out toilet paper and hygiene products. To wash yourself or your dishes, carry water 200 feet from streams or lakes and use small amounts of biodegradable soap. Scatter strained dishwater.

4. **Leave What You Find.** Cultural or historical artifacts, as well as natural objects such as plants and rocks, should be left as found.

5. **Minimize Campfire Impacts.** Cook on a stove. Use established fire rings, fire pans, or mound fires. If you build a campfire, keep it small and use dead sticks found on the ground.

6. **Respect Wildlife.** Observe wildlife from a distance. Feeding animals alters their natural behavior. Protect wildlife from your food by storing rations and trash securely.
7. **Be Considerate of Other Visitors.** Be courteous, respect the quality of other visitors' backcountry experience, and let nature's sounds prevail.

For Leave No Trace information and materials, contact the Leave No Trace Center for Outdoor Ethics, P.O. Box 997, Boulder, CO 80306; 800-332-4100 or 303-442-8222; lnt.org.

1 // NORTHERN BERKSHIRES

The northern Berkshires comprise some of the highest and most remote lands in Berkshire County. This region boasts the only true boreal forest in Massachusetts, the only summits above 3,000 feet elevation, craggy outcroppings yielding splendid vistas, and sphagnum-filled bogs. The area contains the longest, most arduous hikes in this guide but also offers moderate outings to scenic vistas, waterfalls, and other attractions.

Mount Greylock State Reservation (Trips 5, 6, 7, 8, 14, 15, and 16), one of the state's iconic recreation destinations, features a sizable section of the Appalachian Trail as well as an extensive network of blue-blazed routes that provide a wealth of options for hikers. The Greylock Range beckons hikers with many fine trails that range in difficulty from easy to strenuous. In addition to Mount Greylock, Massachusetts's loftiest peak, numerous interesting natural and historical features include waterfalls, old forests, Stony Ledge, former farm sites, and the Hopper, a dramatic cirque, or ravine, carved by glaciers. South of Mount Greylock, the Appalachian Trail leads to Cheshire Cobbles and Gore Pond (Trip 17).

Facing page: The highest point in southern New England, Mount Greylock's summit features views of portions of five states and colorful foliage in autumn.

Hopkins Memorial Forest and Taconic Crest Trail (Trip 2) and Berlin Mountain (Trip 4) run along the spine of the Taconic Range, which extends along New England's western border with New York. The northernmost hikes, including Mountain Meadow Preserve (Trip 1) and Pine Cobble and East Mountain (Trip 3), traverse summits and ridges that are an extension of Vermont's Green Mountains. On the Hoosac Range, which rises east of a marble valley in North Adams, Hoosac Range Trail to Spruce Hill (Trip 9) and the Mohican–Mohawk Recreational Trail: Clark and Todd Mountains (Trip 13) follow portions of the long-distance Mohican–Mohawk Trail, an original American Indian route along the Mohawk Trail corridor. Expansive Savoy Mountain State Forest offers a shorter trip to Spruce Hill via Busby Trail (Trip 10) and features a ravine with two of the region's most striking waterfalls: Tannery Falls and Parker Brook Falls (Trip 11). Dunbar Brook (Trip 12), a tributary of Deerfield River, cascades past old-growth woodlands in Monroe State Forest.

1 MOUNTAIN MEADOW PRESERVE

Straddling two states, this string of connected loop trails begins with one of the most evocative panoramic views in the Berkshires. The Greylock and Taconic ranges are stunning backdrops to a meadow that in summer is filled with colorful wildflowers and butterflies. A few short, steep climbs and the ruins of former habitations add interest.

Features
Location Williamstown, MA; Pownal, VT
Rating Moderate
Distance 4 miles round trip
Elevation Gain 690 feet
Estimated Time 2.5 hours
Maps USGS Williamstown; The Trustees of Reservations map: thetrustees.org/wp-content/uploads/2022/02/mountain-meadow-trail-map.pdf
GPS Coordinates 42° 44.314' N, 73° 12.452' W
Contact The Trustees of Reservations, 617-542-7696, thetrustees.org/place/mountain-meadow-preserve

DIRECTIONS
From the intersection of US 7 and MA 2 in Williamstown, proceed north on US 7 for 1.7 miles, crossing the Hoosic River and Broad Brook along the way. Turn right onto gravel Mason Street and follow it 0.1 mile to where it terminates at the preserve entrance and parking area.

TRAIL DESCRIPTION
A kiosk with a large trail map stands just beyond the parking area; paper copies of maps may also be available here. Trail intersections are signed. Follow an obvious mowed connecting path across a field of goldenrod, yellow hawkweed, and robin plantain, bordered by autumn olive, apple trees, honeysuckle, and dogwood. Autumn olive, now considered an invasive exotic, was planted to control erosion. Its yellowish blossoms fill the air with a sweet perfume in late spring. The trail rises into a wooded strip and then enters another small field. Quaking aspens and cottonwoods line the left perimeter. As the trail steepens, young white ashes with compound leaves appear, as well as white pines.

TRIP 1 // MOUNTAIN MEADOW PRESERVE

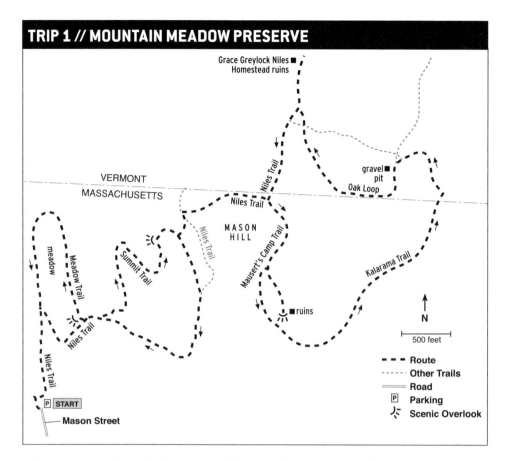

Turn right at the trail split onto red-blazed Niles Trail, which follows a mowed path along the margin of a large meadow, the preserve's namesake. At this low end of the hillside meadow, various field flowers add dashes of color from late spring to fall. The 20-acre grassland is alive with a bountiful array of butterflies in summer. The wood satyr—a small, brown butterfly with a row of black bull's-eye spots—is abundant in late spring. The path soon bears left and climbs the modest slope. The panoramic vista of the Greylock Range to the right is without a doubt the highlight of this hike. Glance over your shoulder and be treated to a view of the Taconic Range.

Turn right to enter the forest on Niles Trail and cross a short boardwalk over a trickling flow. At a trail junction at 0.4 mile, turn left off Niles Trail onto clearly signed Summit Trail. White pine, red maple, witch hazel, and striped maple predominate. Oaks are present, too. Reach a low stone wall of water-tumbled quartzite and travel along it, keeping it to your left. The narrow trail becomes steeper and passes a spreading white oak with three trunks. (White oak leaves have rounded lobes, unlike the bristle-tipped lobes of red and black oaks. White oak acorns are sweet and mature in the fall of their first year, but red and black oaks require two years to mature.) After passing the three-trunked oak, the trail climbs the slope on switchbacks. The last 200 yards are at quite an acute angle, leading to the 1,120-foot summit at 0.8 mile. This U-shaped hill is the result of glacial deposition. Wild geraniums bloom pink in late spring along the ridgeline path. Only a limited view is possible due to encroaching trees. An interesting small tree here is a multitrunked hop hornbeam, with thin, light brown, shredding bark. Hop hornbeam wood is extremely hard and durable.

Bear right and descend to an intersection on the left. Turn left and descend past low maple-leaf viburnum shrubs under a canopy of oaks and red maples. At a junction with a woods road, bear left onto the road to rejoin red-blazed Niles Trail, and then almost immediately turn right at the preserve's boundary, in the direction of the preserve's Vermont parking area. Mature red pines, characterized by scaly pinkish bark, were probably planted along the road, which skirts Mason Hill, during the Great Depression. Enjoy the wide path that parallels the Vermont state line for a brief time. At a green metal gate along the preserve boundary, continue straight ahead to another green metal gate. Walk around it to reach a T intersection with another woods road. Turn right onto yellow-blazed Kalarama Trail.

During damp conditions in late spring and summer, be alert for fiery-orange-red efts traversing the route. The eft, the terrestrial stage of the aquatic red-spotted newt, spends between two and seven years roaming woodlands before returning to water as a breeding adult. The red skin warns potential predators that the eft is poisonous when eaten. Young regenerating trees and decaying stumps speak of past logging here. Watch for a patch of wild geraniums on the left in late spring.

Panoramic vistas of Mount Greylock, the Taconic Range, and colorful wildflowers unfold across the fields of Mountain Meadow Preserve.

Bear left at the intersection with a short side path that leads to the remains of Mausert's Camp, a rustic family retreat that was destroyed by fire in the 1970s. All that is left are two stone chimneys at either end of a clearing. Indigo buntings nest along the edges of the clearing.

Retrace your steps to the intersection and turn left to rejoin Kalarama Trail at 1.5 miles. Descend on an old road cut into the side slope past a gravel borrow pit. Black birches and oaks with lowbush blueberries below dot the rising slope. A couple of beech trees on the right show faint black scars from having been climbed by bears that relish the nuts. Cross a pile of quartzite cobbles (*cobble* is a New England word for "hill") gathered during field clearing, and marvel at the huge twin-trunked oak on the right that exhibits the scars of a wire fence. Watch out for a bit of poison ivy that borders the path before it bisects a handsome patch of spinulose wood fern and then stroll easily downhill.

Look for a cluster of delicate maidenhair fern on the left shortly after the trail climbs again. Before long, reach a junction on the right with a narrow path. Two dogwood trees at this intersection sport large, four-petaled white blossoms in spring, but young white birches are generally more noticeable near the trail. Continue on Kalarama Trail, which leads down to a shallow hemlock ravine cut by a modest brook. Reach a woods road and bear left to remain on Kalarama Trail, and soon turn right to cross the brook. After the crossing, a yellow marker on the right indicates the boundary of Williamstown conservation land. A massive white pine towers behind it.

Bear left and climb past nearly 5-foot-tall bracken fern to an intersection with another woods road at the end of Kalarama Trail. You are now in Vermont. Bear left on orange-blazed Oak Loop, which follows an old road that is cut into the slope. Arrive at the clearing and bear left through an old gravel pit, where rock was removed for road and railroad bed construction in the 1950s and '60s. White pines and quaking aspens, species that thrive in human-disturbed areas, colonized the edge of the pit, which is now carpeted by grass. Reenter the woodland of oaks and a variety of birches on a gravelly track. This was once a multilayered forest dominated by white pines and American chestnuts. Pass through another small old gravel pit by a glacial boulder on the left, along Loop Trail, before emerging into a meadow where boxes provide nesting spaces for bluebirds. Follow the mowed path across the meadow.

At a T intersection with the upper portion of red-blazed Niles Trail, turn right for a brief walk to the old concrete foundation of the Grace Greylock Niles Homestead on the left at 2.3 miles. Begin the return by retracing your steps on Niles Trail south past the intersection with Oak Loop. At the junction with Kalarama Trail, turn right to continue on Niles Trail and retrace your steps along the base of Mason Hill to the intersection with Summit Trail. But rather than return to the summit, turn left to stay on Niles Trail, descending moderately along the ridgeline under a canopy of oaks. White pines soon become numerous above a sapling layer of maples, beeches, and birches. In summer, listen for the sweet, languid trill of pine warblers high in the pine boughs.

Continue walking steadily downhill, steeply at times, on Niles Trail, and bear right as the trail levels out in closely spaced pine groves. Pass the path on the right leading to the summit, and when you reach the large meadow (1.0 mile from the Niles homestead site), turn right to explore the north end of the field on Meadow Trail, which follows an obvious grass path around the field's perimeter. Here, you have a second chance to admire the stunning views and numerous butterflies, and you might see tawny-coated white-tailed deer in summer. A rusty hay rack sits idly along the path. When you reach the intersection with Niles Trail at the end of the meadow loop, bear right to return to your vehicle.

DID YOU KNOW?

The botanist and author Grace Greylock Niles, a native of Pownal, wrote *Bog-Trotting for Orchids* (1904) and *The Hoosac Valley: Its Legends and Its History* (1912). She died in 1943 at age 78.

MORE INFORMATION

Open sunrise to sunset, year-round. Access is free; membership in and donations to The Trustees of Reservations are welcome. Dogs must be leashed at all times. Mountain biking, horseback riding, motorized vehicles, hunting, and firearms are not permitted.

NEARBY

Boat access to the nearby Hoosic River is available at Lauren's Launch in Williamstown, about 3.1 miles away from Mountain Meadow Preserve. Paddlers can travel 4.8 miles north (downstream) to Clayton Park in Pownal. Some tricky rips lie along the route (see hoorwa.org/recreation/paddling-the-hoosic for details). From the junction of US 7 and MA 2 at the Williamstown rotary (traffic circle), proceed 1.2 miles on US 7 to an unnamed road on the left at a sign for Hoosic River access. Follow the unnamed road for 0.2 mile, across railroad tracks, to a sign for Lauren's Launch. Park in the pullout opposite the transfer station entrance.

2 HOPKINS MEMORIAL FOREST AND TACONIC CREST TRAIL

This excursion features monumental hardwood trees, babbling brooks, a pleasant walk along the Taconic Mountain ridge, and a geological curiosity: the Snow Hole, a 50-foot chasm where snow and ice may linger throughout the year.

Features
Location Williamstown, MA; Petersburg, NY; Pownal, VT
Rating Strenuous
Distance 10.4 miles round trip
Elevation Gain 1,650 feet
Estimated Time 5.5 hours
Maps AMC Massachusetts Trail Map 1: B1; USGS Williamstown, USGS Berlin, NY; Hopkins Memorial Forest map: hmf.williams.edu/public/trail-map/?dts=1
GPS Coordinates 42° 43.408' N, 73° 13.402' W
Contact Hopkins Memorial Forest, hmf.williams.edu

DIRECTIONS
From the intersection of US 7 and MA 2 at the rotary in Williamstown, follow US 7 north 0.4 mile to Bulkley Street on the left. Drive down Bulkley Street for 0.75 mile and then turn right onto gravel Northwest Hill Road. Proceed 0.1 mile, bearing left to enter Hopkins Memorial Forest. Park in the small gravel lot on the left, which has room for roughly eight vehicles.

TRAIL DESCRIPTION
Amble up the gravel drive between apple trees and a small meadow, where tree swallows and bluebirds nest in boxes that have been erected for them. The Rosenburg Center (once a carriage house) serves as forest headquarters. Excellent trail maps are available at the kiosk here, which also features a posted trail map and historical information. Bear right past Buxton Garden onto a gravel carriage road. The relocated former Moon Farm barn stands on the left.

Following the combined north branch of Lower Loop Trail and Carriage Road Trail (unblazed but obvious), tread beneath a canopy of sugar maple, black locust, and white ash. Pass a maple sugar processing shed on the left and a field that hosts the forest's main weather station. (*Note*: Numerous research projects are under way on the

TRIP 2 // HOPKINS MEMORIAL FOREST AND TACONIC CREST TRAIL

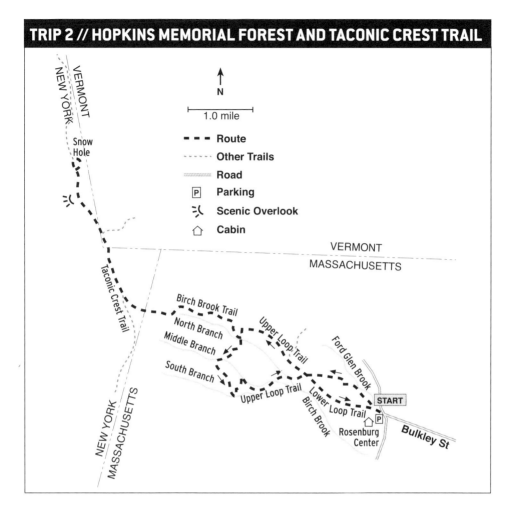

property's 2,600 acres; please stay on trails and do not interfere with research sites.) Continue above Ford Glen Brook, which soon reveals itself 60 feet below in the ravine to your right. The forest changes after the road bears left, with the addition of black birch, beech, oak, and hop hornbeam—easy to identify by its flaky, tan bark.

As you bear right, a tree canopy walkway may be partially visible. The 65-foot-high walkway (off-limits to visitors; see hmf.williams.edu/research-facilities for details) enables scientists to reach a world usually hidden from human eyes. Soon, gigantic oaks dating from the 1860s tower above; their first branches start 40 feet up. As you continue, beeches, yellow birches, and black birches increase in a younger forest. Starflower and Canada mayflower bloom here in spring, while lowbush blueberry, prince's pine, and shining and cedar club mosses spread largely by runners in the acidic soil. In June, watch for pink lady's slipper orchids just before reaching a four-way intersection with Upper Loop Trail at a stone bench and interpretive sign, at 0.9 mile.

Turn right onto the north fork of Upper Loop Trail (unblazed). As the trail climbs gently, a forest of red maple changes to one dominated by oak. At 0.2 mile from the

En route to the Snow Hole, Taconic Crest Trail passes a shrubby area with westerly views toward the Catskill Mountains.

intersection, continue straight at an intersection where Carriage Road Trail branches right. Tiny lowbush blueberry shrubs thrive beneath the trees. A significant number of the oaks here have more than one trunk—a sure sign that these woods were logged. (*Note*: Paint marks on the trees are not blazes; these demarcate forest study plots, which visitors should avoid.) At a junction adjacent to a footbridge over the North Branch of Birch Brook, bear right onto signed and blue-blazed Birch Brook Trail at 1.8 miles.

Now the real hiking begins with a 1.5-mile ascent of the Taconic Mountain ridge's east slopes. Follow Birch Brook Trail past the end of a fallen stone wall indicating former pasturing. Then bear right and pass knee- to waist-high blueberry and huckleberry bushes. The grade of this old woods road increases under mixed northern hardwoods and oaks. On a more moderate slope, notice the dying paper birches—pioneering trees that sprouted after logging and were later shaded out by species whose seeds required less sunlight to germinate. About three-quarters of the way to the ridge (1.3 miles from the junction with Upper Loop Trail, 3.1 miles overall), the route crosses into New York.

Log steps help hikers ascend the eastern slope past glades of yellow-green ferns—most notably hay-scented fern, also called boulder fern, which characteristically forms dense stands. Hopkins Forest scientists have studied alleopathy—a process by which plants secrete chemicals that inhibit growth of other plant species—of hay-scented ferns. The path along the ferns ends at the signed junction with Taconic Crest Trail, blazed with a white diamond in a blue square, at 3.3 miles. Turn right (north) onto Taconic Crest Trail, a well-trodden, long route that traverses undulating terrain along the spine of the

Taconic Range for 35 miles. The Snow Hole is 1.5 miles north of the junction. Up here, where soils are shallow, the forest is reduced in height but boasts a thick sapling layer, consisting mostly of prolific-sprouting American beech.

Enter a former timber harvest site, where much of the small, woody vegetation was cut to create an early successional habitat for species not able to live in dense woodland. At a three-way intersection in a waist-high fern glade, continue straight. Shortly after the trail leaves Hopkins Memorial Forest property and passes onto New York State Forest land, walk through several shrubby areas. Shiny-leafed bilberry and less common huckleberries thrive in the sunny gaps, as do a few red spruces. Though vegetation largely screens several former lookouts, the northernmost shrubby section affords a partial westerly perspective across hills on the western side of the Taconic Range. Reenter the woods, where many beech trees have black bark lesions, symptoms of beech bark disease.

At approximately 4.8 miles, reach two intersections (the first of which is unmarked) with side paths on the right that lead to the Snow Hole, a geological and meteorologic wonder. Continue to the second junction, where a signed trail leads downhill past patches of shining club moss for about 250 feet to the narrow entrance on the right. Old graffiti—some dating to 1865—is carved into the relatively soft phyllite bedrock near the entrance. If you descend into the crevice to explore it from within, watch your footing, as the rock may be slick. Immediately you'll feel a drop in temperature, especially during the summer months. Mosses, wood sorrel wildflowers, and ferns soften the tilted, wafer-thin layers of phyllite, while yellow birches clutch the rim. It feels a bit like a giant, cave-like terrarium. Even on the hottest days of summer, you may find snow and ice here.

Retrace your steps back to the signed intersection, or bear right from the Snow Hole to make a short loop back to Taconic Crest Trail via the first side path, which is marked with periodic red blazes. Turn left when you rejoin Taconic Crest Trail and retrace your steps to Birch Brook Trail on the left. Descend back to the junction with Upper Loop Trail at 7.9 miles. Turn right to cross a wooden bridge over the brook. This section of woodland contains all four common birch species—white, gray, black, and yellow, all separable by specific bark true to their names. Soon reach the Middle Branch of Birch Brook, lumpy with mossy stones, and cross it via another wooden span. Descend easily on a wide path.

Bear left in an arc to drop down close to the South Branch of Birch Brook. Shade-casting hemlocks—some sizable—populate the slope. In summer, shade-tolerant woodland butterflies, such as the northern pearly eye, may make an appearance, although they can be difficult to see when they alight because their coloring blends in with forest vegetation. This eye-spotted species rarely visits flowers, preferring to sip tree sap and other fluids. Soon meet the Middle Branch again, and cross a wooden bridge. Continue along Birch Brook under oaks, beeches, birches, and maples.

Gaze into the depths of clear pools to look for native brook trout. A significant number of monumental oaks dominate this woodland—a 3½-foot-diameter specimen stands on the right. Cross the North Branch of Birch Brook on a bridge built to accommodate vehicles and climb easily back to the four-way intersection with Lower Loop Trail at the stone bench at 9.6 miles. Turn right to begin the final segment, on the south side of Lower Loop Trail along the dividing line between two watersheds—Ford Glen Brook and Birch Brook.

Walk through more fern glades, where an interpretive panel describes the possible chemical warfare waged by hay-scented fern against its competitors. Another informs readers that club mosses are more common in formerly pastured earth. All four local species—prince's pine, shining club moss, cedar club moss, and staghorn club moss—can be seen on this hike. Although capable of reproducing via spores, slow-growing club mosses rely mostly on cloning themselves.

Stride by a dark stand of Norway spruces planted by the U.S. Forest Service, which operated the forest from 1935 to 1968. Amble downhill past an ancient oak with rotting heartwood. Exotic plants along the margins presage your return to the Rosenburg Center.

DID YOU KNOW?

The Taconic Mountains, a narrow, 150-mile-long range, one of North America's oldest at 440 million years, runs from Brandon, Vermont, to the Hudson Highlands of New York. Taconic Crest Trail follows this ridgeline for 35 miles from Hancock, Massachusetts, to Petersburg, New York. Many historians believe *Taconic* is a derivation of an Algonkin word meaning "in the trees."

MORE INFORMATION

Open dawn to dusk, year-round. Access is free. Public restrooms and drinking water are available at the Rosenburg Center, open 7 a.m. to 6 p.m. Pets must be leashed. Hunting is prohibited, except for deer hunting by special permit in the Massachusetts portion of the property during the two-week shotgun season in late November and early December, during which the forest is closed to other users. Skiing is allowed. Horseback riding is permitted on designated trails. Camping, fishing, mountain bikes, and vehicles are prohibited. Collecting fauna and flora is prohibited; do not disturb research sites.

NEARBY

The Williams College Museum of Art, on the college's campus at 15 Lawrence Hall Drive in Williamstown, houses 13,000 objects that span the history of art. This teaching museum is open free of charge to the public (10 a.m. to 5 p.m. Tuesday to Sunday; call 413-597-2429 or visit artmuseum.williams.edu for more information). Construction of a new museum began in 2024; the facility is scheduled to open in 2027. See artmuseum.williams.edu/wcma-in-transition for visitor information during the transition.

3 PINE COBBLE AND EAST MOUNTAIN

A partial loop hike up East Mountain, the southern terminus of the Green Mountains, on sunny slopes covered with oaks and sheep laurel, leads to a summit studded with quartzite and pitch pines, offering some of the most stunning views in the region.

FEATURES

Location Williamstown and Clarksburg, MA
Rating Moderate
Distance 4.8 miles round trip
Elevation Gain 1,340 feet
Estimated Time 3 hours
Maps AMC Massachusetts Trail Map 1: B3; USGS Williamstown; Williamstown Rural Lands Pine Cobble Preserve map: rurallands.org/wp-content/uploads/2021/02/WRL_Map_Pine_Cobble_Hike.pdf
GPS Coordinates 42° 42.963′ N, 73° 11.116′ W
Contact Williamstown Rural Lands, 413-458-2494, rurallands.org/property/pine-cobble
Williams Outing Club, 413-597-2304, woc.williams.edu

DIRECTIONS

From the junction of MA 2 and US 7 at a rotary in Williamstown, proceed east on MA 2 for 0.6 mile to Cole Avenue on the left. Follow Cole Avenue for 0.75 mile (crossing the Hoosic River) and turn right onto North Hoosac Road. Drive for 0.4 mile to Pine Cobble Road on the left, and follow Pine Cobble Road for 0.1 mile to a gravel parking area on the left (space for six or seven vehicles).

TRAIL DESCRIPTION

From the parking area, cross Pine Cobble Road diagonally, walking uphill for about 100 feet to the signed trailhead on the right. The path initially parallels the road and passes a wooden sign on the left erected by the Williams Outing Club. The sign indicates that this blue-blazed trail leads 1.6 miles to Pine Cobble summit, 2.1 miles to the Appalachian Trail (AT) junction, and 3.4 miles to the Vermont border. Turn left at this sign to enter an oak woodland. White and red oak predominate, but black cherry, red maple, American beech, black birch, ironwood, tulip tree, and hop hornbeam add

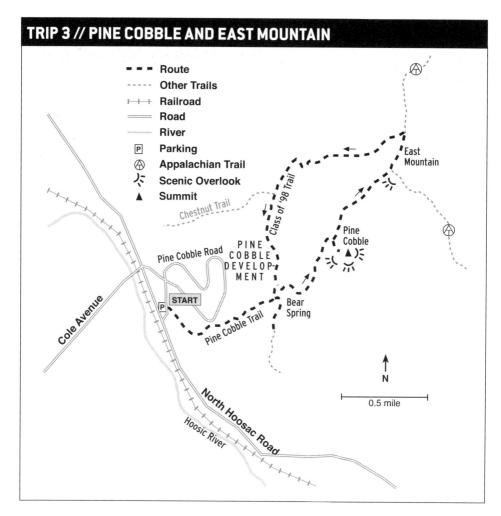

variety. Distinguish white oak by its flaky, light gray bark. Rounded quartzite boulders litter the trail.

Striped maple appears as the trail gently climbs, along with chestnut oak, smooth-skinned black birch, and multitrunked witch hazel. The trail steepens, and lowbush blueberry thrives in the acidic soil under the tannin-rich oak. This section of the route is thought to be the ancient shoreline of Lake Bascom, a glacial lake that once extended along the Hoosic River valley from southern Vermont to Pittsfield. To the north, its waters were 500 feet deep. Sheep laurel, another indicator of acidic soil, first shows up near here and grows about 2 feet high, becoming abundant later. (It is said to be poisonous to livestock.) After another 0.25 mile, near a gray boulder, watch for an unmarked side path on the right that leads about 300 feet toward a dark green wall of eastern hemlocks and Bear Spring.

Bear Spring, at the base of a resistant quartzite cliff, is the only surface water on this south-facing slope. The cooler microclimate here fosters sapling yellow birch and striped maple, both northern hardwood species. Ferns are more noticeable, too, including common polypody on quartzite boulders. Rejoin the main trail, walk uphill past luxuriant growths of shiny-leafed wintergreen, and soon reach a signpost at the 0.8-mile mark, where Class of '98 Trail heads left. You'll return by this route, but for now continue straight. The nutrient-poor soils here host a variety of heath family species, including blueberry, huckleberry, and the Massachusetts state flower: trailing arbutus, or mayflower. Its leaves have a sandy texture, and its delicate spring flowers are pale pink.

As you gain elevation, the oaks and other hardwoods decrease in height while the shrub layer thickens. Chestnut oaks, with wavy-margined leaves and deeply furrowed trunks, are now far more prevalent. The trail steepens again as you reach a sign, surrounded by a mat of moss, proclaiming, "Welcome to Pine Cobble, a unique natural area owned by the Williamstown Rural Lands Foundation and maintained for hiking and enjoyment of nature." As you hike through a small boulder field of gray, angular hunks of quartzite, notice low sheep laurel shrubs.

Sassafras trees, which do well in sandy soils, become common. Their leaves have one, two, or three lobes and emit a spicy aroma when crushed. Continue the steady climb amid white birches, young red maples, and chestnut oaks. Marvel at the wooden bowl formed by a triple-stemmed oak—the result of cutting long ago—that collects and holds rainwater.

After a rocky climb, look for a signpost indicating that the Pine Cobble summit is to the right, and the AT and Class of '98 Trail are to the left. Follow the side path right to excellent vista points at the Pine Cobble summit (elevation 1,893 feet). The Williams College campus is visible from a perch atop rounded quartzite on the right of the summit. Beyond the campus lies the spine of the northern Taconics, with Berlin Mountain (Trip 4) as its most prominent feature. A bit farther, on the other side of the ridge, are views to the east of the nestled town of North Adams. Roughly 6 miles due south is the summit of Mount Greylock, complete with the Massachusetts Veterans War Memorial Tower.

The smooth, gray stone on the top of Pine Cobble is Cheshire quartzite. Six hundred million years ago, it was beach sand. The pure silica of this rock type was once the raw ingredient in Sandwich glass. Some broken rock faces show a rusty tinge of iron.

When ready, return to the main trail and turn right to continue another 0.5 mile to the AT junction. After mostly level walking through oak, gray birch, red maple, witch hazel, lowbush blueberry, sheep laurel, and wintergreen, climb moderately over schist, a metamorphic rock that glistens due to its high mica content. Watch for a metal anchor point in the rock that once helped support a fire tower. The route levels out through a shrubby growth of birches and leaves the forest for an open, rocky promontory. The trail is marked with rock cairns and blue blazes on stones.

The views improve as you climb higher (especially after leaf fall). This boulder field is the perfect place to enjoy the Taconic panorama. The surrounding pitch pines are mostly 12 feet tall. Taller, longer-needled white pines are also present, and a few red spruces stand among the light gray quartzite slabs. Follow the rock-strewn treadway to its junction with the AT at 2.1 miles (elevation 2,050 feet), marked by a signpost on the summit of East Mountain. A mountain azalea shrub stands to the left. Turn left onto the white-blazed AT and continue to the intersection with Class of '98 Trail, marked with blue blazes.

Nestled in the Hoosic River valley to the east, North Adams is visible from the quartzite summit of Pine Cobble.

Turn left and follow Class of '98 Trail downhill through deciduous woodland. Dense understory and stumps indicate fairly recent logging. A Caution sign marks a tricky descent over talus, but after a set of stone steps there are fewer rocks. The route parallels angular quartzite boulders—some capped by ferns—until it reaches the three-way junction with Chestnut Trail. Turn left to remain on Class of '98 Trail. Before long, a dramatic 40-foot cliff catches your eye. Be sure to follow the blue blazes past side paths until you reach Pine Cobble Trail. Turn right to return to your vehicle.

DID YOU KNOW?
Glacial Lake Bascom—which covered the Hoosic River valley from present-day Cheshire, Massachusetts, to the Vermont border for 800 years—and Bascom Lodge on Mount Greylock are both named for John Bascom (1827–1911). The Williams College alumnus and faculty member was one of the first Greylock Reservation commissioners, appointed in 1898.

MORE INFORMATION
Open year-round; access is free. The site has no restroom facilities. Pine Cobble Trail traverses lands owned by Williams College, Williamstown Rural Lands, the Massachusetts Department of Conservation and Recreation, and private owners. The trail is maintained by members of the Williams Outing Club and the Williamstown Rural Lands.

NEARBY

The highly acclaimed Clark Art Institute (413-458-2303; clarkart.edu), at 225 South Street in Williamstown, sits on a 140-acre campus of expansive lawns, meadows, and walking trails. The museum is best known for its extraordinary collection of French impressionist paintings. It is open Tuesday through Sunday (daily in July and August), 10 A.M. to 5 P.M., and closed Mondays and major holidays. The walking trails are open year-round. A $20 admission fee is charged (free for visitors 21 and younger and students; see the website for other free admission opportunities).

CAT O' TALL TALES

At the peril of leaping, figuratively at least, from the tangible to the mysterious, consider the controversy surrounding the presence, real or imagined, of mountain lions in the Berkshires. Many folks have reported sightings of mountain lions; some accounts may be hoaxes, and others are doubtless simple cases of mistaken identity. (Bobcats, which are common in western Massachusetts, are smaller than mountain lions and have much shorter tails.)

Mountain lion, cougar, puma, panther, or catamount—many terms describe this fabled creature. Local place names (such as the Catamount Ski Area) harken back to a time when these large felines did indeed inhabit western Massachusetts. The last known sighting, an individual that was shot in the wild in Hampshire County in 1858, occurred when the amount of forested landscape was significantly less than it is today. The mounted body of that mountain lion now resides at Mass Audubon's Arcadia Wildlife Sanctuary in Easthampton.

Several reports have occurred at Quabbin Reservoir in central Massachusetts, just 40 miles east of the Berkshires. An experienced naturalist (a person with a no-nonsense, scientific approach to observations) reported a mountain lion crossing a road in front of him as he rounded a corner on his bicycle while coasting down a hill. Scat found in 1997 by a professional wildlife tracker at a predator–beaver kill at the reservoir's northern end tested positive for mountain lion DNA.

Published distribution maps reveal the nearest breeding population of this predator to be no closer than the Florida Everglades, although verified reports of sightings do exist from elsewhere in the eastern states. For example, a young male mountain lion was killed on a Connecticut highway in 2011. (DNA detective work traced the cat's origin all the way to South Dakota's Black Hills!)

If indeed a wild population exists in New England—and that is yet unproven—the question of origin remains. Some claim that escaped or released pets are the genesis of local cougar sightings. That may indeed be correct, but could there be more to it? The catamount's chief prey are deer. Southern New England's large and thriving deer population would provide ample sustenance to support at least a few mountain lions. And other animals, such as black bear, moose, and fisher, have reclaimed much of their former ranges in southern New England.

Although sighting reports surface regularly, incontrovertible proof—a body or bona fide photograph—is still lacking. But the intriguing possibility exists that these big cats, long absent from this region, may once again roam the Berkshire forests in the future.

4 BERLIN MOUNTAIN

A challenging loop route heads straight up the east face of the Taconic Range to its highest peak in Massachusetts. Views of Mount Greylock from Berlin Mountain's flat summit are particularly pleasing, and an enchanting little waterfall adds enjoyment at the end of the hike.

FEATURES

Location Williamstown, MA; Berlin, NY
Rating Strenuous
Distance 4.7-mile loop
Elevation Gain 1,545 feet
Estimated Time 2.5 to 3.5 hours
Maps AMC Massachusetts Trail Map 1: C1; USGS Berlin, USGS Williamstown
GPS Coordinates 42° 42.153′ N, 73° 16.231′ W
Contact Williamstown Rural Lands, 413-458-2494, rurallands.org/the-berlin-road-trail-system
Williams Outing Club, 413-597-2304, woc.williams.edu
New York Department of Environmental Conservation, 518-402-8044, dec.ny.gov

DIRECTIONS

From the intersection of MA 2 and US 7 in Williamstown, proceed west on MA 2 for 0.3 mile to Torrey Woods Road on the left. Follow Torrey Woods Road (which becomes Berlin Mountain Road where the pavement ends after approximately 0.5 mile) for 2.1 miles to a small gravel parking area on the left (space for three or four vehicles).

TRAIL DESCRIPTION

Signs at the parking area read "Class of '33 Trail" (Williams Outing Club students cut the trail in 1933) and "WRLF Loop Trail" (Williamstown Rural Lands). Walk back down the gravel road that you just drove on for approximately 300 feet and look for the signed trailhead on a white birch tree to the right. Enter a forest of mostly young white and yellow birches, red spruces, and red and striped maples; follow blue blazes as you descend easily. Oaks and American beeches soon appear.

As the descent becomes steeper, listen for Haley Brook, a clear, fast-flowing stream that, according to an interpretive sign, is home to native brook trout and rare Appalachian brook crayfish.

TRIP 4 // BERLIN MOUNTAIN

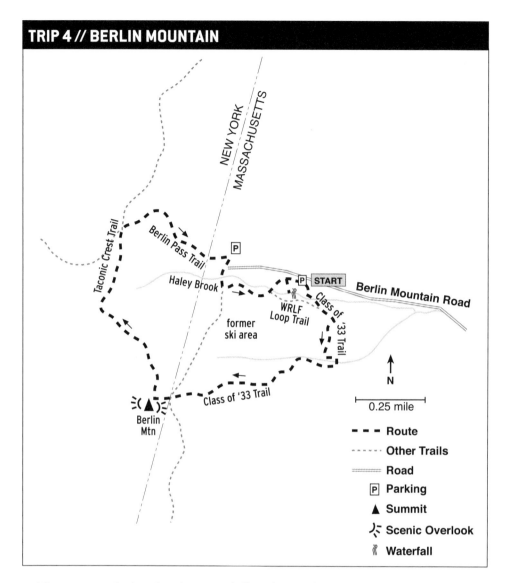

After crossing the brook, advance uphill under northern hardwoods and soon arrive at a signed intersection. Turn left to remain on blue-blazed Class of '33 Trail (WRLF Loop Trail turns right). The abundance of young trees indicates fairly recent harvesting, and the remnants of former logging roads are still visible. The grade, initially level, soon increases and follows a trench-like former skid road with scattered hemlocks and spruces. Some of the hemlocks are considerably older than the hardwoods—beech, birch, and oak. Most of the beeches suffer from the beech bark disease that is prevalent throughout the region.

The path bears left away from the road, winds down rather abruptly, and then levels out among mature yellow birches and hemlocks. A recently rebuilt campsite on the left (open to the public, no fee or registration required) features two tent pads, a picnic table, a fire ring, and a moldering privy. An intertwined hemlock and yellow birch provide a curiosity on the right. Turn sharply right and follow the contour under hemlocks for a short, sloping descent to a nameless brook that has exposed phyllite bedrock. Use caution when crossing on the slick, wet stones, and give the stinging nettles a wide berth.

This section of the trail starts on an old road. The next mile or so represents one of the most challenging ascents of any hike covered in this guide. A nearly relentless series of steep climbs is moderated only by an occasional less exhausting grade, permitting you to catch your breath. When you stop, note that the slope up to your left has more mature timber than the one below you to the right. (Many neotropical migrant birds feel at home on this eastern face of the Taconics, including the black-and-yellow Canada warbler, black-throated green warbler, ovenbird, and rose-breasted grosbeak.)

At one point, pass a fallen hemlock. Once you see the root ball, it's easy to envision how heavy rain and high winds might have separated the tree's shallow root network from the bedrock. The sunny gap created has enabled shade-intolerant species to gain a foothold. Hay-scented ferns have colonized other light-filled gaps.

The trail remains steep but is well blazed with blue, traveling through dense northern hardwoods and finally reaching an unmarked junction on the right with the old Williams College Ski Trail at the Massachusetts–New York border. The ski trail is not maintained and is even steeper than the route you just ascended, so it is not recommended for a return. Bear left to gain the mostly flat open summit of Berlin Mountain (elevation 2,818 feet), 2.0 miles from the trailhead.

The views of the Greylock Range, about 7 miles to the southeast, are splendid, but summit trees are growing taller, and vistas are limited. Red spruces ring the circular open area where a fire tower once stood. Crumbling concrete footings are all that remain. Sunshine has encouraged raspberry, bilberry, and lowbush blueberry to proliferate.

The return route follows a portion of Taconic Crest Trail (TCT), blazed by a white diamond in a blue square (the section in New York also has blue disks), to Berlin Pass. Tire tracks make it obvious that ATVs frequently use this trail, so be on the lookout. Follow the wide, rocky track downhill to the right, passing through numerous fern glades. White birch trees, also known as paper birch, look especially attractive in this setting of yellow-green ferns. The broad path, steep at times and filled with lots of loose stones, is eroded to phyllite bedrock. As a result, side paths have been created. Juneberry (shadbush) trees are among the members of the low-stature ridgeline forest, producing white flowers in April before their leaves emerge.

After experiencing moderately steep descents alternating with level stretches along the wooded crest for 1.2 miles, arrive at a four-way intersection in a shrubby depression, or saddle, called Berlin Pass, at 3.2 miles overall. Leave the TCT, which continues straight toward Petersburg Pass; and turn right onto pink-blazed Berlin Pass Trail. Opposite this trail, the old Boston to Albany Post Road descends to Berlin, New York. The treadway is wide, rutted, and damp in spots but easy to follow. Note the excellent examples of wafer-thin, layered phyllite bedrock in the trail. This rock began as clay deposits, rich in mica, in a shallow sea, which were then metamorphosed by great heat and pressure to produce a rock with grain size between shale and schist.

After you hike downhill for a while, the dry south-facing slope to your left sports lowbush blueberries, mountain azaleas, and a little member of the snapdragon family with the intriguing name of cow-wheat, which bears modest, trumpet-like yellow flowers in summer. It draws its nourishment from the roots of oaks. As the route proceeds rather steeply down the rocky trail, oaks indeed become more common, and haircap moss softens the margins. Finally, bear right in an arc and emerge into a large gravel parking lot, where the trail meets Berlin Mountain Road. You could turn left and walk down the road 0.4 mile to your vehicle, but more fun awaits.

If you decide to extend your hike here, turn right. Still visible on the left slope are the runs of the old Williams College Ski Area, built in 1960. At the end of the gravel lot, turn left to head down a grassy track toward the base of the ski slope. Yellow-blazed Bullock Trail is on your right, but turn left onto red-blazed WRLF Loop Trail. Haley Brook tumbles out of a large culvert and down a ravine on your left. A canopy of maples, ashes, birches, and beeches shades striped maples and patches of delicate maidenhair fern. Spring wildflowers called blue cohosh—forming solid stands—and wild leeks are profligate on this moist, nutrient-rich slope. Wild leek's twin leaves have an unmistakable onion fragrance; they wither away completely by the time the leek's globes of white flowers emerge in summer.

Hikers pass through a lush hay-scented fern glade just below the flat summit of Berlin Mountain.

At the intersection, turn left onto Haley Brook Cutoff (also blazed red), and amble down to cross the stream. Briefly ascend a steep slope through deciduous woodland and bear right. At a wooden bridge outfitted with a wire mesh treadway, turn right onto a side path that leads steadily and then more steeply down, past a beech snag on the right pitted with big pileated woodpecker excavations, to a small viewing platform. The enchanting waterfall consists of cascades and a horsetail for a total drop of at least 30 feet. The auditory aspect of this experience is to be appreciated as well. In late spring and early summer, listen for the exuberant song of the winter wren. After returning to the main trail, turn right and cross the wooden bridge. Berlin Mountain Road and your vehicle are a short distance ahead.

DID YOU KNOW?
To obtain use of a 41-acre site at the end of Berlin Road for a ski area, Williams College exchanged portions of a farm between MA 2 and Berlin Road with Williamstown, which wanted the farm acreage for campsites. The college ski team now trains at Jiminy Peak in Hancock.

MORE INFORMATION
Open year-round; access is free. No restroom facilities or potable water sources are available. The route crosses property owned by Williamstown Rural Lands, the town of Williamstown, Williams College, the New York Department of Environmental Conservation, and private owners. The Taconic Hiking Club (taconichikingclub.org) maintains Taconic Crest Trail. The Williams Outing Club manages the Class of '33 and Berlin Pass trails. WRLF Loop Trail is maintained by Williamstown Rural Lands and the New York Department of Environmental Conservation.

NEARBY
Sheep Hill, a 50-acre former dairy farm and ski area now owned and managed by Williamstown Rural Lands, features hillside trails offering expansive views of Mount Greylock and surrounding features. The entrance is approximately 1.2 miles south of Williamstown Center at 671 Cold Spring Road (US 7/MA 2). The property is open year-round for passive recreation and public programs on natural history and rural heritage (413-458-2494, rurallands.org/property/sheep-hill).

5 GREYLOCK RANGE TRAVERSE

This long, strenuous day hike spans four summits, including the state's highest peak, and features arguably the most sensational panoramic vista in the entire commonwealth—one of six spectacular viewpoints along the route. It's the most exhilarating hiking the Berkshires has to offer!

FEATURES

Location Williamstown, Adams, and North Adams, MA
Rating Strenuous
Distance 12.1-mile loop
Elevation Gain 2,390 feet
Estimated Time 6.5 to 8 hours
Maps AMC Massachusetts Trail Map 1; USGS Williamstown; Massachusetts Department of Conservation and Recreation map: mass.gov/doc/mount-greylock-trail-map/download
GPS Coordinates 42° 39.323' N, 73° 12.325' W
Contact Massachusetts Department of Conservation and Recreation, 413-499-4262, mass.gov/locations/mount-greylock-state-reservation

DIRECTIONS

From the Five Corners area of South Williamstown, where US 7, MA 43, Sloan Road, and Green River Road intersect, turn right onto Green River Road and follow it 2.3 miles to Hopper Road and Mount Hope Park on the right. Turn right, cross the Green River, and drive for 2.1 miles (bearing left at Potter Road) to a large gravel parking area on the right at Haley Farm.

TRAIL DESCRIPTION

From the parking area (elevation 1,100 feet), follow the cobbled road past a farm gate and a state forest gate, between stone walls overhung by sugar maples, to Haley Farm Trail (the return route for this hike) on the right. A panoramic view of the Hopper, a large cirque, or ravine scoured by glaciers, on Mount Greylock's western slopes—unfolds beyond a hayfield. Pass the Hopper Trail intersection on your right and descend gently on blue-blazed Money Brook Trail, where a dense stand of pale touch-me-not blooms in midsummer. Unlike the predominant orange species in this area, though, these flowers are yellow. Amble through a grassy stretch on a mowed

TRIP 5 // GREYLOCK RANGE TRAVERSE

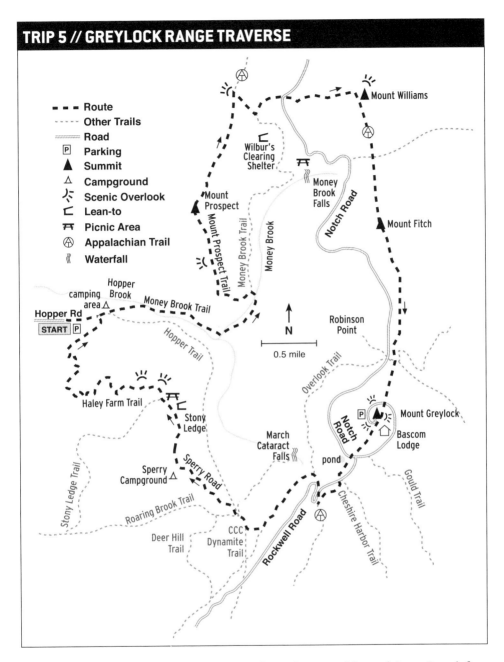

path that skirts Hopper Brook at the boundary of Hopper Natural Area. Bear left to cross a wooden footbridge over the brook's clear water and begin an easy uphill walk along the opposite bank.

At a short reroute, where the raging brook has undercut the trail, bear left up stone steps and along the hillside to rejoin the fast-flowing brook. You are walking along the southern flank of Mount Prospect. Sugar maple, white ash, black birch, yellow birch, beech, and oak shield the path. The eroding force of water is evident at another bend in the brook.

Soon after a stone-lined cellar hole on the right, cross another wooden footbridge over cascading Hopper Brook. At a Y intersection, turn left to remain on spacious Money Brook Trail. At this point, the route parallels Money Brook, a tributary of Hopper Brook, upstream. Magnificent eastern hemlocks rise from the steep slopes as you cross a stream. A wider feeder brook flowing down through the Hopper must be crossed on rocks; use caution when water levels are high in spring or after heavy rain. This is practice for a final crossing on Money Brook via stones a short distance beyond.

After 1.4 miles on Money Brook Trail, begin to ascend rocky Mount Prospect Trail when the path turns left at a signed T intersection and narrows. The grade soon becomes more challenging and winds along a virtual talus slope of schist that requires some use of hands to negotiate (use caution here, especially when the rocks are wet). Soon bear right, under oaks, to climb the prominent spine of Mount Prospect, a subordinate peak of Mount Greylock once known locally as "the Hog's Back." Blueberries and huckleberries both offer sweet morsels in midsummer. Know huckleberry by its rough leaves. The challenging climb is interrupted now and again by more moderate sections, but the overall trek is relentlessly upward. Red maples, shad trees, and mountain azaleas join the oaks on this dry, south-facing slope. At a viewpoint on the left, pause to admire a wonderful panorama of the Taconic Range and Haley Farm. Some moderate uphill stretches remain until the wooded high point, where a rock cairn marks the 2,690-foot summit of Mount Prospect at 2.7 miles.

An easy-to-moderate descent leads through ferns, under yellow birches, maples, beeches, and a few red spruces, and over gneiss (pronounced "nice") bedrock, alternately leveling out and dropping. One mile beyond the cairn, after passing dark stands of young spruces, emerge onto bedrock and enjoy fabulous vistas of the northern Taconics and Vermont's Green Mountains beyond. Turn sharply right here to follow the white-blazed Appalachian Trail (AT) south over a needle-cushioned treadway down a spruce-covered east slope to the intersection with Money Brook Trail. (A sign notes that Wilbur's Clearing Lean-To is 0.3 mile down the trail to the right.) Continue straight on the AT and traipse over bog bridges through a damp spruce stand.

Cross Notch Road and begin your ascent of Mount Williams, still following the white-blazed AT. Mature spruces are reproducing well here. Later, hobblebush and beech form a dense understory. The hike becomes more challenging as you climb rocky "steps," but switchbacks make ascending the west slope of Williams manageable. After leveling off in a low-stature woodland, the AT bears left to reach the 2,951-foot summit of Mount Williams—named for Ephraim Williams Jr., the founder of nearby Williams College—at 4.8 miles. Limited views to the northeast are a welcome respite from climbing. Bear left at the lookout to continue south on the AT. Contorted bedrock along the initially level path shows the effects of the tremendous heat and pressure created by continental collision hundreds of millions of years ago.

At a four-way intersection with Barnard Farm Trail and Old Summit Road Trail, remain on the AT to begin an easy but rocky climb to Mount Fitch, where you may detect the aroma of balsam firs. You will most likely have crested the 3,110-foot summit of Mount Fitch and dropped slightly in elevation again before you realize that you passed over it. The roughly 3 miles of trail between Mount Williams and Bellows Pipe Trail wend through pleasant woodland. More than a mile beyond Mount Fitch, Bellows Pipe Trail (Trip 8) goes left. It's only another 100 yards to steep Thunderbolt Trail—one of the Northeast's pioneering downhill ski runs—on the left. Just beyond Thunderbolt Trail, a side path leads right, to Notch Road and Robinson Point, but continue upward on the AT, which in May is festive with wildflowers.

Blackberry canes fill a linear gap through which the trail passes on its somewhat rocky ascent past low beech, birch, and cherry trees. You'll have your first glimpse of the globe atop the Massachusetts Veterans War Memorial Tower here, if not obscured by clouds or fog. Tread up flagstone steps to paved Notch Road. Look back to admire a spectacular panorama that includes the rocky spine of Ragged Mountain and the Hoosic River valley. Cross the paved auto road and climb over bony outcroppings to arrive shortly at Thunderbolt Shelter, which is available for day use only. The summit, topped by the iconic granite memorial tower, rises just a short distance ahead at 7.2 miles. A relief map near the tower depicts the Greylock Range. A web of trails encircles the summit, which is enlivened in summer by the clear, plaintive whistles (*Old-Sam-Peabody-Peabody-Peabody*) of white-throated sparrows.

For fabulous scenery eastward, bear left on a universally accessible path that leads to an overlook where all promontories are identified on a granite tableau. Restrooms and drinking water are available at Bascom Lodge (open late May to mid-October), built in 1938 by the Civilian Conservation Corps. When you're ready to depart, return to the AT beyond the tower. Stroll through bluish conical firs and cross the paved road again near the lofty radio antenna. Descend steeply over rock amid red spruce and firs to the next auto road crossing. Turn right and follow the AT along the road for 100 feet; then reenter the woods on the right, remaining on the white-blazed AT. After a brief descent, follow bog bridges to a scenic human-built pond—once the lodge's water supply and headwater for Hopper Brook. At 0.7 mile from the summit, leave the AT and stay right, heading downhill on blue-blazed Hopper Trail toward Sperry Road. Bear right at paved Rockwell Road and descend on a wide, rocky path, following Hopper Trail left at the junction with Overlook Trail on the right.

The grade is moderate as you continue down the slope under a canopy of beech and birch trees with red spruces mixed in. After leveling out and passing a shielded spring on the right, turn right at a T intersection to follow Hopper Trail at a steeper grade along an unnamed brook to gravel Sperry Road. Turn right and stroll down through the campground, passing junctions for several other trails—including Hopper Trail on the right—and toilet facilities. Continue west on Sperry Road, which begins to climb, easily at first, then moderately, through mixed forest. At 1.1 miles from the campground (roughly the hike's 10-mile mark), reach the road's end at Stony Ledge (elevation 2,560 feet), where some of the state's most breathtaking scenery awaits.

Directly across the 1,500-foot-deep chasm of the Hopper glacial cirque is Mount Greylock's summit, roughly 1,000 feet higher. From left to right, an impressive panorama encompasses all the peaks you scaled today—Prospect, Williams, Fitch, and Greylock. Picnic tables invite a long pause. Hopper Brook is audible, and the flutelike voices of thrushes spiral up from the extensive forest below in late spring and summer. When you're ready to continue, find the "Stony Ledge Group Site" sign at the trailhead on the far end of the gravel turnaround. At the Y split, follow the sign left for Stony Ledge and Haley Farm trails. Make a fairly steep descent through hardwoods and spruce to the junction with blue-blazed Haley Farm Trail.

Turn right onto Haley Farm Trail to begin the last segment, a 2.1-mile descent to the trailhead. A final splendid vista, this one north toward Williamstown and Vermont's Green Mountains, is yours at the end of a short path on the right. Haley Farm Trail descends among beech, maple, cherry, and yellow birch and then through an oak-covered slope that shows signs of selective logging from previous decades. Switchbacks lead down, quite steeply, through two small bowl-like depressions. Continue through a forest of well-spaced large sugar maples, beneath which understory growth seeks sunlight. (Sugar maples thrive in such nutrient-rich soils.) Reach level ground at last among birches and arrive at the hayfield you gazed across hours ago at the start of your trek.

Beyond the summit of Mount Prospect, hikers emerge onto bedrock offering fabulous vistas of the northern Taconics and Vermont's Green Mountains beyond.

Mount Prospect looms ahead. Stroll through the meadow and turn left on the old road toward the parking area to end a rewarding day.

DID YOU KNOW?
After Captain Ephraim Williams Jr. died in battle during the French and Indian War in 1755, his estate provided funds for a free school in West Township—later Williamstown. The school would eventually become world-renowned Williams College.

MORE INFORMATION
Mount Greylock State Reservation is open dawn to dusk, year-round. Admission is free. A parking fee ($5 Massachusetts residents, $10 out of state) is charged only on the summit from May to October. Mountain bikes, skiing, and leashed dogs are allowed (bicycles are prohibited on the AT). Hunting is prohibited from May 20 to Columbus Day/Indigenous Peoples' Day and is never permitted within War Memorial Park. Toilet facilities are at the summit, Bascom Lodge, the campground on Sperry Road, and Stony Ledge. Carry in, carry out rules apply. The visitor center, at 30 Rockwell Road in Lanesborough, is open 9:00 A.M. to 4:00 P.M. daily (closed Thanksgiving and Christmas).

NEARBY
According to the Williams College archives, Captain Ephraim Williams Jr. supervised the completion of Fort Massachusetts in 1745, which was strategically situated by the Hoosic River, between the present towns of North Adams and Williamstown. A plaque in the parking lot of a former supermarket along MA 2 in North Adams marks the site.

AN IMMENSE AND AMAZING GRANDEUR: MOUNT GREYLOCK'S HISTORY

Famously described by the writer Herman Melville as "Most Excellent Majesty," Mount Greylock boasts a long and rich cultural history. In precolonial times, the 11-mile-long Greylock Range stood as a prominent landmark for the Mohican and Hoosac tribes that inhabited western New England and upstate New York. (Artifacts indicate Indigenous presence in the Hoosac Valley region dates back at least 4,000 years BCE.)

European settlers arrived in the mid-eighteenth century and subsequently transformed the landscape by clearing forests for agriculture and industries. Jeremiah Wilbur, owner of a 1,600-acre farm at the northern end of the range, created the first trail to the summit. Jones Nose (see Trip 16), so named because it was once the site of a nineteenth-century upland farm owned by Seth Jones, offers a glimpse of the mountain's agricultural past. The former farm fields, now maintained as meadows, provide habitats for wildlife, including monarch butterflies and black bears.

Streams and brooks on the range's steep slopes powered early sawmills, gristmills, textile mills, and cider mills. Money Brook's name derives from counterfeiters who illegally forged coins in its secluded ravine in the late 1700s.

Mount Greylock became a popular tourist and recreation destination during the nineteenth century. Williams College students and faculty cut the present Hopper Trail route (Trip 6) in 1830 and built two observation towers on the summit. Members of the Alpine Club, founded in 1864, subsequently helped form the Appalachian Mountain Club. A small summit house, which provided meals and lodging for summer visitors, opened in 1875.

Some of America's most prominent writers drew inspiration from Mount Greylock. Explorer, preacher, and Yale University president Timothy Dwight, who ascended to the summit with Jeremiah Wilbur in 1799, described the view as "immense and of amazing grandeur" in *Travels in New England and New York*, a four-volume account of his observations in the region. A midnight hike in 1838 motivated Nathaniel Hawthorne's short story "Ethan Brand," in which the main character operates a limestone furnace on Mount Greylock.

In 1844, Henry David Thoreau climbed Bellows Pipe Trail (see Trip 8) and spent a night on the summit. In his first book, *A Week on the Concord and Merrimack Rivers*, (self-published in 1849) he chronicled waking up above clouds and fog that shrouded the surrounding hills. Herman Melville's view of snowcapped Mount Greylock from Arrowhead, his studio and farm in Pittsfield, reputedly inspired the fabled white whale in his classic *Moby Dick*, published in 1851. Melville dedicated his novel *Pierre; or, The Ambiguitie*s, completed in 1852, to Mount Greylock.

Unregulated logging, spurred by industries such as lime kilns, iron furnaces, and railroads, denuded nearly all the Greylock Range's forests by the late nineteenth century. Deforestation and charcoal burning caused numerous environmental consequences, including wildlife habitat loss, soil erosion, landslides, fires, and air pollution.

Conservation efforts began in 1885 when the Greylock Park Association (GPA), a group of local business owners, purchased the summit and surrounding 400 acres. In 1898, the Commonwealth of Massachusetts acquired the land and established Mount Greylock State Reservation, the state's first public wilderness park. An 11½-mile section of the Appalachian Trail, which traverses the crest of Mount Greylock's summit ridge, opened in 1928.

First erected at the summit in 1932, the Massachusetts Veterans War Memorial Tower serves as a monument to the state's military personnel. NBC Radio broadcast the tower's dedication to a national audience. After weather damage led to the removal of the original tower in the 1960s, the 92-foot-high granite structure was rebuilt in 1975. Rustic Bascom Lodge, constructed by Civilian Conservation Corps (CCC) workers with stones and spruce timber harvested from Mount Greylock's slopes, opened in 1936. The CCC also built hiking trails and shelters, improved the auto roads, and created Thunderbolt Ski Trail.

From 1935 through the 1940s, Thunderbolt Ski Trail hosted races such as the 1938 Eastern United States Downhill Championship, which attracted international participants and an estimated 7,000 spectators. The Thunderbolt Ski Runners, a volunteer organization, revived the trail and hosted several races and events after 2010.

A series of controversial development proposals sparked intensive debates during the late twentieth century. The Mount Greylock Protective Association successfully opposed plans for an aerial tramway and ski resort on the east slopes during the 1960s. A resort company subsequently began construction of an elaborate facility with ski trails, a golf course, condominiums, and a convention center in 1973 at Greylock Glen, a 1,063-acre parcel at the base of the mountain in Adams; financial problems and environmental concerns halted the project before the planned opening. Other proposals, including a casino, shopping center, and housing development, also never came to fruition. After the state acquired Greylock Glen in the 1980s, discussions about its future continued into the twenty-first century. Greylock Glen Outdoor Center, a multipurpose recreation and conservation education facility that opened in 2024, features a variety of amenities, such as exhibits, a dining room, and educational programs led by Mass Audubon.

6   HOPPER TRAIL TO MOUNT GREYLOCK SUMMIT

Arguably the most scenic route to the summit of the state's highest peak, and among those requiring the greatest elevation gain, Hopper Trail leads from Haley Farm through lush woodland to a campground on Sperry Road, the Appalachian Trail (AT), the state's only true boreal forest, and the summit. The descent on Overlook Trail and Money Brook Trail adds variety.

FEATURES

Location Williamstown and Adams, MA

Rating Strenuous

Distance 9 miles round trip

Elevation Gain 2,390 feet

Estimated Time 5 to 6 hours

Maps AMC Massachusetts Trail Map 1; USGS Williamstown; Massachusetts Department of Conservation and Recreation map: mass.gov/doc/mount-greylock-trail-map/download

GPS Coordinates 42° 39.323' N, 73° 12.325' W

Contact Massachusetts Department of Conservation and Recreation, 413-499-4262, mass.gov/locations/mount-greylock-state-reservation

DIRECTIONS

From the Five Corners area of South Williamstown, where US 7, MA 43, Sloan Road, and Green River Road intersect, turn right onto Green River Road and follow it 2.3 miles to Hopper Road and Mount Hope Park on the right. Turn right, cross the Green River, and drive for 2.1 miles (bearing left at Potter Road) to a large gravel parking area on the right at Haley Farm.

TRAIL DESCRIPTION

At the trailhead, where a map is posted at the kiosk, enjoy a fine view of the Hopper, which is a cirque, or ravine, scoured by glaciers—so named because of its resemblance to a grain hopper. Begin by following the farm road past machinery, livestock, hayfields, and pastures of the functioning Haley Farm—a bucolic setting. The angular mound of Mount Prospect rises to your left. Pass a sign with park regulations and a brown metal barway. Stone walls and overarching sugar maples line the route, which is

TRIP 6 // HOPPER TRAIL TO MOUNT GREYLOCK SUMMIT

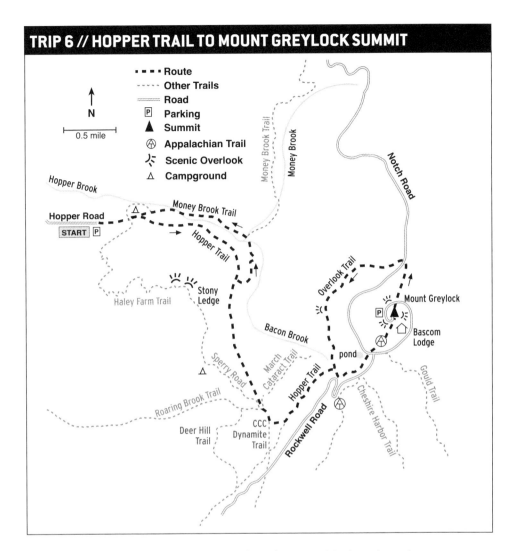

marked with blue blazes. When you reach Haley Farm Trail on the right, step out into the hay meadow for a fabulous vista of the Hopper, but then continue straight on Hopper Trail. A bit farther, Hopper Brook Loop Trail leads off to the left.

At a three-way intersection where Money Brook Trail branches left, bear right on Hopper Trail, which follows a narrow path up through prickly Japanese barberry, multiflora rose (which blooms in June), and honeysuckle shrubs—all invasive exotics characteristic of human disturbance. Before long, enter a maple and white birch woodland and traverse bog bridges across seepages. Hopper Brook is audible. If you're wearing shorts, give a wide berth to stinging nettles lining the path. A steeper climb over a rocky path begins soon after you enter the Hopper—a 1,600-acre National Natural Landmark.

After 1.0 mile on Hopper Trail, pass the intersection with a cutoff to signed Money Brook Trail on the left. You'll take this trail on your return, but for now continue uphill on Hopper Trail. Shiny schist with high mica content litters the route, which travels through sugar maple, white ash, and American beech woodland. Work your way up a grade that exceeds 25 degrees in places. Yellow birch, another northern hardwood forest indicator, becomes numerous. From late spring to midsummer, male black-throated blue warblers, black-throated green warblers, ovenbirds, American redstarts, red-eyed vireos, and hermit thrushes sound off to attract mates and announce their claims to nesting territories.

Pass sugar maples with an understory of sapling beech, striped maple, and hobblebush. Sharp-needled red spruce becomes dominant as you approach the campground on gravel Sperry Road (elevation 2,400 feet), 2.4 miles from the trailhead. The road was named for William H. Sperry, the longest-serving Greylock Reservation commissioner (1900–1938). Turn left to follow Hopper Trail along Sperry Road, and pass another gravel road on the right that leads to both Roaring Brook Trail and Deer Hill Trail and Shelter. (On the north side of Sperry Road, March Cataract Trail offers an optional out-and-back side trip to scenic March Cataract Falls). An interpretive sign relates the history of the Civilian Conservation Corps (CCC), which at its zenith employed workers throughout the United States, including 100,000 men in 68 Massachusetts camps. Based here from 1933 to 1942, crews of 200 men rotated every six months. The region continues to benefit from their fine work.

Continue past two gushing high-gradient streams—the first bounces over schist steps. About 100 yards past the campground entrance, turn left to continue on Hopper Trail. Native stone steps lead up through mixed woods of beech, birch, and spruce to a T intersection with an old carriage road—Deer Hill Trail. Turn left to remain on Hopper Trail, which continues on a gentle grade, past the source of a spring below. Striped maple and hobblebush, with paired, heart-shaped leaves, are abundant. Black-throated blue warblers construct cup nests among the hobblebush's pliable branches. Cross a few small flowages and maneuver over bedrock outcroppings that are often slick underfoot. The evocative aroma of balsam may soon be apparent.

In some spots, the layered bedrock serves as a handy staircase.

At 0.7 mile from Sperry Road (3.2 miles overall), turn sharply right at the junction with Overlook Trail and continue uphill on Hopper Trail, which becomes rocky. Follow the path left when it nears paved Rockwell Road. Turn left to follow the signed path to the Appalachian Trail (AT). The narrow treadway climbs into the balsam fir zone—part of the circumspect boreal forest in Massachusetts. Here, at 3,000 feet above sea level, blackpoll warblers breed among the stunted yellow birches and firs. These small, black-capped, black-and-white birds are abundant in the vast boreal forests of Canada but are virtually unseen in the United States outside upper Greylock in Massachusetts. Their sibilant, vibrating notes are insect-like.

At the intersection with the white-blazed AT, continue straight ahead on the AT, following a line of bog bridges to a serene pond that once supplied drinking water to Bascom Lodge. On clear days, the 200-foot radio tower with a 70-foot TV antenna is visible across the pond—the summit is but a few hundred vertical feet away. The AT follows the shoreline briefly, leads up over a staircase ledge, and reaches Rockwell Road

A landmark of Mount Greylock's summit since the 1930s, rustic Bascom Lodge provides meals and accommodations for hikers and travelers.

near its junction with Notch Road (leading to North Adams and MA 2) and Summit Road. (The three roads collectively form the Mount Greylock Scenic Byway.)

Follow the AT left for about 100 feet past the intersection and then turn left and make a final ascent on the AT through low-stature beech, yellow birch, mountain ash, and young balsam. The soil is thin at this elevation, and the growing season is short. Some trees show signs of stress, both from the harsh climate and from acidic deposition. Cloud droplets contain an elevated level of atmospheric pollutants, sulfuric acid among them. Although the terrain is mostly exposed bedrock, *Clintonia* manages to thrive in pockets of soil. Its yellow flowers transform into dark blue berries that are the source of its other moniker—blue-bead lily.

Finally, step out onto pavement near the summit garage and radio tower, 4.1 miles from the trailhead. (*Note*: In winter, chunks of windblown ice from the structure can be hazardous to anyone below.) Rustic Bascom Lodge, constructed mostly by the CCC in the 1930s and named for John Bascom, an original member of the Greylock Commission, stands a short distance to the right. The lodge offers restroom facilities, meals, and accommodations. A water spigot at the back of the building is for hikers' use when the lodge is open (see More Information). Walk straight ahead, cross the access road, and continue on the AT through clumps of firs to the Massachusetts Veterans War Memorial Tower, erected in 1932. A bronze relief model of the Greylock Range invites examination just after you cross the roadway again at the entrance to the summit parking area. Ahead, the 93-foot granite tower may be ascended via a spiral staircase. From a paved path on the other side of the tower, enjoy excellent views north, east, and south, including the bare summit of Mount Monadnock in New Hampshire. Porcelain plaques interpret key landmarks. In summer, listen for the signature plaintive whistle of the white-throated sparrow—*Old-Sam-Peabody-Peabody-Peabody*—at these heights.

From the summit, retrace your steps and bear right, around the end of the radio tower, to blue-blazed 1.6-mile Overlook Trail. Descend under the dense shade of low spruce and fir. Listen for Swainson's thrushes and golden-crowned kinglets in early summer. The trail becomes rutted and passes shrubby mountain maples before crossing paved Notch Road; it then leads easily down past gnarled and diseased beech trees. Many mature yellow birches hug the trail, which is also lined by the hobblebush that covers the slope. Listen for the melodious, flutelike calls of hermit thrushes in spring and summer. At a wide spot in the trail, a spur leads right 80 feet to a view west to the Hoosic Valley and the Taconics beyond, and north to nearby Mount Prospect and ridgelines in Vermont. Back on mostly level Overlook Trail, tread bog bridges until you hear the sound of flowing water.

Cross narrow Hopper Brook above March Cataract Falls and ascend fairly steeply for a short distance to the familiar junction with Hopper Trail. Turn right and retrace your steps through the campground and down Hopper Trail 0.9 mile back to the connecting path to Money Brook Trail (which you passed on your ascent) on the right. Turn right onto the connecting path and amble downhill under a canopy of sugar maple and ash. Sharp-lobed *Hepatica* (one of the earliest bloomers in April), red trillium, baneberry, jack-in-the-pulpit, mitrewort, and foamflower make this a fine wildflower trail in spring. Maidenhair fern adds to its charms in summer. Red oaks appear as you descend toward rushing Bacon Brook; the path turns left at a flat spot under hemlocks. Pass large oaks and descend to Bacon Brook after crossing a shallow feeder stream on stones.

Bear left, walk 90 feet, and turn right to cross a wooden bridge over Bacon Brook. Bear left again on a short, level section and then cross another wooden span. At the T intersection on the far side, turn left onto Money Brook Trail, following energetic Money Brook and blue blazes downstream to the confluence with Bacon Brook; the merged streams then flow west together as Hopper Brook. An old cellar hole on the left is all that remains of a former farmstead. Red-flowering raspberry thrives in a seepage area and blooms in late June. The lower segment of Money Brook Trail, which follows an old woods road adjacent to Hopper Brook, winds downhill easily over stones—a pleasing finale to this mountain excursion.

The erosive force of flowing water is evident where Hopper Brook has cut deeply into the bank. Cross a wooden bridge over the brook and then walk through a couple of small, grassy clearings. Reenter woods and ascend gradually to the intersection with Hopper Trail, which enters from the left. Retrace your steps past Haley Farm to return to your vehicle.

DID YOU KNOW?

A small population of Bicknell's thrushes once bred on Mount Greylock, wintering on the Caribbean island of Hispaniola. Never exceeding two dozen, they had dwindled to only a handful by the 1960s. The last one was spotted in 1972. Degradation of their wintering habitat, climate change, and a catastrophic storm may have played a role in their disappearance from Greylock.

MORE INFORMATION

Open dawn to dusk, year-round. Access for hikers is free. A parking fee ($5 Massachusetts residents, $10 out of state) is charged at the summit from May to October. The Massachusetts Veterans War Memorial Tower is open daily from Memorial Day to Columbus Day/Indigenous Peoples' Day; contact the visitor center for other dates. Bascom Lodge is open Wednesday to Sunday from late May to late October as of 2024 (see bascomlodge.net for more information). Skiing and leashed dogs are allowed. Mountain bikes are not allowed on the AT, but are allowed on other trails. Hunting is prohibited from May 20 to Columbus Day/Indigenous Peoples' Day and is always prohibited within War Memorial Park. The visitor center, at 30 Rockwell Road in Lanesborough, is open 9:00 A.M. to 4:00 P.M. daily (closed Thanksgiving and Christmas).

NEARBY

The Williamstown Historical Museum, in the South Center School building at 32 New Ashford Road in Williamstown, offers an interesting glimpse into local history. The museum, founded in 1941, is open Friday and Saturday, 10 A.M. to 2 P.M., and by appointment. Admission is free (413-458-2160, williamstownhistoricalmuseum.org).

OLD-GROWTH CHAMPIONS

Robert Leverett, an amiable, soft-spoken native North Carolinian, is a recognized authority on old-growth forests in Massachusetts. Leverett has, more than once, bushwhacked up and down just about every rugged hillside that could possibly hide ancient trees. To be sure, almost all old-growth stands exist on steep, virtually inaccessible slopes that defy logging. Finding them has been a career-long challenge and a labor of love for Leverett, who has served as the executive director and cofounder of the Eastern Native Tree Society and the president and cofounder of Friends of Mohawk Trail State Forest; many of the state's oldest and largest trees reside in this forest.

In Massachusetts, approximately 2,700 acres of old-growth forest remain out of a statewide forested expanse of 3 million acres. The two largest stands are only 200 acres each, and most are far smaller. To be considered old growth, a stand must cover at least 5 acres and hold at least eight trees per acre that are a minimum of 150 years old. One would think this is not a high threshold to meet, but in Massachusetts, which was 75 percent deforested by the mid-1800s, meeting even those standards is not an easy proposition.

The largest Berkshire old-growth forest is in the Hopper, a federally designated 1,600-acre National Natural Landmark on the western flanks of the Greylock Range. Those 115 acres and another 60 in Mount Greylock State Reservation still hold 200-year-old red spruce. Six parcels totaling almost 100 acres remain in southwestern Berkshire County, in Mount Washington State Forest, and in Mount Everett State Reservation, including Bash Bish Falls (Trip 43), Mount Race (see Trip 44), Mount Everett (Trip 45), Alander Mountain (Trip 46), and Sages Ravine and Bear Mountain (Trip 49). Additionally, several stands of 20 acres or more exist in Monroe State Forest, including groves on Dunbar Brook (Trip 12). Mohawk Trail State Forest (see Trip 13), the western portion of which lies in Berkshire County, is home to the greatest concentration of old-growth forest in Massachusetts, as well as giant second-growth pines.

But old-growth forest is much more than aged trees sporting eye-popping statistics. Old growth is a climax forest type; by definition, that means it is self-perpetuating. For that to occur, the mature trees must regenerate, or the entire stand would eventually succumb to old age. Trees have natural life spans; for example, the eastern hemlock can live about 600 years and the red spruce about 400. In addition to trees of every age class, old-growth forests host a myriad of other species. Nothing can compare with standing in the dim light beneath 150-foot-high old-growth giants and listening to the ascending flutelike notes of a Swainson's thrush.

7 STONY LEDGE VIA HALEY FARM TRAIL

This short but fairly steep hike in Mount Greylock State Reservation leads to one of the most scenic panoramas in the entire commonwealth. The return is by way of one of the reservation's most popular trails along the southern slope of the bowl-shaped Hopper.

FEATURES

Location Williamstown, MA

Rating Moderate to Strenuous

Distance 5.1-mile loop

Elevation Gain 1,460 feet

Estimated Time 2.5 to 3 hours

Maps AMC Massachusetts Trail Map 1; USGS Williamstown; Massachusetts Department of Conservation and Recreation map: mass.gov/doc/mount-greylock-trail-map/download

GPS Coordinates 42° 39.323′ N, 73° 12.325′ W

Contact Massachusetts Department of Conservation and Recreation, 413-499-4262, mass.gov/locations/mount-greylock-state-reservation

DIRECTIONS
From the Five Corners area of South Williamstown, where US 7, MA 43, Sloan Road, and Green River Road intersect, turn right onto Green River Road and follow it 2.3 miles to Hopper Road and Mount Hope Park on the right. Turn right, cross the Green River, and drive for 2.1 miles (bearing left at Potter Road) to a large gravel parking area on the right at Haley Farm.

TRAIL DESCRIPTION
Walk past the Haley Farm barn and a gate bordered on both sides by hayfields and go around a state forest gate. Continue along an old cobbled lane under a canopy of sugar maples for a couple hundred yards to the signed Haley Farm Trail intersection, which offers a fine easterly view to the Hopper. Turn right and follow blue-blazed Haley Farm Trail through a hayfield and up into the forest. The path, initially level as it passes through the shade of maple, birch, and white ash, steepens before bearing left on the first of a series of four major switchbacks that take you up the slope. As you ascend, the terrain becomes steeper and rougher.

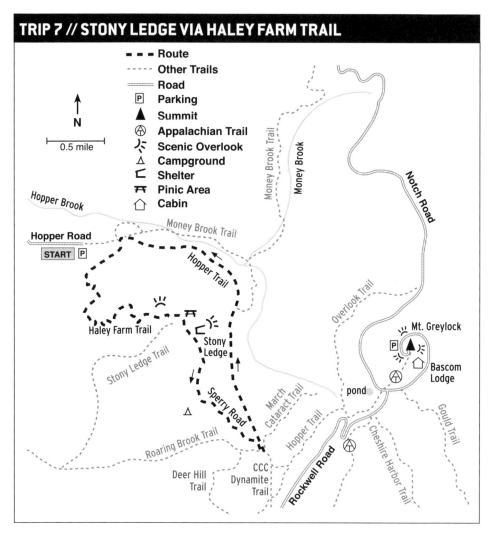

The first of numerous patches of maidenhair fern graces the verge after a right turn. Proceed on quite an incline; diagonal trenches (water bars) shunt water off the treadway. Under sugar maples—characteristic of rich woods—a profusion of ferns flourish, including spinulose wood, Christmas, glade, and maidenhair. Climb a series of stone steps at the steepest section to arrive at a small saddle; turn left and continue the ascent. Younger forest here is a clue to past logging, as are the rotting stumps you'll encounter farther on. Oak and American beech now join the deciduous woodland mix, and a few hemlocks make an appearance amid rockier ground. Oaks predominate as the grade eases, but gone are the lush ferneries in this drier environment. Instead, wild sarsaparilla and prince's pine enliven the forest floor. Pass through a small cleft in a low ledge and enter northern hardwoods again—sugar maple and yellow birch, joined by hop hornbeam, a small understory tree. At the end of a narrow gap, turn right and continue ascending over rocks and a network of surface roots. Easy switchbacks lead through woodland with abundant undergrowth to a fine viewpoint on the left at approximately

1.4 miles; enjoy the vista of farm fields and the buildings of Williams College, all against the backdrop of southern Vermont's verdant ridges. The Dome, a rounded quartzite peak that serves as a local landmark, is clearly visible at the Vermont state line. Note the deep green patch of conifers ringing its summit.

Continue on a relatively easy grade up through dense fern growth. Note the outcropping on the right, cushioned by a thick mat of yellow-green sphagnum moss. Just beyond, the first short red spruces appear. The path levels out under deciduous trees and arrives at a signed T intersection with Stony Ledge Trail, a former ski trail built by the Civilian Conservation Corps in the 1930s. Turn left onto this trail and proceed up a steep section toward Stony Ledge Shelter and Stony Ledge. The wooden lean-to group shelter stands on the left just before you emerge from the shade of the forest at a brown metal bear box into an open area with a picnic site at Stony Ledge (elevation 2,560 feet) at 2.1 miles, where a spectacular panorama of the Greylock Range and the Hopper awaits. From left to right, Mounts Prospect, Williams, Fitch, Greylock, and a portion of Saddle Ball Mountain are all visible. From a nearby bench or picnic table, you can hear the distant roar of March Cataract Falls and Money Brook some 1,000 feet below.

To continue, follow gravel Sperry Road for about 1 mile on an easy downhill jaunt from the picnic area to Sperry Road Campground under spruces and native hardwoods. Numerous ephemeral wildflowers, including Canada violets, color the road's edge in mid to late spring. Pass two composting toilets opposite a wooden picnic shelter just before reaching Hopper Trail, your return route, at a signed intersection at approximately 3 miles. Turn left onto Hopper Trail and begin a descent of

Stony Ledge, once called Bald Mountain, offers arguably the most spectacular vista in Massachusetts.

approximately 2 miles to the Haley Farm trailhead. The level, blue-blazed path initially leads through young spruce growth and mostly deciduous woods, with an abundance of hobblebush, common in cool, moist forests. In late summer, this plant's paired, palm-sized, heart-shaped leaves morph from green to maroon, and its coral-red berry clusters ripen to blue-black. The grade increases as you drop down along the southern flank of the Hopper, and the sound of flowing water is much more evident than it was from Stony Ledge. Many wildflowers, including red and painted trilliums and white violets, bloom in the ravine's rich soils in late May.

The angle of descent becomes more acute and rockier. Eastern hemlocks are more numerous on this north-facing slope, which, in turn, lowers the temperature. After leaf fall, a fine view through the trees on the east side of the Hopper is possible as the sound of rushing water gains volume. Shortly after the descent eases, pass the intersection with Money Brook Trail on the right. Remain on Hopper Trail as it leads under a canopy dominated by sugar maple, with some white ash (now threatened by the emerald ash borer). Copses of stinging nettle and yellow jewelweed alternately impinge on the path; avoid contact with the nettle.

The route crosses a few intermittent drainages, levels out, and soon traverses a series of bog bridges. After the last set, invasive Japanese barberry—a sign of human disturbance—makes an unwelcome appearance. Walk through a small clearing and reach the cobbled roadway that leads back to Haley Farm. Turn left, walk past the junction with Haley Farm Trail at the end of the loop at 4.9 miles, and retrace your steps to the trailhead.

DID YOU KNOW?

The Haley and Greene families sold their farmland to the commonwealth in 1990, protecting the access and approach to the scenic and biologically significant Hopper. The Massachusetts Department of Conservation and Recreation and Williamstown Rural Lands together created Haley Farm Trail as a shorter route to Stony Ledge in 1997.

MORE INFORMATION

Open dawn to dusk, year-round. Access is free. Mountain bikes, skiing, and leashed dogs are permitted. Hunting is not allowed from May 20 to Columbus Day/Indigenous Peoples' Day. The visitor center, at 30 Rockwell Road in Lanesborough, is open 9:00 A.M. to 4:00 P.M. daily (closed Thanksgiving and Christmas).

NEARBY

Mount Hope Park in Williamstown—at the intersection of Green River Road and Hopper Road (see trip directions on page 39)—is a scenic and pleasant place to have a picnic after your hike or to do some fishing (Massachusetts fishing license required). The high-gradient and coldwater Green River is a trout stream that tumbles and gushes over rocks as it flows through the small, well-kept park.

8 MOUNT GREYLOCK AND RAGGED MOUNTAIN VIA BELLOWS PIPE TRAIL

Spring wildflowers grace the mixed woodlands along this historic route followed by Henry David Thoreau in 1844. A side path leads to Ragged Mountain and a magnificent view of Mount Greylock's east face.

FEATURES

Location North Adams and Adams, MA

Rating Strenuous

Distance 8.6 miles round trip

Elevation Gain 2,140 feet

Estimated Time 5 hours

Maps AMC Massachusetts Trail Map 1: D5; USGS Williamstown; Massachusetts Department of Conservation and Recreation map: mass.gov/doc/mount-greylock-trail-map/download

GPS Coordinates 42° 40.404′ N, 73° 08.325′ W

Contact Massachusetts Department of Conservation and Recreation, 413-499-4262, mass.gov/locations/mount-greylock-state-reservation

DIRECTIONS

From MA 8 (State Street) and MA 2 in downtown North Adams, follow MA 2 (West Main Street) west 1.1 miles and turn left onto Notch Road at the brown-and-white Mount Greylock State Reservation sign. Follow Notch Road for 1.2 miles to where it turns sharply left near Mount Williams Reservoir. After turning left, proceed straight ahead to the Mount Greylock State Reservation parking area on the right, approximately 100 yards from the trailhead.

TRAIL DESCRIPTION

From the parking area, walk back down Notch Road and turn right at a trail sign onto blue-blazed Bellows Pipe Trail, which leads south along an old gravel road under an inviting canopy of sugar maples. This initial portion of the route passes through the North Adams watershed. Planted Norway spruces, impressive red oaks, and white ashes border the raised path that likely follows a road built by pioneering farmer Jeremiah Wilbur in the late 1700s. Notch Reservoir is visible down to your left. The gravel road soon crosses a feeder stream confined to a culvert. In all, about twenty water crossings (some merely a trickle) exist in the first 2 miles, but none pose a problem for hikers. Wildflowers, such as wild ginger, foamflower, false Solomon's seal, and jack-in-the-pulpit, grace the verge here.

Three mills once operated along Notch Brook, down to the left. Old trees now border the roadway's left flank. Iconoclastic naturalist and transcendental thinker Henry David Thoreau tramped this route toward the summit just days after his 37th birthday. Of it he wrote, "My route lay up a long and spacious valley called the Bellows, because the winds rush up or down it with violence in storms, sloping up to the very clouds between the principal range and a lower mountain." That lower mountain is Ragged Mountain. Trees now hem in Thoreau's "spacious valley." In his day, the landscape was virtually devoid of trees, and the half-pipe shape of the Bellows would have been much more discernible.

The path steepens and becomes rockier, leading past small ravines carved by feeder streams; in spring, some sections of the trail may be wet. Also during spring, the lacy leaves and heart-shaped white flowers of squirrel corn are common. (Squirrel corn is the natural version of bleeding heart, a cultivated plant.) False Solomon's seal is also numerous among the ashes, maples, and birches. As you continue your ascent, trees of a typical northern hardwood forest soon appear—American beech and yellow birch, with striped maple in the understory. Wildflowers grow lush in these rich woods, blooming in spring—among them are mitrewort, named for the traditional bishop's headdress; *Clintonia* (blue-bead lily); and wild sarsaparilla. Trout lily (also called adder's tongue because of its tongue-shaped leaves) blankets the steep slopes. Solomon's seal, rose twisted stalk, cucumber root, violets of various hues, and Canada mayflower delight the eye as well. You may notice that wildflowers that have begun to set seed in the valley, such as red trillium, are in full bloom at higher elevations. You're literally following spring up the mountain.

The path soon becomes narrower and more eroded. The trail splits briefly immediately after you cross a flowing brook and turns sharply left (avoid an eroded path here). A mill once stood at the head of the brook. (Watch out for the stinging nettle that borders the route.)

The trees are of shorter stature here due to the harsher growing conditions and less fertile soils. Stay left where the trail temporary splits again. Spring beauty, with five delicate, pink-veined, whitish petals, blooms in profusion here. As the slope moderates, young deciduous growth is common, along with planted spruces and red pines. After a brief, steep climb, reach the 0.4-mile side path to Ragged Mountain South Peak on the left at 2.2 miles, just before the remnant of a stone wall. (*Note*: Pay close attention here; this intersection can be easily missed.) Turn left to follow a narrow woodland path under Norway spruces. The undulating route reaches a stone wall that once bordered sheep pasture and turns left to parallel it for a short stretch. Bear left and commence climbing quite steeply through semi-open birch, beech, and maple woods.

Reach a schist ledge on the right, perhaps 15 to 20 feet high. Stunted trees, mountain ash, and azalea convey the effects of elevation. At the upper end of the ledge, watch for the sharp right turn that takes you up the steep and rocky trail via switchbacks—it's easy to miss. Shiny fragments of schist dot the treadway. After a second sharp right, an attention-getting view of Mount Greylock's east face presents itself—especially after

TRIP 8 // MOUNT GREYLOCK AND RAGGED MOUNTAIN VIA BELLOWS PIPE TRAIL

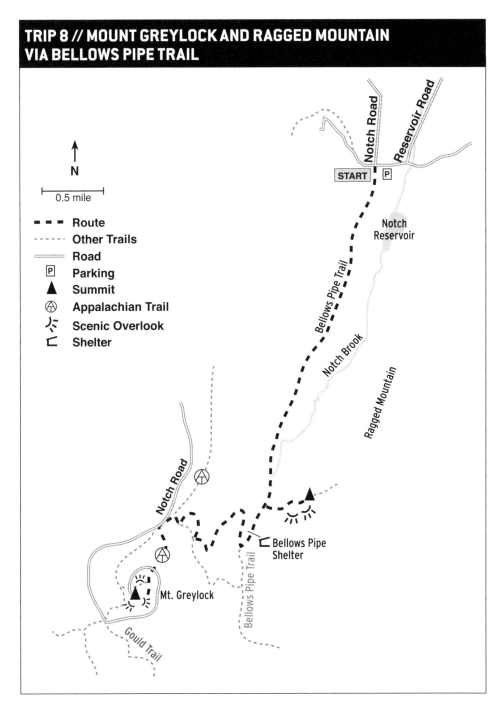

leaf fall. Notice the flaky brown rock tripes (lichens) attached to the outcropping a bit farther on the right. Watch for a side path on the right that leads 40 feet to an open ledge fringed with lowbush blueberry, where a truly stunning vista of the Greylock Range awaits. Ahead lies the Hoosic River valley.

From the vista, retrace your steps along the out-and-back path back to blue-blazed Bellows Pipe Trail and turn left on the mostly level old road. Jewelweed carpets the forest floor in late spring. Yellow birch with brassy and peeling bark dominates, along with sugar maple and gray birch. Reach a signed intersection and turn right to continue on the upper portion of Bellows Pipe Trail, ascending moderately on a rockier path. From here, it is approximately 1 mile to the Appalachian Trail (AT) and 1.5 miles to the summit. Pass Bellows Pipe Shelter on the right. In spring, watch for native small white butterflies—West Virginia white and mustard white. The trail alternately rises and levels out and then becomes steeper. In May, white-blooming hobblebush brightens this slope.

Among the stunted gray beeches and rocky outcroppings, the golden stars and glossy leaves of trout lilies glorify the hillside in spring, along with abundant spring beauties and red trilliums. At the three-way intersection with the AT (4.2 miles overall, including the side trip to Ragged Mountain), bear left (southbound) on the white-blazed AT. To the left is a shed with first-aid supplies for Thunderbolt Trail skiers. You'll soon arrive at intersections with Thunderbolt Trail (the pioneering downhill ski trail) on the left and a short trail leading to Notch Road on the right, but continue straight ahead and ever uphill on the AT. The treadway is firm, and the sweet, spicy aroma of balsam fir permeates the mountain air. The plaintive *Old-Sam-Peabody-Peabody-Peabody* tune of white-throated sparrows is emblematic of this bit of boreal forest. Yellow-rumped

The scar produced by the 1990 landslide on Greylock's eastern face seems relatively close at hand from a perch on Ragged Mountain.

warblers and dark-eyed juncos (sparrows that are slate-gray above and snowy white below) also breed at these heights.

The beacon on the top of the Massachusetts Veterans War Memorial Tower comes into view ahead, appearing as a huge crystal sphere. Stone steps lead up to Summit Road. Cross the road and climb the last angular section over a ledge to the restored Thunderbolt Shelter on the right. Follow the paved path to skirt the summit parking area and find yourself among 15- to 20-foot-tall pyramidal balsams before arriving at the granite tower on the commonwealth's highest summit at 3,491 feet. The memorial tower is at the center of a web of summit paths leading to various lookout points that offer views northeast to New Hampshire's Mount Monadnock and many other points 60 miles or more distant. Water, restrooms, meals, and trail merchandise are available at nearby Bascom Lodge, constructed by the Civilian Conservation Corps (CCC) in the 1930s.

When you're ready to return, walk back to Thunderbolt Shelter and the AT to begin the 3.9-mile descent to the trailhead along the same route. Enjoy the lofty view of Ragged Mountain after you cross Summit Road.

DID YOU KNOW?

The Thunderbolt Ski Trail, built in 1934 by the CCC, was one of America's premier expert downhill ski runs. Its 2,175-foot vertical drop served as the site of numerous sanctioned races until the mid-1950s. A proposed ski area was never built, and the trail gradually became overgrown. A few years ago, a group of Thunderbolt aficionados restored the trail and reinstated an annual ski race. The Thunderbolt Ski Runners now maintain the route and offer an annual hike and ski race on Thunderbolt (thunderboltski.com).

MORE INFORMATION

Open dawn to dusk, year-round. Access is free. The Massachusetts Veterans War Memorial Tower is open daily from Memorial Day to Columbus Day/Indigenous Peoples' Day; contact the visitor center for other dates. Skiing and leashed dogs are allowed. Mountain bikes are not allowed on the AT, but are allowed on other trails. Hunting is prohibited from May 20 to Columbus Day/Indigenous Peoples' Day and is always prohibited within War Memorial Park. Bascom Lodge is open Wednesday to Sunday from late May to late October as of 2024 (see bascomlodge.net for details). The visitor center, at 30 Rockwell Road in Lanesborough, is open 9:00 A.M. to 4:00 P.M. daily (closed Thanksgiving and Christmas).

NEARBY

The Massachusetts Museum of Contemporary Art (MASS MoCA), housed in a sprawling nineteenth-century mill complex on 13 acres, is one of the world's premier centers for making and showing modern art. With an annual attendance of 120,000, it ranks among the most visited institutions in the United States dedicated to cutting-edge art. MASS MoCA is at 1040 MASS MoCA Way, North Adams, MA 01247 (413-662-2111, massmoca.org). See the museum's website for information about fees and visiting.

PINECONE JOHNNIES

As you hike Berkshire trails, take a moment to appreciate the efforts of the Civilian Conservation Corps (CCC), which built or improved many of the region's recreational facilities. The CCC is one of President Franklin Delano Roosevelt's enduring legacies. Created during the Great Depression, a time of national economic calamity, the CCC provided meaningful employment for thousands of young men. They built roads; countless trails, ponds, and dams; various park facilities; and even such noteworthy structures as Bascom Lodge atop Mount Greylock (constructed between 1933 and 1937). Much of their handiwork is still serviceable today. Certainly our public lands had never before seen such an infusion of labor directed at creating and improving recreational facilities nor have they seen it since.

At the height of the CCC's involvement in Massachusetts, approximately 100,000 men worked in camps statewide. Of these camps, fourteen operated in the Berkshires. Monuments to the CCC's work are everywhere, which is especially amazing because it has been more than 75 years since the workers left the woods. At Sperry Road Campground in Mount Greylock State Reservation and at the Benedict Pond dam in Beartown State Forest, wayside exhibits relate some of the fascinating history made by the recruits. We owe these "Pinecone Johnnies," as they were known, a debt of gratitude.

In his gripping book *Berkshire Forests Shade the Past* (Attic Revivals Press, 2007), local historian Bernard A. Drew relates the tale of two CCC companies that operated in Beartown State Forest on one site from June 1937 until October 1941. According to Drew, each camp was assigned some 200 men, most in their early 20s and all hailing from Massachusetts. Fort Devens, northeast of Worcester, served as their boot camp. The U.S. Army was responsible for the operation of the camps, while the U.S. Forest Service was charged with overseeing the work. Local men were hired as foremen. At Beartown, the workers' accomplishments included building and fortifying roads, adding approximately 6 miles of trails, and constructing two dams—one of which expanded the size of Benedict Pond to 35 acres. In fact, the Beartown companies were among the most active in all of New England.

9 HOOSAC RANGE TRAIL TO SPRUCE HILL

A largely out-and-back hike on a portion of the fabled Mohican–Mohawk Recreational Trail follows the spine of the Hoosac Range to a stunning vista atop Spruce Hill. This is a longer but less traveled option to Spruce Hill than via Busby Trail (Trip 10).

FEATURES

Location North Adams, MA
Rating Moderate
Distance 5.4 miles round trip
Elevation Gain 540 feet
Estimated Time 2.5 to 3.5 hours
Maps USGS North Adams; Berkshire Natural Resources Council map: bnrc.org/fileadmin/files/Maps/BNRC_Hoosac_Range_2023_FINAL.pdf
GPS Coordinates 42° 41.789′ N, 73° 03.886′ W
Contact Berkshire Natural Resources Council, 413-499-0596, bnrc.org/reserves/hoosac-range
Savoy Mountain State Forest, 413-663-8469, mass.gov/locations/savoy-mountain-state-forest

DIRECTIONS
From the intersection of MA 8 and MA 2 (Mohawk Trail) in downtown North Adams, follow MA 2 east uphill past the "Hairpin Turn" for 4.7 miles to a gravel parking area on the right (0.9 mile beyond the Hairpin Turn).

TRAIL DESCRIPTION
From a kiosk with a posted trail map, begin on the northern end of Hoosac Range Trail, marked by red-on-white blazes, at an elevation of more than 2,000 feet. Walk up into the fern-rich forest of northern and southern hardwoods—American beech, red maple, birch, and oak. Hobblebush (viburnum) thrives in the understory along the mostly level trail, and oaks soon become abundant. It's an interesting mix of forest types: northern hardwoods versus oaks with southern affinities. Goldthread, lowbush blueberry, and other northern forbs (herbaceous flowering plants) grace the forest floor. Notice also the small spruces; oddly, they are the only ones along the entire route.

TRIP 9 // HOOSAC RANGE TRAIL TO SPRUCE HILL

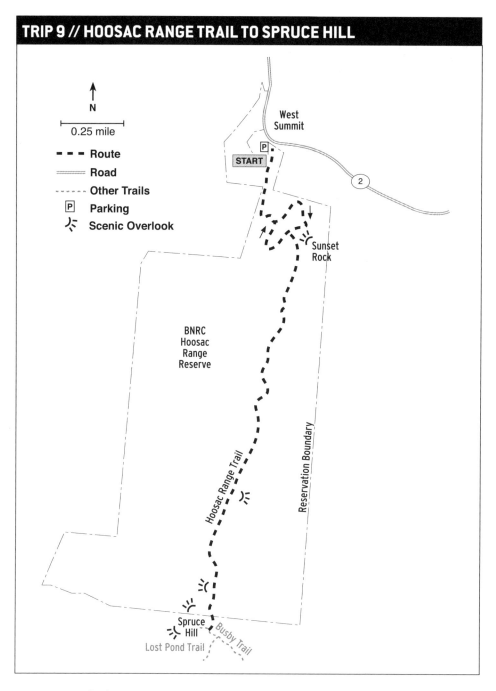

Begin a gradual ascent on a treadway with a few protruding quartzite rocks. Virtually all the beech trees (many appear young) show signs of disease—a fungus has disfigured their normally smooth, gray trunks. Beneath the trees, 4-inch-tall, bottle-brush-like stalks of shining club moss form soft mats. This trail is well constructed, as evidenced by the stone steps that lead to the first switchback. At a signed intersection where the

Just before reaching the Spruce Hill summit, hikers enjoy an expansive vista westward beyond the Hoosic River valley to the Greylock Range.

trail splits to form a loop to the Sunset Rock outlook, stay straight for the most direct route to the view. You'll return via the other fork later; both are 0.3 mile.

Yellow birch joins the beech and red maple. The path is littered with chunks of glistening, mica-rich schist. As you near the ridgetop, the trees become shorter. Hedge bindweeds (with white and pink morning glory–like flowers in summer) and raspberry canes blanket the forest floor under breaks in the canopy. In shady spots, some tree trunks are cushioned with mosses. More stone steps and easy switchbacks bring you to Sunset Rock (elevation 2,253 feet) and a nearly 180-degree view—from west to northeast—of the Hoosic River valley, downtown North Adams, and the rolling hills beyond at 0.8 mile. A wooden bench, dedicated to Tad Ames (former Berkshire Natural Resources Council president), offers a suitable place for a snack. When you're ready, continue about 100 feet to a signed intersection at the loop's upper end and follow the left branch of Hoosac Range Trail to head toward Spruce Hill, 1.9 miles away. (For a 1.6-mile round trip, turn right to return to the trailhead.)

Amble up through woodland marked by open patches nearly smothered in hedge bindweeds and raspberries. Through gaps in the foliage, catch a glimpse of wind turbines along a ridgeline to the left. Ascend the modest slope under more hardwoods, including black cherry, with beech sprouts forming a fairly dense understory. Parasitic flowering plants called beechdrops draw nourishment from beech roots and produce inconspicuous, orchid-like purple-brown blossoms in early fall. For nearly the rest of the route, the path undulates, using stone steps, through a low-stature forest with occasional canopy breaks. A notable old yellow birch—hollow at the base—fronts a moss-adorned ledge more than 100 feet long that walls in the treadway. In midspring, enjoy profuse blooms of trout lilies, spring beauties, and other wildflowers.

Bear left away from the ledge; you'll encounter more yellow birches later on. These trees are adept at gaining a foothold, and mosses cushion the hard stone, helping them along. In fact, another one is on the left here, flecked with the leafy lichens known as rock tripe.

A short wooden span leads over an intermittent brook, the only one along this ridgeline route. The walking is easy as you stroll past expansive patches of shining club moss and hobblebush. The paired, heart-shaped leaves of hobblebush turn shades of maroon in late summer, and its berry clusters turn from red to blue-black. Reach a signed intersection with a 250-foot side path to a viewpoint on the left. The landscape of rolling hills to the east is worth a look. Return to the main trail and continue past more ledge outcroppings.

Emerge into a narrow, linear clearing—a power-line cut. You are standing directly above the Hoosac Tunnel, the 4.75-mile railroad tunnel bored through the heart of the range in the late nineteenth century, a quarter-mile beneath your feet! The tunnel opened a crucial rail line to markets in New York and beyond, but nearly 200 people died during its construction. Reenter forest, walk past more ledge outcroppings, and pass an unmarked trail on the left. Arrive at a short path on the right leading to an expansive vista—bordered by blueberries and hay-scented fern and rimmed with mountain ash—across bedrock westward over the valley to the Greylock Range. Mountain ash glows with coral-red berry clusters in late summer. Return to the main trail and turn right to hike the last 0.2 mile to Spruce Hill.

After walking through two more small clearings and past more ledges, arrive at a point where a couple of well-worn paths on the right lead steeply up over bedrock to the summit; take the wider second path. From here, the route (now Busby Trail in Savoy Mountain State Forest) is blazed blue. Look back for a view of two sets of wind turbines on a ridgeline several miles away. Bear left to follow a narrow path a short way to the open summit of Spruce Hill, marked by two U.S. Geological Survey benchmarks, at 2.7 miles. Atop this cliff, enjoy a variety of scenic perspectives in virtually all directions—especially south and west—but be sure to watch your footing as you maneuver for that perfect photo. The southern Green Mountains of Vermont are visible to the north, and the Mount Greylock range rises high above the valley to the west. The quarry at the foot of Mount Greylock is distinguished by its brilliant white color. Spruce Hill is one of the region's finest places to view migratory raptors, especially in autumn. When you're ready, scramble down the short, steep bedrock and retrace your steps along the ridge to the T junction near Sunset Rock at approximately 4.6 miles. Turn left for a slight variation (both routes are 0.3 mile) back to the start of the loop. Descend to the lower junction and turn left to return to the parking area.

DID YOU KNOW?
The Hoosac Range is a southward extension of Vermont's Green Mountains. *Hoosac* (also spelled Hoosic, Hoosick, and Hoosuck) is an Algonkin word that means "place of stones."

MORE INFORMATION
Hoosac Range Trail is open during daylight hours and is free of charge. The route traverses portions of a 989-acre reserve owned and managed by Berkshire Natural Resources Council (BNRC) and 11,118-acre Savoy Mountain State Forest. Mountain bikes, skiing, and dogs are allowed. Motorized vehicles, fires, camping, littering, and cutting or removing plant material are prohibited. Open to hunting in season.

NEARBY
Savoy Mountain State Forest offers camping (mid-May through mid-October) and many miles of recreational trails. From the BNRC trailhead, follow MA 2 east less than 0.5 mile and turn right onto Central Shaft Road. Travel 2.8 miles to the park headquarters, 3.3 miles to the North Pond day-use area, and 3.7 miles to the campground.

The famous Hairpin Turn on the Mohawk Trail Highway (MA 2), renowned for sweeping views of the Taconic Mountains and Hoosic Valley, is approximately 1 mile west of the BNRC trailhead.

10 SPRUCE HILL VIA BUSBY TRAIL

This trip offers perhaps the best views after a short hike in the entire region. An old road leads past an early-nineteenth-century cellar hole to a rocky perch with stunning vistas of the eastern face of the Greylock Range and the Taconic Range beyond, as well as points north and south.

FEATURES

Location Florida and North Adams, MA
Rating Moderate
Distance 2.6 miles round trip
Elevation Gain 670 feet
Estimated Time 1.5 to 2 hours
Maps USGS North Adams; Massachusetts Department of Conservation and Recreation map: mass.gov/doc/savoy-mountain-state-forest-trail-map/download
GPS Coordinates 42° 39.477' N, 73° 03.351' W
Contact Savoy Mountain State Forest, 413-663-8469, mass.gov/locations/savoy-mountain-state-forest

DIRECTIONS
From the intersection of MA 8, MA 2, and MA 8A in downtown North Adams, follow MA 2 (Mohawk Trail) east for approximately 5.1 miles (via the Hairpin Turn). Turn right onto Central Shaft Road just after the Florida town line and continue 2.1 miles to a fork. Bear right to stay on Central Shaft Road and drive an additional 1.0 mile (passing the Savoy Mountain State Forest headquarters on the right) to a roadside parking area at the Busby Trail trailhead on the right.

TRAIL DESCRIPTION
From the kiosk, where trail maps may be available, walk up into a forest of birch, maple, and beech, with a few red spruce. After about 150 feet, reach blue-blazed Busby Trail, which follows a dirt woods road that may bear evidence of off-road vehicle use in spite of these vehicles being prohibited. Turn right onto the level path bordered and shaded by sugar and striped maples, white and gray birches, and hobblebush shrubs. Cross a power-line clearing filled with raspberry canes, gray birches, and red maple saplings. Chestnut-sided warblers whistle their *pleased, pleased, pleased to meetcha* breeding refrain and nest in shrubs here from May through July.

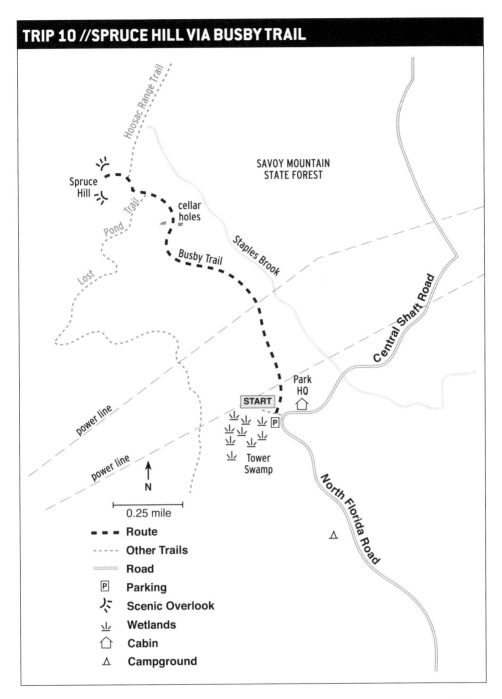

Back in the forest, Busby Trail bypasses the rutted and often wet road to the left for a couple hundred yards and continues through a northern hardwood forest of birch, beech, maple, and hemlock. Patches of the Massachusetts state flower, trailing arbutus (more commonly known as mayflower), grace both sides at one point, their pale pink blossoms emerging for a short time in early May. More common are the little paired leaves of partridgeberry and the heart-shaped leaves and tiny white blossoms of Canada mayflower. Soon the road rises a bit and becomes drier and more pleasant.

Traverse another power-line cut, filled with arrowwood (note the straight branches), bilberry, raspberry, and birch, at 0.4 mile. The cut—devoid of mature trees—reveals the lay of the land as it dips and then rises to a ridgeline on the right. Ignore a short side path that branches off Busby Trail from the right a bit farther along and begin a gradual ascent. So far, you've expended little effort.

During the 1930s, the renowned Civilian Conservation Corps planted groves of Norway spruce here and at many other locations. These trees provide habitat for birds and mammals that prefer conifer stands, such as black, white, and fiery-orange Blackburnian warblers; impish red squirrels feast on bird eggs, spruce seeds, and fungi. Spruce Hill itself has virtually no spruces, and nearly all that you encounter along the trail have been planted.

Listen for the sound of flowing water to your right and soon gaze upon a small brook. The stone remnants of former bridge abutments are visible along the far bank, as is a stone wall. White ash trees here are identifiable by their crosshatched bark; they do well in moister ground. In fact, other than the spruce plantations, deciduous trees predominate. The clean white trunks of paper birch here are most attractive. Continue an easy climb, bear right, and cross a narrow drainage (wet in spring). At one point, flowing water has eroded a gully, exposing rock and forming a modest falls during wet seasons. Watch your step.

A bit farther, tread up and over bedrock steps; the remains of an unmortared wall stand on your left. The old road becomes rockier before you arrive at a jumble of rectangular cut blocks of schist on the left at the site of a former foundation at 1.0 mile. A few feet farther and on the opposite side gapes a well-preserved cellar hole. A yellow birch threatens to cleave the stones of the right wall. (It's interesting to contemplate what farm life would have been like here some 200 years ago.)

Busby Trail now turns sharply left, where the shiny, pointed leaves of trout lily carpet the ground profusely in late spring, and begins to climb. The terrain becomes briefly sandy under a canopy of black cherry, ash, birch, and beech and sparkles with flecks of the mineral mica. Here is where you'll finally have to exert yourself. Cross a stone wall built of large schist blocks—moving them into place would have been no easy chore. A bench sits on the right. Continue straight up the slope. A luxuriant growth of skunk currant about 18 inches high fills the sunny forest floor where you turn left, and shining club moss forms a patch of green "bottle brushes" on the right.

The path winds up through attractive woodland. Listen for the *beer, beer, bee* songs of tiny black-throated blue warblers in late spring and early summer as you approach ledge outcroppings. These birds nest low among the wiry branches of hobblebush, which in spring are lovely with bunches of white flowers resembling doilies. At a junction where Lost Pond Trail (part of the long-distance Mohican-Mohawk Recreational Trail) branches left, follow Busby Trail right.

Pass through a swale, or gap between the rocks, and climb a steep but well-built stone staircase up the ledge. A bouquet of exquisite painted trillium—three petals, three leaves—clamors for attention partway up in May. Bear left and continue a more moderate climb under stunted beech trees into a wonderful spring wildflower garden. *Clintonia* (blue-bead lily), bunchberry (a tiny, ground-hugging dogwood), wild oat, and lowbush blueberry have turned this into a fairyland forest. The paired, heart-shaped leaves and flat, white flower clusters of hobblebush are abundant. The tiny, fertile flowers produce red berries, and in late summer and fall, the leaves turn lovely shades of maroon.

After a few short switchbacks, reach the junction with the southern end of Hoosac Range Trail (Trip 9), which leads 2.7 miles to MA 2. Turn left for one last ascent over a ledge outcropping and emerge into the open. Follow the blue blazes left over bedrock and through a hobblebush thicket for the best views from exposed, slanted schist bedrock at an elevation of 2,566 feet, 1.3 miles from the trailhead. What a fantastic vista from this perch on the Hoosac Range! The Greylock Range sprawls to the west, with Ragged Mountain lying below, and the Taconics loom beyond Greylock. North Adams lies in the Hoosac Valley to your right, with Pine Cobble poking up beyond. To the left is the town of Adams. At your feet, lowbush blueberry crowds the perimeter and shows bell-shaped, creamy white blossoms in spring, while a few wind-trimmed mountain ashes hold forth to the right.

Linger here and soak in all the stunning scenery. (The spectacular fall foliage is a great reason to visit in October.) When you're ready to leave, retrace your steps back to the parking area.

From vantages near Spruce Hill's summit, hikers enjoy vistas to Mount Greylock, the Hoosic River valley, and the southern Green Mountains of Vermont.

DID YOU KNOW?
From mid-September to early November, be on the lookout for southbound migrant hawks heading for wintering grounds in Central America. You are most likely to observe broad-winged hawks (sometimes in "kettles" of dozens of birds in September), sharp-shinned and Cooper's hawks, turkey vultures, and ospreys.

MORE INFORMATION
Open sunrise to sunset, year-round. Access is free. Leashed dogs, mountain bikes, and skiing are permitted; hunting is allowed in season. The state forest campground has 45 sites in an old orchard and 4 log cabins at South Pond. Motorized off-road vehicles and alcoholic beverages are prohibited.

NEARBY
Mass Audubon's West Mountain Wildlife Sanctuary, in Plainfield, near the boundary of Berkshire, Hampshire, and Franklin counties, protects 1,835 acres on the slopes of West Mountain. A 1.3-mile loop trail leads to a beaver pond, cascading streams, and northern hardwood and spruce-fir forests. The roadside entrance is on Prospect Street off MA 116, west of the town center (massaudubon.org/get-outdoors/wildlife-sanctuaries/west-mountain).

PATHWAY TO HISTORY: THE MOHICAN–MOHAWK RECREATIONAL TRAIL

For thousands of years, travelers have followed a route that links the Connecticut and Hudson rivers via the Deerfield, Cold, and Hoosic rivers, as well as the imposing Hoosac Range. American Indian tribes, Colonial armies, industrial traders, and well-known figures, including Benedict Arnold and Henry David Thoreau, all trod this highly scenic and historically significant route, which evolved over time to accommodate modern transportation. The Mohican–Mohawk Recreational Trail is now being developed as a long-distance trail along the corridor, connecting a wealth of natural and cultural features.

The region's American Indian tribes, including the Pocumtuck of the Pioneer Valley, the Mohawk of upstate New York, and the Mohican of New York and western Massachusetts, created and used the original trail for trade, hunting, fishing, and war. After the Mohawk defeated the Pocumtuck in a 1664 battle, the passage eventually became known as the "Mohawk Trail," a term coined in the twentieth century to market the region for tourism.

European settlers relocated and widened the narrow footpaths to facilitate travel by horses and wagons. After serving as a key military route during the French and Indian War and the American Revolution, the corridor became a vital commercial link between Massachusetts and New York during the nineteenth century.

The Mohawk Trail Highway, one of New England's iconic scenic roads, opened to automobiles in 1914. The region quickly became a popular tourist destination, thanks to the sweeping views from outlooks such as the fabled Hairpin Turn and Whitcomb Summit. The highway roughly parallels the original American Indian paths, but there is likely little actual overlap.

The Mohican–Mohawk Recreational Trail began to take shape in 1992, when Williams College students researched the historical route and opportunities to develop the trail. Thanks to the efforts of the Massachusetts Department of Conservation and Recreation, Berkshire Natural Resources Council, Deerfield River Watershed Association, and many other regional organizations, landowners, and volunteers, approximately 40 miles of the proposed 100-mile route are open, including 30 miles of foot trails and a 10-mile paddling segment on the Deerfield River.

Heading east from North Adams, the Mohican–Mohawk Recreational Trail follows a portion of a historical turnpike up to Western Summit and then continues on Hoosac Range Trail (Trip 9) along the ridge to Spruce Hill (Trip 10). After traversing several existing trails in Savoy Mountain State Forest, the route crosses steep-banked Cold River and MA 2 in Drury. On the north side of the valley, it joins the original American Indian footpath over Clark and Todd mountains (Trip 13), passing by and through old-growth forest, groves of 150-foot white pines, and meadows at the confluence of the Cold and Deerfield rivers.

East of the Hoosac Range, the Deerfield River offers a scenic paddling route from Charlemont to Buckland. The foot trail resumes near Shelburne Falls, paralleling the river through portions of South River State Forest to a historical truss bridge at Bardwell's Ferry (a short section on private land was closed as of this writing). The trail's eastern end follows the abandoned New Haven and Northampton Railroad grade past the stone remains of a giant railroad trestle at the South River crossing, now spanned by a fiberglass hikers' bridge. Three side paths loop along the Deerfield River's wooded banks, offering opportunities to see barred owls and other wildlife. From the Hoosac Road trailhead in Deerfield, lightly traveled country roads lead to the official eastern terminus at Historic Deerfield, an outdoor museum that features twelve well-preserved antique houses in an eighteenth-century village.

Future plans include developing the route's western segments from North Adams and Williamstown to the Hudson River. For more information and updates, visit mass.gov/location-details/mohican-mohawk-trail.

11 TANNERY FALLS AND PARKER BROOK FALLS

The twin cascades of Tannery Falls and Parker Brook Falls share the same enchanting ravine in Savoy Mountain State Forest. Several trails and roads loop to Balance Rock and hemlock-lined Ross Brook, upstream from the falls.

FEATURES

Location Savoy, MA
Rating Easy to Moderate
Distance 0.6-mile round trip (waterfalls), 4.5-mile loop (circuit)
Elevation Gain 200 feet (waterfalls), 615 feet (circuit)
Estimated Time 30 minutes (waterfalls), 2.5 hours (circuit)
Maps USGS Windsor, USGS North Adams; Massachusetts Department of Conservation and Recreation map: mass.gov/doc/savoy-mountain-state-forest-trail-map/download
GPS Coordinates 42 37.328′ N, 73 00.304′ W
Contact Savoy Mountain State Forest, 413-663-8469, mass.gov/locations/savoy-mountain-state-forest

DIRECTIONS

From the junction of MA 2 and Black Brook Road in Savoy (1.7 miles west of the Florida town line), follow Black Brook Road uphill for 2.6 miles, bearing right at a fork after 1.3 miles. Turn right and follow dirt Tannery Road for 0.2 mile to the state forest boundary and then continue downhill 0.5 mile to the parking area on the right, opposite Tannery Pond. Tannery Road is unmaintained in winter beyond the last residence. (*Note*: It is possible to reach the trailhead from the Savoy Mountain State Forest main entrance on Central Shaft Road, but the dirt roads are often rutted and potentially difficult for low-clearance vehicles.)

TRAIL DESCRIPTION

This hike combines the popular out-and-back walk to Tannery Falls and Parker Brook Falls with a 4.5-mile circuit on Tannery Trail, Tannery Road, and Ross Brook Trail. To reach the falls, start from the back of the parking area and follow the unnamed blue-blazed trail north into the woods between Parker Brook (Tannery Pond's outflow) and Ross Brook. Eastern hemlock, a fire-intolerant species, thrives in wetlands and sheltered

TRIP 11 // TANNERY FALLS AND PARKER BROOK FALLS

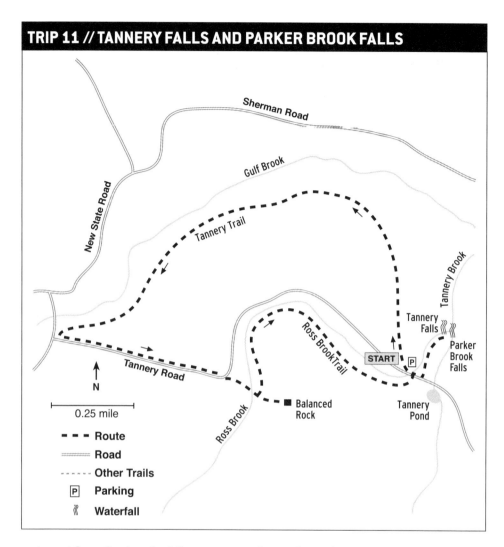

ravines. After a few hundred feet, continue along a fence above Ross Brook, which cascades through a narrow gorge scoured through the bedrock.

At 0.2 mile, the trail bends right, opposite the crest of Tannery Falls (also known as Ross Brook Falls). Wood and rock steps provide a steep but safe passage to the bottom of the ravine. At the base of the descent, Parker Brook Falls is on your right. Distinctive, jagged mossy walls line the 60-foot cascade in a gorge of angular bedrock, with several smaller drops along its base.

Tannery Falls is a quick 100-foot walk from the steps. Pass water gliding over smooth rock at the top of the falls on the left before reaching a dead-on view of the 80-foot waterfall at the trail's end. Roughly dividing the two main drops is a small, shelflike pool. Ross Brook and Parker Brook merge at the base of the falls, forming Tannery Brook, which empties into Cold River about a mile downstream. All these waterways are part of the Deerfield River watershed. (*Note*: Swimming and rock climbing are prohibited at the waterfalls.) The steep slope below the falls shelters a 120-acre grove of old-growth hemlock, spruce, sugar maple, and birch. In May, look for a patch of flowering hobblebush, Canada mayflower, and painted trillium on the bedrock between the two waterfalls. After enjoying the views and the sound of the rushing water, retrace your steps to the parking area.

Now that you've seen the falls, begin hiking the loop on the north side of Tannery Pond, which was originally created in the nineteenth century by damming Parker Brook. As the place and trail names suggest, this was once the site of a tannery, where animal hides were converted to leather. Workers immersed the skins in tannic acid to add durability and color. Eastern hemlock was the primary source of tannin in the Northeast, and many of the region's hemlock groves were harvested for use at tanneries in the mid-nineteenth century, when the industry peaked. Civilian Conservation Corps workers rebuilt the dam during the 1930s as part of improvements to the property (the Bog Pond and Burnett Pond dams were also upgraded). A beaver dam and lodge are visible near the pond outlet on the left.

Walk right (when facing the pond) on Tannery Road and cross the bridge over Ross Brook. Turn right onto Tannery Trail, a multiuse trail on an old woods road, marked with periodic orange triangle blazes. Portions of the path may be seasonally wet or muddy (partly due to erosion by off-road vehicles), but the edges are usually passable. After briefly paralleling Tannery Road, the trail bends north through northern hardwoods interspersed with hemlocks and a few white pines, a forest community characteristic of high elevations, such as the Hoosac Range. In autumn, the birches, maples, and beeches display colorful foliage. In spite of the remote location and rocky terrain, these woods were mostly cleared for agriculture in Colonial times. Savoy Mountain State Forest was originally formed by purchases of abandoned farmland in the early twentieth century.

Hobblebush, a common shrub of northern hardwood forests, thrives in the cool, moist environment. The white flowers bloom in May, and the broad leaves offer colorful, sometimes multihued, maroon foliage in autumn. Abundant trout lilies, with narrow, mottled leaves and yellow flowers, line the trail edges in midspring.

Arrive at a shady hemlock grove that indicates a wet area. Note the lack of understory vegetation compared with broadleaf forests. Cross a seasonal stream draining into wetlands on the right. Chestnut-sided warblers frequent the shrubby growths here in spring and summer.

Continue an easy walk on Tannery Trail along the slope high above Gulf Brook, which cascades through a deep valley out of view to the right. A few yellow violets bloom along sunlit trail openings in May and June. Wooded ravines are an ideal habitat for winter wrens, easily identified by their distinctive long, melodious, warbling call. Dark-eyed juncos, which favor mountain settings, are familiar year-round residents. During spring and summer listen for the loud and frequent *teacher-teacher-teacher* call of ovenbirds, which build nests on the ground in mixed broadleaf forests.

The trail narrows in a seasonal wet area, where flexible water bars have been installed to mitigate erosion. Sadly, the ash trees, identified by crosshatched bark, are threatened by the emerald ash borer, which arrived in the northern Berkshires in 2018. Enter another hemlock grove, where intermittent brooks drain the steep slope. Red trilliums

The picturesque cascades of Tannery Falls (shown) and Parker Brook Falls share the same ravine in Savoy Mountain State Forest.

bloom along the embankments in April and May. Juvenile red-spotted newts (or red efts) roam the forest floor before returning to ponds and streams as mature adults.

At 2.3 miles, reach Tannery Trail's western end at the junction with Tannery Road, adjacent to New State Road on the right. Turn sharply left onto Tannery Road, heading uphill along the north side of 2,177-foot Lewis Hill, one of seven prominent Hoosac Range summits within the state forest. Look for more red trilliums along the road edges in midspring.

Reach an interpretive sign at a large forest management area, where trees were cut to promote age diversity, slow the spread of diseases, and create wildlife habitat. Mixed-aged forests enhance resilience to storms, forest pests, and other disturbances. Moose, white-tailed deer, black bears, and other wildlife often feed on regenerating vegetation at harvest sites, while prairie warblers and common yellowthroats nest in young growth. Thanks to its expansive size and remote location, Savoy Mountain State Forest is an ideal habitat for large mammals, including a healthy bear population.

Continue through the timber harvest, past the junction with Lewis Hill Trail on the right. After 0.7 mile on Tannery Road, reach an unmarked but obvious intersection at the edge of the clearing. Turn right (leaving Tannery Road, which bends left at the junction) and descend a woods road to Ross Brook, about 1.4 miles upstream from Tannery Falls. False hellebore, with photogenic green leaves, unfurls along the banks in midspring. Step across the brook and ascend past the unmarked junction with Ross Brook Trail (your return route) on the left. In another 150 feet, reach the intersection with Balance Rock Trail, marked by a sign on the right. Turn left and make a quick 0.1-mile climb to Balanced Rock, 3.2 miles from the trailhead. Rock tripes (lichens) coat this large, angular glacial boulder, perched atop a ledge at an elevation of 1,890 feet.

Return to the junction with blue-blazed Ross Brook Trail and turn right (north) onto it to begin the final 1.1-mile segment, a pleasant descent along the hemlock-lined brook. The narrow footpath is open to hiking and skiing (although maps may show crossings, the trail stays entirely on the brook's southern banks until reaching a footbridge near the trailhead). Eroded portions of the channel are evidence of torrential flooding caused by storms, such as the remnants of Tropical Storm Irene in August 2011.

After about 0.3 mile, the trail briefly bends away from Ross Brook, descending the moderately steep ravine to a dense hobblebush growth. Wild oats (also known as sessile bellwort) display bell-shaped, creamy white or pale yellow flowers in mid to late spring. A few winterberries dot the forest floor. Return to the brook edge at a small cascade, and cross a low knoll where the path levels. Pass a large, old yellow birch and follow the blue markers along Ross Brook's winding banks.

Ross Brook Trail's lower segment leads through another rich wildflower area. Bluebead lilies, sometimes mistaken for much rarer yellow lady's slippers because of their similar elongated leaves and yellow flowers, thrive in cool, acidic woodlands. Look for, but don't eat, the lilies' rather foul-tasting (and mildly toxic) blue berries during summer. Cross a footbridge near Tannery Pond's northwestern corner and complete the circuit at Tannery Road and the parking area.

DID YOU KNOW?

Tropical Storm Irene's torrential rains caused several landslides on the Cold River valley's steep slopes in August 2011. A 6-mile segment of the Mohawk Trail Highway washed out, and Black Brook Road wasn't repaired until 2017.

MORE INFORMATION

Open sunrise to sunset, year-round. Access is free. Mountain biking, skiing, and leashed dogs are permitted; hunting is allowed in season. The state forest campground has 45 sites in an old orchard and 4 log cabins at South Pond. From the intersection of MA 2 and Central Shaft Road, follow Central Shaft Road 2.8 miles to the park headquarters, 3.3 miles to the North Pond day-use area, and 3.7 miles to the campground.

NEARBY

The 7,882-acre Kenneth Dubuque Memorial State Forest, part of a large conservation corridor in the Deerfield River watershed, offers 35 miles of trails. An easy loop around Hallockville Pond leads to an old mill site and dam, and the woods roads are ideal for skiing and mountain biking. The main entrance is on MA 8A (West Hawley Road) at Hallockville Pond (413-339-5504, mass.gov/locations/kenneth-dubuque-memorial-state-forest).

12 DUNBAR BROOK

Old-growth trees, massive boulders, and roaring waters make Dunbar Brook Trail a path of superlatives. A steep slope leads to gravel woodland roads that enable an interesting loop through wild uplands at the northeastern edge of the Berkshires.

FEATURES

Location Florida and Monroe, MA
Rating Moderate to Strenuous
Distance 6.8 miles round trip
Elevation Gain 1,010 feet
Estimated Time 4 hours
Maps USGS Rowe; Massachusetts Department of Conservation and Recreation map: mass.gov/doc/monroe-state-forest-trail-map/download
GPS Coordinates 42° 42.275′ N, 72° 57.161′ W
Contact Monroe State Forest, 413-339-5504, mass.gov/locations/monroe-state-forest

DIRECTIONS
From the intersection of MA 2 and MA 8 (opposite Massachusetts Museum of Contemporary Art) in North Adams, follow MA 2 east past the Hairpin Turn, Western Summit, and Whitcomb Summit to the intersection with Whitcomb Hill Road on the left at 7.5 miles. Follow Whitcomb Hill Road (staying right at the intersection with Monroe Road) for 2.5 miles to the junction with River Road. Turn left onto River Road, proceed to the railroad crossing at the Hoosac Tunnel, and continue another 4.0 miles to a gravel parking area (day use only) on the left, across from the Dunbar Brook Picnic Area.

TRAIL DESCRIPTION
Hiking options at Dunbar Brook include an out-and-back walk on Dunbar Brook Trail or a longer circuit as described here. Foot trails are marked with blue blazes that may be intermittent in places. From the parking area, where a map and recreation rules are posted, follow the rough track up the inclined power-line corridor for about 150 feet. Bear right and follow Dunbar Brook Trail into shady hemlock woods. Do not follow the wooden staircase down to the small concrete dam that spans the brook.

TRIP 12 // DUNBAR BROOK

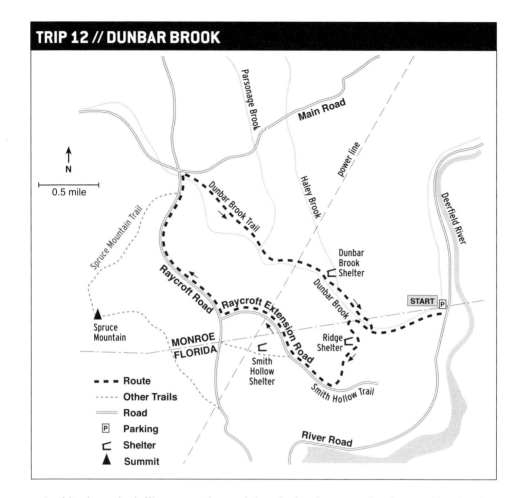

Amble along the hill's contour beneath hemlocks along a rocky slope. Yellow birches rise from the gneiss boulders they firmly grasp. As you descend, the sound of Dunbar Brook, an evocative tributary of the nearby Deerfield River, captures your attention as it cascades over rocks. The brook and forest have a wild, untamed appearance. You'll be struck by the sheer size of some of the boulders in the streambed.

A bordering outcropping drips moisture from its mossy sphagnum coat. More large boulders protrude from the slope; others, rounded by flowing water, litter the brook. Yellow birches soon become more numerous. Along the path, foamflowers, with leaves that resemble those of geraniums, send up frothy white heads of modest blossoms in late spring. Hobblebush also grows here, with paired, heart-shaped leaves and white blossoms earlier in spring.

Bear left and climb rock steps, gradually moving higher above the brook and into a mixed forest. A towering white ash, with crosshatched bark, stands like a sentinel on the right. Big-tooth aspen, red maple, and beech join the deciduous mix along the banks of Dunbar Brook. Yellow violet, red trillium, baneberry, jack-in-the-pulpit, starflower, and wild ginger are among the woodland wildflowers you may spot in spring.

At 0.8 mile, reach the start of the loop at an intersection where stone steps lead down to the brook bank. Turn left onto Smith Hollow Trail to ascend the steep slope (Dunbar Brook Trail, the return route, continues to the right, following a recently constructed plastic bridge over Dunbar Brook). The path undulates, slants up the steep incline, and finally bears right toward the height-of-land. Nearly two-thirds of the hike's total elevation gain occurs here. Some impressive trees dot the slope—sugar maples, yellow birches, and white ashes that escaped the ax thanks to the slope's acute angle.

Bear left just before reaching Ridge Shelter on the right. A privy is 100 yards farther along this old woods road on the right. Blazes are a bit spotty here, but the path is easy to locate on this somewhat-level stretch. A pond on the left, transitioning to a bog, has been virtually filled in with fallen leaves and branches. At 1.5 miles, follow Smith Hollow Trail right on gravel Raycroft Extension Road (a snowmobile corridor in winter). Although technically a road, it is more of a wide, nearly level path through pleasant deciduous woodland that now includes oak and American beech. The voices of neotropical songbirds, such as the scarlet tanager, American redstart, ovenbird, red-eyed vireo, and rose-breasted grosbeak, are audible in late spring and early summer.

White birch—one of the most attractive of the northern trees—abounds along the road, and red spruce soon becomes common at this elevation. In late spring and early summer, listen carefully for the ascending flutelike song of Swainson's thrush, a species found in Massachusetts only at high elevation. At an intersection where Smith Hollow Trail branches left down to Smith Hollow Shelter, continue on Raycroft Extension Road through mixed woods dotted with big gneiss boulders, and a power-line right of way. Back in the forest, plantations of Norway spruce and red pine were established in the 1930s. The 6-inch-long cones of this exotic spruce litter the ground. Some trees have been harvested, allowing deciduous growth—cherry, birch, and raspberry—to fill the sunny void. Canada mayflower and *Clintonia* (blue-bead lily) both bloom in spring along the roadway.

Arrive at a T intersection with unsigned gravel Raycroft Road at 2.6 miles and turn right onto this route—open to motor vehicles seasonally (ATVs are prohibited at Monroe State Forest, but illegal use may occur, especially on summer weekends). Sugar maples and light green hay-scented ferns line the mostly level road; gneiss boulders protrude from the forest floor. The road begins an easy descent and then becomes rougher. Large, platy-barked yellow birches bear little resemblance to youthful, brassy-skinned individuals of the same species. Two brooks flow through culverts under the roadway. Cabin-sized boulders—one characteristically serving as an anchor for a yellow birch on the left—are astonishing. After a short rise, continue the descent, sometimes steeper and in the dense shade of hemlocks, and follow the road as it bends right. On the left, pass the northern end of Spruce Mountain Trail, which leads up to the wooded summit of Spruce Mountain.

As you continue downward on Raycroft Road, the sound of flowing water becomes apparent. More monumental boulders appear—one with a sheer face toward the road. Reach a flat pullout area on the right adjacent to Dunbar Brook and soon cross a modular wooden bridge over the brook at 4.0 miles, near Main Road (where trailhead parking is available). Immediately after the crossing, turn right to rejoin Dunbar

Brook Trail and enter a mixed forest of hemlock, beech, and yellow birch. The roaring, cascading water gushes through tight squeezes between and over rocks, creating an evocative scene. (*Caution*: Be careful if you move closer for a better view, as the rocks are slippery and the current unforgiving!) Note how eons of flow have abraded and sculpted the bedrock. Between here and the parking area, the brook drops some 700 vertical feet.

Look for the stone ruins of a millrace on the left, where diverted water once turned a mill wheel. Pass a feeder stream's rocky tumble where foot-tall American yew bushes (a favorite of deer) thrive. Their needles resemble those of hemlock but are longer and a lighter shade of green. Climb up under a canopy of large hemlocks and northern hardwoods away from Dunbar Brook on a needle-cushioned path. Bear right when you reach a narrow woods road that traverses mature woodland dotted with more boulders. One on the right where the path narrows further is the size of a cottage. Little undergrowth exists except where big trees have fallen to admit light. Look for the cloverlike leaves of wood sorrel. In June, its five-petaled, pink-veined blossoms resemble those of spring beauty.

Now temporarily out of sight of the brook, the trail climbs under hemlocks, undulates, and then follows the grade downward, sometimes with moderate steepness. Glimpse Spruce Mountain through a screen of trees to your right. Watch for the large pink slippers of the moccasin flower in the acidic soil during early June. Red spruce is regenerating very well here, as evidenced by the abundant seedlings and small trees.

Dunbar Brook pours over gneiss boulders polished to a fine patina by the abrasive actions of the swift current.

No doubt the most imposing boulder along the route—verdant with moss and capped by polypody ferns—lies where the trail turns sharply right and skirts its overarching face. Other boulders are a veritable nursery for hemlocks and spruces. Tiny, orange-throated Blackburnian warblers sing their lisping refrains from high in the evergreens during the breeding season.

As you continue a steady and sometimes rather steep descent, the sound of rushing water becomes evident again. The trail levels out just above Dunbar Brook and bears left to parallel it. The rocky streambed, cascades, and crystalline pools beckon the photographer. Walk over level ground where red-backed salamanders hide under logs by day and search for tiny morsels by night, while red efts (juvenile red-spotted salamanders) wander blissfully in broad daylight. Watch for piles of moose droppings. After you cross a log bridge over Parsonage Brook, the delightful trail widens under a leafy canopy on the far bank and turns right. Watch for a boulder with a thick milky quartz intrusion on the right just before the power-line cut.

Raspberry, bush honeysuckle, meadowsweet, interrupted fern, birch, and red maple fill the linear light gap. Back in mixed woodland, you'll be awed by a pair of massive white pines—one twin-trunked—on the right. Tiny prince's pine, a club moss, and lots of ground-hugging partridgeberry, with coral-red berries, create a miniature woodland beneath.

Descend the slope toward Haley Brook, a tributary of Dunbar Brook that enters from the left, near a mammoth split white ash. Cucumber root (which has an edible tuber), false Solomon's seal, and red trillium thrive in the rich soil as you reach Dunbar Brook Shelter. Turn left and walk about 100 feet to cross a wooden bridge over Haley Brook (if the bridge is inaccessible, cross at a nearby shallow spot). Stone abutments indicate that a bridge of higher capacity once spanned the water. Continue to parallel Dunbar Brook's course.

Watch for an old millstone in Dunbar Brook just before you arrive at another pair of giant, straight-boled white pines, more than 100 feet tall. Not surprisingly, Monroe State Forest is known for its old-growth pines. Soon bear right to cross Dunbar Brook on the aforementioned plastic bridge. At the end of the loop, bear left on Dunbar Brook Trail to return to the parking area. Near the end, where the trail splits, be sure to follow the right fork uphill.

DID YOU KNOW?

Old-growth forest in Massachusetts is limited to approximately 2,700 acres statewide. To qualify as old growth, a forest must not have been significantly disturbed for at least the last 150 years. In Monroe State Forest, some 270 acres meet those criteria, including pockets of old-growth hemlock, white pine, red spruce, and associated hardwoods—yellow birch, American beech, and white ash.

MORE INFORMATION

Open sunrise to sunset year-round. Access is free. Skiing, mountain biking, leashed dogs, and hunting in season are allowed. Unpaved roads, including Raycroft Road and Raycroft Extension Road, are ideal for horseback riding. Portable toilets are available at Dunbar Brook Picnic Area across River Road. Privies are available at shelters along the route. Carry in, carry out rules apply to all trash. Snowmobiling is permitted when conditions allow; all-terrain vehicles are not permitted. Trailhead parking area and restroom facilities at Dunbar Brook Picnic Area are owned and managed by Great River Hydro (greatriverhydro.com), a hydropower producer.

NEARBY

The Hoosac Tunnel was an engineering marvel when it was completed in 1875. At 4.75 miles long, it remains the longest active transport tunnel east of the Rockies. It was built at considerable cost in dollars and human lives (193 people died during its construction, which began in 1848). The eastern portal in the town of Florida can be viewed from the railroad crossing on River Road 4.0 miles south of the Dunbar Brook trailhead. This freight line is still active—do not linger near the tunnel entrance or tracks!

13

MOHICAN–MOHAWK RECREATIONAL TRAIL: CLARK AND TODD MOUNTAINS

On a steep valley ridge above the fabled Mohawk Trail Highway corridor, this segment of the Mohican–Mohawk Recreational Trail follows a historical American Indian route that leads to diverse forests, mountain laurel, brooks, and a scenic lookout on Clark and Todd mountains.

FEATURES

Location Florida, Savoy, and Charlemont, MA
Rating Moderate to Strenuous
Distance 8.2 miles round trip
Elevation Gain 2,120 feet
Estimated Time 5.25 to 6.25 hours
Maps USGS Rowe; Massachusetts Department of Conservation and Recreation map: mass.gov/doc/mohican-mohawk-trail-map/download; Mohawk Trail State Forest map: mass.gov/doc/mohawk-trail-state-forest-trail-map/download
GPS Coordinates 42° 39.121′ N, 72° 59.809′ W
Contact Massachusetts Department of Conservation and Recreation, mass.gov/location-details/mohican-mohawk-trail
Mohawk Trail State Forest, 413-339-5504, mass.gov/locations/mohawk-trail-state-forest

DIRECTIONS

From the intersection of MA 2 (Mohawk Trail Highway) and MA 8A in Charlemont, drive west on MA 2 for 3.6 miles to the Mohawk Trail State Forest main entrance. Continue west on MA 2 for 4.5 miles to the intersection with South County Road (just after a large overhead highway sign) in Drury, a village in the town of Florida. Turn right onto South County Road and enter the parking area on the right. Limited roadside parking (not prominently marked) is available on the north side of MA 2 at the Mohican–Mohawk Recreational Trail crossing 0.1 mile south of the junction with South County Road.

TRAIL DESCRIPTION

This historically and ecologically significant segment of the Mohican–Mohawk Recreational Trail (also known as Mohican-Mohawk Trail; see "Pathway to History: The Mohican–Mohawk Recreational Trail" on page 59 for an overview) leads over the

TRIP 13 // MOHICAN–MOHAWK RECREATIONAL TRAIL: CLARK AND TODD MOUNTAINS

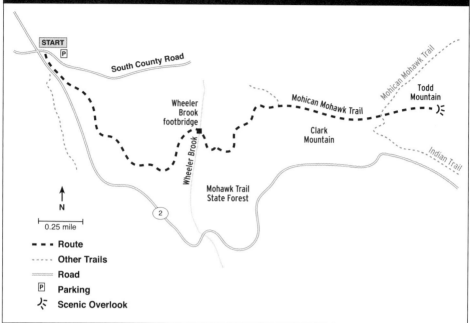

ridges of Clark and Todd mountains in the western portion of Mohawk Trail State Forest. An out-and-back hike is described here; to avoid backtracking, spot a vehicle at Mohawk Trail State Forest's main entrance.

At the South County Road trailhead (elevation 1,580 feet), a kiosk includes a map of Mohawk Trail State Forest. Begin by following a short connecting path on the north side of Manning Brook for roughly 700 feet to the intersection with Mohican–Mohawk Trail near MA 2. A trail sign marks distances: 1.8 miles to Wheeler Brook, 4.1 miles to the Mohawk Trail State Forest campground, and 6.5 miles to the state forest headquarters.

Follow Mohican–Mohawk Trail—marked with white paint blazes and green-and-yellow disks—east along an old woods road on a contour above MA 2. Groves of eastern hemlock initially shade the path. (Although hemlock woolly adelgid has killed many hemlocks in southern New England over the last 25 years, cool temperatures at high elevations, such as the Hoosac Range, impede this insect's spread.) Step across two small brooks and traverse well-placed rocks and a log bridge in a seasonally muddy area. Trout lilies, wildflowers distinguished by yellow petals and narrow leaves with brown mottled spots, emerge in late April. Cross another intermittent brook and continue an easy walk through upland hemlock-hardwood forest.

At the convergence of several brooks, two wooden footbridges lead over channels scoured by flowing water. Torrential rains, such as those associated with Tropical Storm Irene in 2011, have caused erosion and occasional landslides on the Hoosac Range's steep slopes. Follow white blazes through a mix of northern and southern tree species,

A crucial link in the original Mohawk Trail formerly traveled by American Indians, the ridge of Clark and Todd mountains features diverse forest communities.

including red spruces that thrive in high elevations, oaks that favor milder settings, and tall white pines. Songbirds such as American redstarts, scarlet tanagers, black-throated blue warblers, and winter wrens benefit from the extensive unfragmented woodlands. Off the trail to the right, a vernal pool provides breeding habitat in early spring for wood frogs and salamanders.

Ascend at an easy grade through more hemlocks. Mountain laurel shrubs, which display white or light pink flowers in June and early July, become increasingly abundant in the forest understory. Continue climbing through drier upland woods, where beech trees bear evidence of beech bark disease; dense laurel growths nearly obscure the narrow path. From late October through early May, when leaves are down, portions of the south side of the Cold River valley are visible through trees to the right. Bear left in a grove of beech trees and continue climbing at easy to moderate grades to hemlock woods, where the route steepens before reaching a high point of the ridge at approximately 1.3 miles.

Begin descending to the ravine of Wheeler Brook. Follow blazes carefully and watch for fallen trees in this section; trail crews have kept most of the route clear, but there may be recent blowdowns. Diminutive yellow violets emerge in late April and early May. White-tailed deer use hemlock forests as wintering areas, so during that season keep an eye out for their tracks and sign, such as body imprints in snow. Walk through an old spruce plantation littered with many fallen trees and woody debris. The downed logs and evergreen branches provide cover for snowshoe hares.

At the base of the descent, cross a footbridge over Wheeler Brook at 1.9 miles and ascend past tall old pines and dense mountain laurel on Clark Mountain's upper west slopes. After a short switchback, Mohican–Mohawk Trail levels out along the crest of the ridge and leads through more laurel and hardwoods (watch blazes carefully, as fallen leaves or snow may obscure the narrow path). Oaks and beeches, the last deciduous tree species that change color in autumn, display russet foliage from mid to late October. Ascend easily past hemlocks and pines and then bear right near the wooded 1,923-foot peak of Clark Mountain, with additional screened views, especially before trees leaf out. On mild days in early spring, look for butterflies such as diminutive spring azures and mourning cloaks, which emerge from hibernation to bask in sunlit forests.

The rugged ridges and ravines of Mohawk Trail State Forest protect more than 500 acres of old-growth forest, including approximately 200 acres on Clark and Todd mountains, as well as some of New England's tallest trees. Aged hemlocks and oaks on the ridge generally range between 170 and 300 years old; some hemlocks are more than 400 years old.

Bear left and descend the east side of Clark Mountain to a small hollow, staying to the left of a low rock ledge where the trail levels. Look for owl pellets, which often contain undigested feathers, teeth, or bones of prey, beneath roost trees. Amble through more evergreen hemlocks, pines, and laurels. Periodic blue markers delineate the trail, which becomes more prominent as it continues downhill at easy to moderate grades toward Todd Mountain. Pass screened glimpses of ridges to the north and south and a small rock slab with a partial southerly perspective across the Cold River valley. You may hear the distant sounds of trains coming from or heading toward the Hoosac Tunnel on the north side of the range. The rocky slopes and abundant laurels provide habitats for bobcats, which use dense thickets for cover, and eastern coyotes, which often leave droppings on rocks to mark their territories.

At 3.7 miles, reach a signed four-way intersection in the gap between Clark and Todd mountains. Here, Mohican–Mohawk Trail branches left down the north side of the ridge, and Indian Trail, on the right, leads to the Mohawk Trail State Forest campground on the banks of Cold River. From a sign for Indian Lookout, continue straight on an out-and-back spur to the top of 1,687-foot Todd Mountain, where the hike's best views await. At the trail's eastern end, roughly 0.4 mile from the intersection, enjoy scenic perspectives of the steep, wooded gorges of Cold River to the west and Deerfield River to the east.

Return to the intersection and retrace your steps on Mohican–Mohawk Trail. With the exception of moderately steep climbs back up Clark Mountain and Wheeler Brook's ravine, the return route traverses mostly easy terrain, with some minor ups and downs as you head west to the trailhead.

DID YOU KNOW?

Trail planners named Mohican–Mohawk Trail in honor of the Indigenous Mohican tribe that inhabited the region and the Mohawk who used the route to travel between the Hudson and Connecticut River valleys for trade and warfare.

MORE INFORMATION

Open year-round; access is free. Mountain bikes, skiing, and dogs are allowed. Hunting is permitted in season. No facilities exist along the hike route, but restrooms and a campground are available at Mohawk Trail State Forest's main entrance on MA 2 in Charlemont. The campground includes 53 wooded tent sites and 6 log cabins.

NEARBY

Whitcomb Summit, the highest elevation of the Mohawk Trail Highway at approximately 2,185 feet, is 2.9 miles west of the intersection with South County Road. A large bronze elk statue, erected in 1923, honors soldiers who lost their lives during World War I.

14 SADDLE BALL MOUNTAIN

Although it terminates short of the Mount Greylock summit, this challenging hike has its own delights: a flower-filled hillside meadow offering incredible views and a damp boreal forest atop Saddle Ball Mountain, where sphagnum moss carpets the ground.

FEATURES

Location Adams, Cheshire, New Ashford, and Williamstown, MA
Rating Strenuous
Distance 9.6 miles round trip
Elevation Gain 1,675 feet
Estimated Time 6 to 7 hours
Maps AMC Massachusetts Trail Map 1: D4; USGS Williamstown, USGS Cheshire; Massachusetts Department of Conservation and Recreation map: mass.gov/doc/mount-greylock-trail-map/download
GPS Coordinates 42° 36.635′ N, 73° 9.399′ W
Contact Massachusetts Department of Conservation and Recreation, 413-499-4262, mass.gov/locations/mount-greylock-state-reservation

DIRECTIONS

From the south: From Pittsfield at Allendale Center, drive north on MA 8 for 9.1 miles into Cheshire and turn left onto Fred Mason Road. Follow it north for 2.9 miles (it becomes West Road after approximately 1 mile) to West Mountain Road on the left. Turn left and follow West Mountain Road for 1.6 miles, past parking for Gould Trail, to the Cheshire Harbor trailhead.

From the north: Proceed south on MA 8 south to Adams and turn right onto Maple Street at the President William McKinley monument. Follow Maple Street for 0.9 mile and turn right onto West Mountain Road. Follow it for 1.6 miles to the trailhead.

TRAIL DESCRIPTION

This long loop over Saddle Ball Mountain combines several trails on Mount Greylock's southeastern slopes. All Mount Greylock State Reservation trails, except for the white-blazed Appalachian Trail, are blue-blazed. From the parking area (elevation 1,560 feet), follow the gravel roadway to your right (northwest) that leads into a meadow. When leaves are down, look for a view of Mount Greylock's summit at a gap in the treeline as

TRIP 14 // SADDLE BALL MOUNTAIN

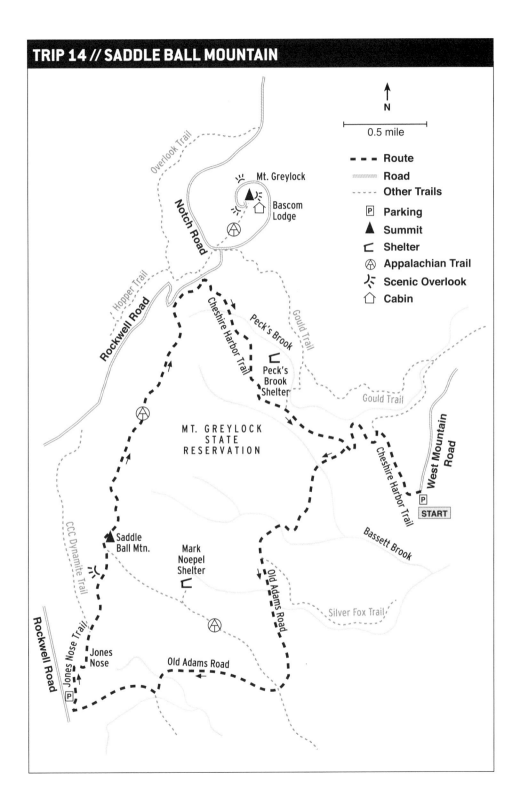

you pass a trail sign. Reach a map board at the woodland's edge. Just before a metal gate, at a sign for Cheshire Harbor Trail, take a short path to the start of blue-blazed Cheshire Harbor Trail, which follows a rocky roadbed past stone walls in a forest of sugar and red maples, black and gray birches, young red spruce, and hemlock. Green-trunked striped maple and American beech fill the understory. Hay-scented fern, New York fern, and spinulose wood fern border the road. Bits of rusty barbed wire embedded in trees hint that livestock grazed on what was once a grassy hill.

Parallel the slope's contour lines uphill; soon cross intermittent brook beds. Watch for old steel culverts held together with rivets—artifacts of a bygone age of engineering. As the route curves sharply left, it passes the junction with a blue-blazed path connecting to Gould Trail on the right. Several switchbacks lead up the slope to the first balsam firs. At 1.0 mile, reach the intersection with Old Adams Road, where the loop begins. Turn left onto this predominantly level route as it contours along the lower slopes of Saddle Ball Mountain, initially on gravel, then on an unimproved surface. These rich woods are fertile ground for wildflowers, including cucumber root, sessile-leafed bellwort, Canada mayflower, red trillium, and *Clintonia* (blue-bead lily).

Stream crossings are an enjoyable feature of this trail. In short order, the route crosses a wide wooden bridge over an unnamed tributary of Bassett Brook. The brook wends through a rocky ravine, producing small cascades en route. Mixed woodland has reclaimed these slopes. Hobblebush and spindly moosewood (striped maple) and beech saplings dominate the understory, while hay-scented ferns soften the road shoulders. Arcing through a deeply cut bank brings you to a hemlock ravine offering a glimpse of a chain of gushing cataracts on another Bassett Brook tributary. On the right, a small vernal pool hosts wood frogs and salamanders that play out age-old breeding rituals in early spring. Cross another wide vehicle bridge and relish a small cataract and horsetail falls a few feet upstream.

Enjoy the easy grade on wide Old Adams Road and soon pass the junction with Silver Fox Trail on the left. Remain on Old Adams Road. Trees with multiple trunks, as well as young regenerating trees, indicate former logging. A third water crossing, the final Bassett Brook feeder stream, lacks the drama of the previous two. Vehicles have gouged muddy swales in the road, which winds through forest dominated by beeches and other hardwoods.

Near the signed intersection with Red Gate Trail on the left, red spruces become more numerous—first 6- to 15-foot-tall trees, then mature ones with boles 2 feet across. Continue straight ahead to cross the Appalachian Trail (AT) at 2.8 miles. Remain on Old Adams Road and head easily downhill through mixed woods and past plush, green schist boulders. Note the remnants of a stone wall that once bounded a sheep pasture. After you pass a multitrunked yellow birch, the trail bends left, and the descent soon steepens on a rougher track. Cross a wooden bridge over the modest headwater of Kitchen Brook and arrive at a signed T intersection. Turn right to stay on Old Adams Road and head upward over thinly layered phyllite rock toward Jones Nose.

Here, the roadway is cut deeply into the earth, and the ascent soon becomes gradual. A few oaks, the first along this route, mingle with beeches, birches, maples, and spruces. Lush undergrowth characterizes this young, spacious forest, which soon gives way to a shrubby clearing of chokecherry, meadowsweet, steeplebush, raspberry, and birch. A grassy path runs through this early growth, where indigo buntings and common yellowthroats reside in summer. The trail splits where a snowmobile route bears left. After 3.2 miles on Old Adams Road (4.2 overall), walk around a metal gate and emerge into the open at the gravel parking lot for the Jones Nose Trail trailhead, along paved Rockwell Road.

Pick up Jones Nose Trail on the right before the kiosk, which has a map of Mount Greylock State Reservation. The blue-blazed route leads up a sharply sloping meadow, resplendent with blooming shrubs in midsummer. In late July and early August, fireweed, steeplebush, and meadowsweet all add splashes of pink to the angular hillside, which is said to resemble the profile of Seth Jones, who once farmed this area. Fireweed colonizes burned sites; its spikes of orchidlike flowers are candy for the eyes. Steeplebush (hardhack) is also well named because this shrub's tiny magenta blossoms form a spire. Meadowsweet, which is related to steeplebush, has frothy, pale pink flowers that attract both bees and beetles.

Chokecherry (with blood-red fruits), goldenrod, and yellow Saint-John's-wort enliven the slope. Scrumptious blueberries may be reason enough to make the climb in midsummer. As you tread the narrow, grassy path, glance over your shoulder to take in an expansive view to the south and west. The Taconic Range forms the border between Massachusetts and New York to the west. As the ascent becomes tougher, a switchback leads up over stone steps into sapling, mountain, and striped maples and over bedrock

A small ledge outcropping on Saddle Ball ridge offers panoramic views south to central Berkshire lakes, Lenox Mountain, and New York's distant Catskills.

outcroppings. A moist glade holds the odd white blossoms of turtlehead, whose leaves compose the diet of the Baltimore checkerspot butterfly caterpillar. The big, coarse fern with bronzy green fronds is Goldie's fern. Hobblebush is abundant here.

At a signed Y intersection with CCC Dynamite Trail, bear right on the upper portion of Jones Nose Trail to continue toward the AT, 0.5 mile distant. The climb increases as you near the summit of Saddle Ball. Hermit thrushes can be heard in summer. An outcropping on the right is a veritable rock garden of mosses, ferns, tree seedlings, and flowers. Reach a small bedrock clearing, bounded by spruce, mountain ash, and birch. A bit farther, an obvious side path on the left beckons you to a panoramic view: from the schist ledge, you can see the central Berkshire lakes, Lenox Mountain, and, on a clear day, the distant Catskills. Back on the main trail, bear right at the blue blaze for a detour. Watch your footing over rocks and roots under wet conditions. The fairly steep path grows serpentine and rocky, undulating as you enter the boreal zone of redolent balsam fir trees.

At the signed AT junction (5.2 miles), bear left on the white-blazed AT and follow it north for 1.9 miles, passing over the level, wooded Saddle Ball summit at 3,247 feet, which is marked with a rock cairn. The spongy ground forms a fertile seedbed for balsam fir. *Clintonia* (blue-bead lily) grows in abundance along the trail in mid to late spring; in midsummer, clusters of dark blue fruits top its flower stalks. Milky quartz pops up here and there. The trail alternately rises and falls, crossing a small brook, its flow stained the color of tea by tannins. The erect stems of shining club moss poke up in luxuriant patches. At this elevation, fog, cloud droplets, and rain produce conditions similar to those of a temperate rainforest. The result: boulders covered with mossy mats. Sphagnum moss, containing dead cells that hold moisture, carpets low areas. Ghost pipes, which rise from the mossy mats, lack chlorophyll and must obtain nourishment from other plants. Thin bog bridges lead through this cool, acidic wetlands section, past ground-hugging bunchberries adorned with clusters of scarlet berries.

Continue on the AT to an S curve on Rockwell Road—a reliable site for nesting blackpolls, warblers found in Massachusetts only on upper Greylock. Turn right on the AT and reenter woodland. This forest is predominately deciduous—featuring beech—and the trail alternates level spots with steep climbs and descents, soon arriving at the intersection with blue-blazed Cheshire Harbor Trail on the right at Rockwell Road. Trees now largely obscure a vista of Greylock's summit before the road crossing. At 7.1 miles, turn sharply right off the AT onto Cheshire Harbor Trail to loop back to the trailhead on this wide, cobbled path under a canopy of northern hardwoods. Begin a moderate-to-steep descent over a well-worn trail that is heavily traveled on good-weather weekends. Stay right at the split, and soon cross a wooden bridge over Peck's Brook.

Pass the signed intersection with Peck's Brook Loop Trail on the left approximately halfway down. Cheshire Harbor Trail levels out amid copious hobblebush and then descends in earnest. At the familiar intersection with Old Adams Road on the right, continue straight on Cheshire Harbor Trail, retracing your steps approximately 1 mile to the parking area at the end of West Mountain Road.

DID YOU KNOW?

Mount Greylock's massif was often historically known as Saddleback Mountain or Saddle Mountain, due to the shape of its profile when viewed from the south.

MORE INFORMATION

Open year-round. Access is free. Skiing and leashed dogs are allowed. Mountain bikes are prohibited on the AT, but are allowed on other trails. Hunting is not allowed from May 20 to Columbus Day/Indigenous Peoples' Day and is never permitted within War Memorial Park. The route has no toilet facilities. Carry in, carry out rules apply.

NEARBY

The Susan B. Anthony Birthplace Museum, at 67 East Road in Adams, celebrates the life of prominent nineteenth-century American civil rights leader Susan B. Anthony. Born at the site in 1820, Anthony was a social reformer, a pioneering feminist, and a suffragist. The museum is open year-round and has a small admission fee. From Memorial Day to Columbus Day/Indigenous Peoples' Day, the site's hours are 10 A.M. to 4 P.M. Thursday to Monday; from Columbus Day/Indigenous Peoples' Day to Memorial Day, the hours are 10 A.M. to 4 P.M. on Monday, Friday, and Saturday, and 11:30 A.M. to 4 P.M. on Sunday (413-743-7121 susanbanthonybirthplace.com).

15 MOUNT GREYLOCK STATE RESERVATION: EAST SIDE

This is one of the shortest routes to the summit of the state's highest peak. Despite the significant elevation gain, anyone in reasonably good physical condition should be able to complete the hike.

FEATURES
Location Adams, MA
Rating Moderate to Strenuous
Distance 6.7 miles round trip
Elevation Gain 1,930 feet
Estimated Time 4 to 4.5 hours
Maps AMC Massachusetts Trail Map 1: D5; USGS Cheshire, USGS Williamstown; Massachusetts Department of Conservation and Recreation map: mass.gov/doc/mount-greylock-trail-map/download
GPS Coordinates 42° 36.635' N, 73° 09.399' W
Contact Massachusetts Department of Conservation and Recreation, 413-499-4262, mass.gov/locations/mount-greylock-state-reservation

DIRECTIONS

From the south: From MA 8 in Pittsfield at Allendale Center, drive north on MA 8 for 9.1 miles into Cheshire and turn left onto Fred Mason Road. Follow it north for 2.9 miles (it becomes West Road after approximately 1 mile) to West Mountain Road on the left. Turn left and follow West Mountain Road for 1.6 miles, past parking for Gould Trail, to a circular gravel parking area where the road ends. The trailhead is on the right.

From the north: Proceed south on MA 8 to Adams and turn right onto Maple Street at the statue of President William McKinley. Follow Maple Street for 0.4 mile and turn left onto West Road. Follow West Road for 0.6 mile to West Mountain Road on the right. Turn right onto West Mountain Road and drive 1.6 miles to a circular gravel parking area where the road ends. The trailhead is on the right.

TRAIL DESCRIPTION

Begin at an elevation of 1,560 feet and follow the gravel road to your right (northwest) that leads through a field. Pass a small sign on the left that reads "Old Adams Rd. to Cheshire Harbor Tr. to Summit 3.5 mi." A map board sits at the woodland's edge. Walk past a metal gate and walk the lower portion of Cheshire Harbor Trail along an old, rocky roadbed.

TRIP 15 // MOUNT GREYLOCK STATE RESERVATION: EAST SIDE

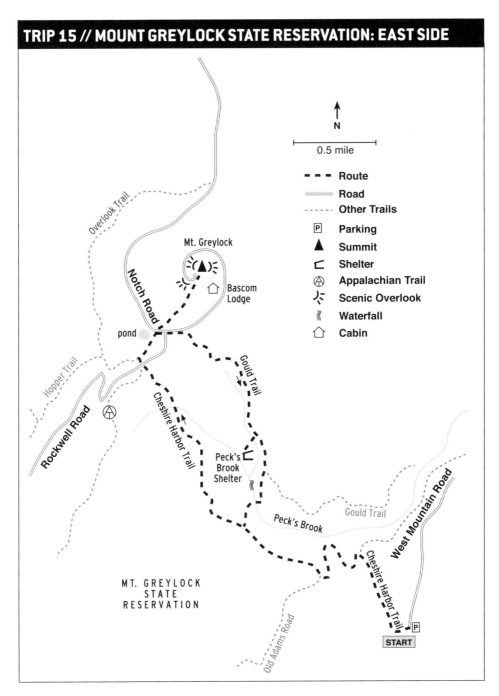

Follow the slope's contour to a sharp left turn. At this point, a narrow connecting path leads down into the forest to Gould Trail, but stay on wide Cheshire Harbor Trail. It splits briefly here but rejoins 50 yards farther up. As the trail curves right, note the first red spruces of the hike. After some twists and turns, reach a signed intersection with Old Adams Road on the left at 1.0 mile, but continue straight on Cheshire

Harbor Trail. The heart-shaped, paired leaves of chest-high hobblebushes provide nest sites low to the ground for black-throated blue warblers. The scoured treadway becomes even rockier; step over ledge outcroppings of metamorphic schist rock. Reach the signed intersection with Peck's Brook Loop on the right (you will return via this way later) and continue straight uphill on Cheshire Harbor Trail. The triangular seed capsules of a patch of sessile-leafed bellwort are notable on the right in autumn. A large, shaggy, three-trunked red maple stands on the left where the surface roots of beech lace the treadway.

The route now leads up through woods of beech and yellow birch. Although some trees are sizable, this forest is generally young. Beeches sprout from roots and form clones of smooth, gray-barked trees. An eye-catching 4-foot-long quartz boulder perches on schist to your left. Mountain maple saplings have taken root among the boulders. Porcupines are fond of their leaves, which are distinguished by sawtooth edges. Hear the sound of flowing water and smell the sweet aroma of balsam fir as you reach Peck's Brook. Cross a wide, wooden snowmobile bridge over the brook (use caution if boards are loose or missing).

On the far side, the trail briefly splits as it ascends; you can follow either fork. Evergreens are now more numerous. When you reach Rockwell Road (2.6 miles), the southbound Appalachian Trail (AT) is on the left, just before the pavement. Cross the road (a sign on a tree indicates the route to the summit) and hike the white-blazed AT north over wooden stairs amid a heavenly balsam fragrance. The AT follows a narrow path as it weaves through stunted spruce, yellow birch, and mountain ash and over bog bridges to reach a T intersection with blue-blazed Hopper Trail on the left. Turn right to continue on the AT over more bog bridges toward the summit.

Stroll through a boreal forest zone, a natural community found in only a handful of locations in Massachusetts, in the company of spruce and fir trees that grow at elevations above 2,600 feet. The zone's climate is equivalent to that of interior Canada. Upper reaches of the mountain are often foggy, and the condensing moisture is acidic, which, when combined with shallow soil and harsh temperatures, negatively affects the growth of woody vegetation. When you arrive at a scenic spring-fed pond, which once supplied water to the summit lodge, the communications tower on the summit is easily visible unless conditions are foggy.

Briefly follow along the pond's shore and soon reach Rockwell Road again, near the intersection with Notch Road and Summit Road. Turn left, walk about 100 feet past the intersection, and then follow the AT's signature white blazes into the woods on a rocky path that soon reaches an asphalt parking area near the communications tower at 3.1 miles. From this point, the 93-foot Massachusetts Veterans War Memorial Tower on the summit is only a few hundred feet across the roadway. Attractively rustic Bascom Lodge—where drinking water, flush toilets, meals, and overnight accommodations are available May through October—stands to the right. Take time to explore the summit (3,491 feet) and, on a clear day, admire the expansive views. Look for the distinctive, low, pyramid-shaped profile of southern New Hampshire's Mount Monadnock, 60 miles to the northeast.

The 93-foot-tall granite Massachusetts War Veterans Memorial Tower, from which five states may be visible, was dedicated in 1933. The bronze relief map in the foreground shows the topography of the Greylock Range.

TRIP 15 // **MOUNT GREYLOCK STATE RESERVATION: EAST SIDE**

When you're ready to descend, return to the AT and retrace your steps (beware of wet or loose rocks) back to the intersection of Rockwell, Notch, and Summit roads. Return via a more interesting and challenging route by using a portion of Gould Trail, which begins at a small gravel parking area at the intersection (3.7 miles). Initially narrow and steep, blue-blazed Gould Trail soon levels out among maple, beech, striped maple, hobblebush, and dense jewelweed. Pass through a stand of yellow birch and fragrant balsam fir. Raspberry canes flourish in the light gaps. At a junction with an almost-unrecognizable overgrown trail, bear left to continue descending. Sugar maples predominate in the now-deciduous woodland. Cross a couple of intermittent streambeds, using a wooden span over the first one. Mosses line the bedrock channel of the second one. Gould Trail leads through dense spruce regeneration on the fairly steep slope and then widens to become a rocky roadway.

After walking roughly 1.2 miles from the summit (4.9 miles overall), reach a short, signed path on the right that crosses the brook to Peck's Brook Shelter. The lean-to nestled on the hillside above the tumbling brook is well worth the short detour of less than 5 minutes, especially for the waterfall that flows there during wet seasons. Return to Gould Trail, which turns right and levels out under hardwoods. Bear right at a wide, overgrown path and reach a signed Y intersection. Turn right toward Cheshire Harbor Trail and Peck's Brook, leaving Gould Trail, which continues left down to West Mountain and Gould roads. The path descends gently past prince's pine, shining club moss, and wildflowers, such as *Clintonia* (blue-bead lily), Canada mayflower, and wild sarsaparilla. Bear right and proceed toward the sound of cascading water. A series of switchbacks down the steep slope deposits you at the exceedingly rocky Peck's Brook. Briefly follow the brook downstream through a narrow ravine. Clear pools in this idyllic spot provide abodes for brook trout and spring salamanders.

Across the brook, watch for a blue blaze on a maple on the far side. Follow the blue-blazed trail, eroded in places, steeply up stone steps and short switchbacks. Continue through a hobblebush thicket to the intersection with Cheshire Harbor Trail at the end of the loop. Turn left to follow Cheshire Harbor Trail back to the intersection with Old Adams Road on the right. From here, retrace your steps on Cheshire Harbor Trail for 1.0 mile. After the series of switchbacks, reach the parking area.

DID YOU KNOW?

The name Cheshire Harbor Trail does not derive from a body of water; rather, it refers to a former settlement, midway between Adams and Cheshire, that reputedly served as a way station on the Underground Railroad, which assisted formerly enslaved people who had escaped.

MORE INFORMATION

Open year-round; access is free. A parking fee ($5 Massachusetts residents, $10 out of state) is charged at the summit from May to October. Skiing and leashed dogs are allowed. Mountain bikes are not permitted on the Appalachian Trail, but are allowed on other trails. Seasonal restrooms are available at the summit. Hunting is not allowed from May 20 to Columbus Day/Indigenous Peoples' Day and is never permitted within War Memorial Park. Carry in, carry out rules apply. The visitor center, at 30 Rockwell Road in Lanesborough, is open 9:00 A.M. to 4:00 P.M. daily (closed Thanksgiving and Christmas).

NEARBY

Berkshire Outfitters in Adams is a full-service outdoor sports store offering both sales and rentals. Call 413-743-5900 or visit berkshireoutfitters.com for hours and other information. The store is on MA 8 (169 Grove Street), 1.2 miles north of the intersection of Fred Mason Road and MA 8.

16. MOUNT GREYLOCK STATE RESERVATION: JONES NOSE AND ROUNDS ROCK

A delightful ramble along Greylock's middle slopes—an alternative to the longer and more difficult summit trails—features stunning vistas, wildflower meadows, and prolific blueberry barrens.

FEATURES

Location Cheshire and New Ashford, MA

Rating Easy to Moderate

Distance 2.9-mile loop

Elevation Gain 235 feet

Estimated Time 1.5 to 2 hours

Maps USGS Cheshire; Massachusetts Department of Conservation and Recreation map: mass.gov/doc/mount-greylock-trail-map/download

GPS Coordinates 42° 36.102′ N, 73° 12.023′ W

Contact Massachusetts Department of Conservation and Recreation, 413-499-4262, mass.gov/locations/mount-greylock-state-reservation

DIRECTIONS

From Park Square in the center of Pittsfield, drive north on US 7 (North Street) for 6.6 miles to North Main Street in Lanesborough. Turn right onto North Main Street, bearing right at Scott Road at 0.7 mile. The reservation's visitor center is 1.0 mile farther along Rockwell Road on the right. Continue past the visitor center an additional 3.8 miles to a large gravel parking lot at Jones Nose on the right.

TRAIL DESCRIPTION

At the parking lot (2,420 foot elevation), a kiosk details the history of Jones Nose, site of a former upland farm. Cross Rockwell Road and begin the loop on blue-blazed Northrup Trail. The mowed path leads through a meadow filled with goldenrod, dewberry, meadowsweet, and steeplebush, which all bloom in summer. Luxuriant growths of hay-scented fern surround clumps of cherry, mountain ash, and gray birch. Indigo buntings and chestnut-sided warblers sing in summer from treetops and shrubs. At the T junction, turn left to continue on Northrup Trail (Stage Trail is on the right), which descends easily into deciduous woods, dominated by sugar maple and white ash. The path undulates through fern glades, where you can hear the songs of red-eyed vireos, ovenbirds, and rose-breasted grosbeaks in spring and early summer.

TRIP 16 // MOUNT GREYLOCK STATE RESERVATION: JONES NOSE AND ROUNDS ROCK

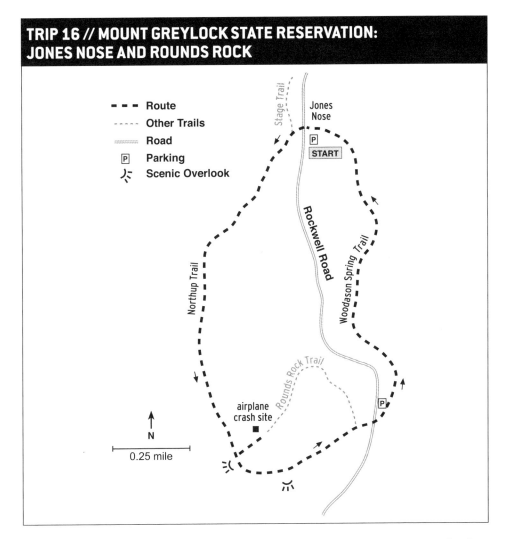

Cross a small brook and continue through forest where American beech and yellow birch—two important northern hardwoods—form a canopy over hobblebush shrubs as you follow the contour of a hillside that drops off steeply to the right. Prickly raspberry canes fill light gaps as you pass a garden of wildflowers; red trillium, blue cohosh, and various violets bloom in spring before the forest canopy blocks out the sun. In late spring and summer, the mature woodland hosts breeding migratory songbirds, including hermit thrushes and both black-throated green and black-throated blue warblers.

After about 0.5 mile, reach a ledge outcropping on the left and a series of angular boulders. Mosses, polypody fern, and sapling yellow birches cap one impressive slab. The presence of wild ginger, wild leek, and maidenhair fern all indicate nutrient-rich soil. Pass an unmarked trail on the left and continue south on Northrup Trail. At 1.0 mile, turn sharply left onto a signed connecting path to Rounds Rock Trail. Climb easily under more hardwoods—especially beech, which fills the understory with sprouts and laces the footpath with its roots. Traverse a series of springs and seeps along this slope and continue through a younger forest of numerous low, deformed trees to a blueberry-and-fern-filled barren, dotted with clumps of mountain holly, white (paper) birch, and mountain ash at the signed intersection with Rounds Rock Trail.

Follow the left branch of Rounds Rock Trail on a short out-and-back detour (about 250 yards) to the site of an August 12, 1948, airplane crash. An interpretive sign, rusted wreckage, and a memorial to the deceased pilot, John Newcomb, tell the tragic tale. Backtrack to the intersection and continue on Rounds Rock Trail for about 75 feet to a short side path on the right that leads to an excellent vista of the Taconic Range, Jiminy Peak ski area, a ridgeline capped by white wind turbines, and New York's Catskill Mountains beyond.

Return to Rounds Rock Trail and turn right to continue through more blueberries (ripening in July and August), ferns, and pyramidal red spruces. Eastern towhees skulk in the brush. At 1.7 miles, turn right onto another side path and walk down some 200 feet to a clifftop perch with a fantastic view of Lenox Mountain and the central Berkshire lakes. Retrace your steps to Rounds Rock Trail and turn right. Conical red spruces stand sentinel-like amid the blueberries and ferns—a scene reminiscent of Maine. Back in the deep woods, North Country wildflowers, such as goldthread, appear. Beech trees soon replace spruces, and Canada mayflower carpets the ground as you reach a gray granite marker, erected in 1912, indicating the boundary between New Ashford and Cheshire.

A portion of Rounds Rock Trail leads through a blueberry barren with colorful fall foliage.

Continue on Rounds Rock Trail as it bends left through mixed woods and a grove of spruces and under a canopy of yellow birch, black cherry, sugar maple, and spruce with lush undergrowth. At a junction at the northern end of the Rounds Rock Trail loop, continue straight ahead toward the Rockwell Road trailhead (an optional starting point for a shorter hike on Rounds Rock Trail). At 2.1 miles, cross Rockwell Road and turn left (north) on Woodason Spring Trail to head back toward Jones Nose. Creeping partridgeberry blooms here in early summer; its coral-red fruits are edible but virtually tasteless. Beeches sprout prolifically; the understory is predominantly beech, but hobblebush shrubs are numerous and head high. Many American beech trees in these woods are diseased, their normally smooth gray bark disfigured by the *Nectria* fungus. *Clintonia* (blue-bead lily), sessile-leafed bellwort, and Canada mayflower thrive beneath the trees.

The winding path parallels gurgling Kitchen Brook for a stretch, traverses it and several other small waterways in rapid succession, and then enters younger forest. Emerge from the woods at a savannah with a view of Jones Nose (the southern end of Saddle Ball Mountain). From early summer to midsummer, enjoy pink fireweed blooms just before you return to the parking lot and your vehicle.

DID YOU KNOW?

Jones Nose took its name from Seth Jones, and Rounds Rock was named for Jabez Rounds. Both worked their mountain farms in the 1790s. Forty-two farmers once tended the land that is now Mount Greylock State Reservation. Sheep grazed at the Rounds farm, which was added to the reservation in 1915.

MORE INFORMATION

Open dawn to dusk, year-round. Access is free; summit parking fee ($5 Massachusetts residents, $10 out of state). Mountain biking, skiing, and leashed dogs are allowed. Alcoholic beverages are not permitted. Hunting is not allowed from May 20 to Columbus Day/Indigenous Peoples' Day and is never permitted in War Memorial Park—a 0.75-mile radius around the Massachusetts Veterans War Memorial Tower at the summit.

NEARBY

Before or after your hike, stop at the Mount Greylock State Reservation visitor center at the mountain's base (30 Rockwell Road, Lanesborough). Features include an orientation film and exhibits on the cultural and natural history of the mountain. The visitor center is open 9:00 A.M. to 4:00 P.M. daily (closed Thanksgiving and Christmas). For more information, call 413-499-4262 or visit mass.gov/locations/mount-greylock-state-reservation.

A BEAR IN THE WOODS

Few local creatures engender as much trepidation or excitement as black bears. You're more likely to come upon one while motoring toward the trailhead, but trail encounters do occur. Like moose, white-tailed deer, fishers, and beavers, bears have recovered strongly from past population declines caused by historical forest clearing and unregulated hunting.

Black bears are formidable beings; an adult male—or boar—generally weighs in at 250 pounds in Massachusetts, but record-sized individuals have tipped the scales at 600 pounds or more. In rare instances (unlikely in New England), individuals may have brown or blond coloration. The considerably larger grizzly bear does not dwell in the eastern United States.

Healthy black bears are rarely aggressive toward humans. They generally detect our scent or hear us coming and make a hasty exit. If you do meet one, remain calm, back off, and allow the bear to retreat. You can thrill about the encounter once the animal has departed. A mother bear with cubs or yearlings merits special concern, but do not panic. Giving the animals a wide berth is the best action.

Many bears, unfortunately, have learned to associate humans with food, and this is potentially dangerous—especially for the bear. Bears that are coaxed near human habitation by garbage, birdseed, farm animals, or even deliberate handouts are far more apt to become nuisance animals, to be struck by automobiles, or even to be shot. And a diet of human food is certainly not a recipe for good bear health. Sadly, as bear populations expand into suburban areas and more people choose to live in proximity to bear habitats, the odds are that conflicts will continue to increase.

Black bears are now quite common in western and central Massachusetts and are rapidly expanding their range in the eastern part of the state; several have even reached Cape Cod. While an estimate of only 100 individuals roamed the state's woodlands in 1978, the current population likely exceeds 4,500, according to the Massachusetts Division of Fisheries and Wildlife. Several factors seem to be at work. The fact that our woodlands have come of age after historical land clearing and timber harvesting is probably foremost. In addition, a breeding nucleus was always present in northern New England, and as that population increased, competition forced animals south.

If you spend much time on the trail, you will find bear "sign"—a polite word for fecal matter. An ample pile of large-diameter, dark, blunt-end droppings is almost certainly of bear origin, especially if major constituents are seeds and berry pits. Coming upon bears, or their tracks and scat, is a tangible reminder that we share this land with some rather amazing creatures—what conservationists like to refer to as "charismatic megafauna."

17 CHESHIRE COBBLES AND GORE POND

A fantastic vista and the solitude of a scenic pond are the major rewards of this out-and-back hike along the Appalachian Trail.

FEATURES

Location Cheshire and Dalton, MA
Rating Moderate
Distance 7.6 miles round trip
Elevation Gain 1,250 feet
Estimated Time 4 hours
Maps AMC Massachusetts Trail Map 1; USGS Cheshire; Appalachian Trail Conservancy online map: appalachiantrail.org/explore/hike-the-a-t/interactive-map
GPS Coordinates 42° 33.745' N, 73° 09.399' W
Contact AMC Western Massachusetts Chapter Massachusetts AT Committee, amc-wma.org/appalachian-trail-management-committee
Appalachian Trail Conservancy (New England Regional Office), 802-281-5894, appalachiantrail.org/explore/explore-by-state/massachusetts

DIRECTIONS

From the junction of MA 9 and MA 8 in the Allendale section of Pittsfield, travel north on MA 8 for 7.3 miles to a traffic signal at Church Street in Cheshire. Turn right onto Church Street and follow it 0.4 mile, just past the post office on the right to the Ashuwillticook Rail Trail parking area on the right.

TRAIL DESCRIPTION

The first 0.4 mile of the route is on pavement. Walk left (north) on Ashuwillticook Rail Trail to the Appalachian Trail (AT), which runs along Church Street (note the white blazes on utility poles). Turn right at Church Street, following the AT south, and cross the Hoosic River. Reach the intersection of Main and East Main streets. Walk up East Main Street 150 feet to Furnace Hill Road on the right. Turn right onto Furnace Hill Road and head up, following white-blazed utility poles for almost 0.25 mile, at which point the AT turns left into the forest at a private drive.

Begin the ascent following white, rectangular blazes under hemlocks and a few Norway spruces. Hardwood companions include black birch, red maple, and American beech. Cross a short wooden span and stride up railroad ties through a mixed hemlock and hardwood forest. Soon the hemlocks yield entirely to hardwoods, including

TRIP 17 // CHESHIRE COBBLES AND GORE POND

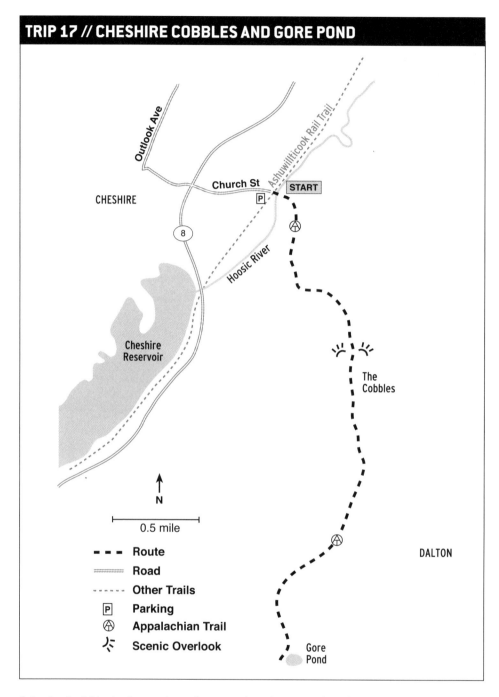

flaky-barked black cherry. At a clearing, the AT turns sharply right along an old tote road. Pass through a gap in a fallen stone wall built of tough quartzite and then turn left off the tote road. After leaf fall, the rounded hump of Mount Greylock is visible to the left from the undulating trail. After the AT turns left, white birches appear.

Multitrunked hardwoods indicate former logging. The tiny evergreen shoots of primitive club mosses—prince's pine, shining, and cedar—soften the forest floor.

The trail now steepens a bit, traversing a number of old tote roads in the process; follow the white blazes at junctions. White ash, yellow birch, and, in the understory, striped maple join the woodland mix with the increasing elevation. Beneath the trees spreads a luxuriant cover of evergreen spinulose wood fern. At a junction with a well-traveled path, follow the AT as it turns right to wend up the slope.

Constructed water bars, edged with rock, shunt water off the treadway; a jumble of quartzite boulders defines the slope. Over eons, the rocks have eroded to sand that now whitens the path. Pass massive boulders on the left—some capped by polypody fern. Crevices between the boulders invite porcupines and other creatures to den. As you walk, look ahead to the looming, iron-stained Cobbles, which are hills formed of quartzite. Mountain laurel wreathes their base. The terrain roughens as you continue past the impressive cliff face and climb stone steps to the crest of the Cobbles at 1.3 miles. Bear left at a protruding rock on a short, blue-blazed side path among laurel and hemlock, and walk through a sort of "secret passageway" hemmed in by evergreen laurel to emerge onto exposed bedrock that offers an expansive vista. (Watch your footing.)

From atop this rocky perch—composed of 500-million-year-old Cheshire quartzite—look southwest to Cheshire Reservoir, northwest to the hamlet of Cheshire just below, and north to Mount Greylock with Ragged Mountain to its right—approximately 10 miles distant. The Hoosac Range lies farther right, studded with wind turbines. These fine views make the Cobbles a popular destination for hikers. When you're ready, return to the AT on the blue-blazed side path and continue straight (south) to begin a moderate ascent through mixed woodland to a U.S. Geological Survey (USGS) marker embedded in the bedrock. The AT follows the cliff edge for a distance, passing another USGS marker and screened views of the reservoir. Gray birches, blueberry shrubs, and a few mountain ashes flank the bony ridgeline.

Reach a small, attractive grassy clearing dotted with diminutive red maples and reindeer lichen and then begin an easy descent over glacially grooved bedrock and through more hardwoods—birch, beech, maple, and cherry. Clumps of hobblebush sport clusters of white flowers in May. The route undulates, crosses a grassy woods road, and uses stepping-stones to span a brook. Climb moderately again and traverse modest flows three more times in fairly short order. Then cross an old logging road and bear left to remain on the AT. Pass a grove of white ash trees that has suffered heavily from emerald ash borer infestations. The trail winds among stands of raspberries in light gaps—former pastures. The climb steepens somewhat and leads into a level landscape of young beech trees in an area damaged by a storm. Walk across a damp, hummocky area under hemlocks with some red spruces. Goldthread grows here—a low wildflower sporting shiny, rounded leaves, delicate white flowers, and telltale orange roots.

Climb steadily up the slope of North Mountain, passing a boulder reminiscent of an overstuffed couch. After cresting the wooded summit at 2,211 feet, begin descending and cross another woods road. The path leads into the shade of a hemlock grove alongside beaver wetlands and then turns right to traverse Gore Brook over a series of split-log bridges and stones. Beaver dams on the left hold back the flow, and another pond is

From the crest of Cheshire Cobbles on the Appalachian Trail, panoramic views of the 6-mile-long Mount Greylock massif reward hikers.

visible to the right. Follow the AT over a few more split logs to the west shore of Gore Pond on the left at 3.8 miles. Under the shade of hemlocks, enjoy the pond's tranquil beauty and look for a beaver lodge to the left. This is the turnaround for the hike, so linger a bit before retracing your steps northward.

DID YOU KNOW?
The Cheshire quartzite of the Cobbles is almost pure quartz and was once used to make glass. A glass industry was established in the local area, but much of the quartzite was shipped east to Cape Cod for use in making the renowned Sandwich glass.

MORE INFORMATION
The National Park Service administers the Appalachian National Scenic Trail (AT). Motorized vehicles, mountain bikes, and hunting are not permitted within the 1,000-foot-wide AT corridor, but hunting is allowed in season on some adjacent properties. Camping is permitted only at designated sites. Volunteers from the Appalachian Mountain Club's Western Massachusetts Chapter maintain approximately 90 miles of the AT in Massachusetts.

NEARBY
A replica of the Cheshire Cheese Press stands at the intersection of Church and School streets, adjacent to the AT message board, just a short walk from the Ashuwillticook parking area. A bronze plaque from 1940 commemorates the Baptist elder John Leland, of Massachusetts and Virginia, who presented the Big Cheshire Cheese, weighing 1,235 pounds, to President Thomas Jefferson on January 1, 1802. The people of Cheshire had voted unanimously for Jefferson in the election of 1800.

2 // CENTRAL BERKSHIRES

The central Berkshires are home not only to Berkshire County's most populous city (Pittsfield, with a population of around 45,000) but also to Massachusetts's most expansive state forest, October Mountain State Forest, which covers nearly 16,000 acres, as well as other conservation lands. The central Taconic Range extends along the border with New York on the west; to the east, the high, undulating, and sparsely settled Berkshire Plateau stretches for mile after forested mile. Between the range and plateau, the Housatonic River carves a wide valley through relatively soft marble bedrock.

For the most part, the high points are not as lofty as those in the northern or southern Berkshires, but excellent vistas exist nonetheless. Several trips in this region, such as Old Mill Trail (Trip 21) and Shaker Mountain (Trip 23), offer outstanding combinations of historical and natural attractions. Ashuwillticook Rail Trail (Trip 18), a former railroad bed, provides a universally accessible route with fine views of Cheshire Reservoir and adjacent wetlands teeming with life. A significant number of hikes have moving or still water as a major focal point. These include spectacular Schermerhorn Gorge (Trip 28), Finerty Pond (Trip 29), and tranquil, scenic Upper Goose Pond (Trip 30). Summit vistas are available, too. Among the hikes with a long view are Pittsfield State Forest (Trip 19), Warner Hill on the Appalachian Trail (Trip 20), and Pleasant Valley Wildlife Sanctuary (Trip 25). At Windsor State Forest and Notchview (Trip 22), diverse settings include a brook ravine in a steep valley and expansive hilltop meadows on an old farm site. Several Berkshire Natural Resources Council properties, including Mahanna Cobble (Trip 24) and Yokun Ridge South (see Trips 26 and 27), are part of the High Road, a recently established trail and conservation corridor that is planned to be a long-distance route linking natural areas and communities.

Facing page: Mahanna Cobble lies within a large network of contiguous conservation lands in the central Berkshire Hills.

18 ASHUWILLTICOOK RAIL TRAIL: LANESBOROUGH TO CHESHIRE

Ashuwillticook Rail Trail's southernmost section passes through biologically rich wetlands that host a panoply of birds and ends at picture-perfect Cheshire Reservoir. The elevation gain is negligible; the "moderate" rating is based on distance.

FEATURES

Location Lanesborough and Cheshire, MA
Rating Easy to Moderate
Distance 7.4 miles round trip
Elevation Gain 20 feet
Estimated Time 3 hours
Maps USGS Cheshire, USGS Pittsfield East; Massachusetts Department of Conservation and Recreation map: mass.gov/doc/ashuwillticook-rail-trail-map/download
GPS Coordinates 42° 29.331' N, 73° 12.220' W
Contact Massachusetts Department of Conservation and Recreation, 413-497-7003, mass.gov/locations/ashuwillticook-rail-trail

DIRECTIONS

From the south: From the intersection of MA 8 and MA 9 in Pittsfield (at Allendale Shopping Center), drive north on MA 8 for 2.5 miles to Berkshire Mall Road in Lanesborough on the left. A large paved parking lot straddles the road. The trailhead is to the right.

From the north: From the intersection of MA 8 and Maple Street at the statue of President William McKinley in the center of Adams, drive south on MA 8 for 10.9 miles to Berkshire Mall Road on the right.

TRAIL DESCRIPTION

This 10-foot-wide, paved, universally accessible trail, built on a historical railroad line, serves a variety of recreational users, including bicyclists, inline skaters, walkers, runners, and bird-watchers. The trail is extremely popular, and the parking lot is often filled with vehicles by late morning. For the best chance of spotting wildlife, arrive early in the morning, when many species are most active. Binoculars are recommended for this hike as the many open wetlands offer opportunities to see a variety of birds and

TRIP 18 // ASHUWILLTICOOK RAIL TRAIL: LANESBOROUGH TO CHESHIRE

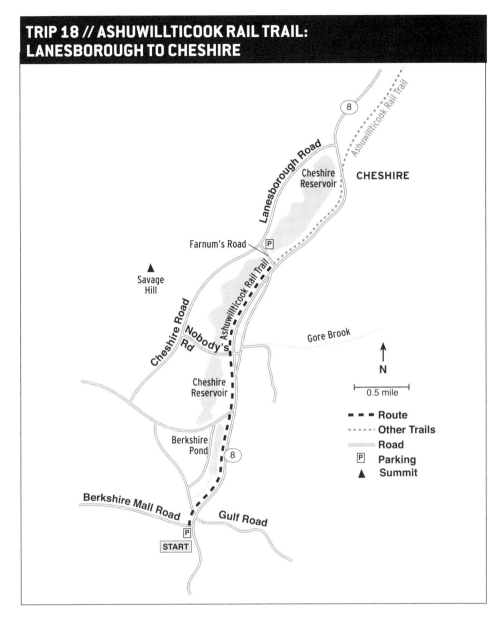

other wildlife. Basic rail-trail etiquette mandates that users stay to the right. When you stop, be sure not to block the path. Bicyclists and inline skaters approaching from behind usually call out that they are passing on the left or ring a bell to alert you to their presence. Because courtesy is the rule, user groups on Ashuwillticook encounter little conflict.

Begin by heading north toward a brick restroom building. Just beyond it on the left stands a kiosk where trail maps may be available. Walk through a gap in a green metal gate and immediately peer into a wooded swamp with skeletal white pines and ribbon-leafed cattails on the left—just the sort of habitat favored by many aquatic and

Cole Mountain borders the northern basin of Cheshire Reservoir as seen from Farnams Road.

semiaquatic creatures. The swamp is the headwater of the Hoosic River, a northward-flowing tributary of New York's mighty Hudson River.

During the warm months, you're apt to observe familiar mallards, elegant wood ducks, Canada geese, and perhaps a great blue heron. Spring and summer are prime times for seeing a wide range of species, including various waterfowl, wading birds, and migratory songbirds. Smaller birds include feisty eastern kingbirds, skulking gray catbirds, olive-drab warbling vireos, male red-winged blackbirds flashing their scarlet epaulets, and crested cedar waxwings. Look for painted turtles basking on logs and various species of camouflaged frogs, including bellowing bullfrogs and green frogs. Green frogs can be distinguished by their call, which sounds like the note of a plucked banjo.

Seek out smaller creatures as well. Butterflies are numerous in summer. Darting darners and skimmers—dragonflies—are hard to miss. Some to watch for are the common whitetail, ebony jewelwing, and widow skimmer. And don't worry; they are harmless. Extensive patches of bullhead lilies blanket sections of the wetlands, their stalks rooted in the muddy bottom 3 or 4 feet down. Their yellow flowers never seem to fully open.

Continue along the paved trail and soon stride beneath an overpass and enter a shaded section bounded by oaks, maples, black birches, ashes, and white pines. Shrub swamps and marshy sloughs continue on both sides of the asphalt. Trees felled by North America's largest rodent, the beaver, are in evidence in the red maple swamp. Red maples are among the most tolerant of trees. They thrive in poor, dry soils and in saturated ones, in bottomlands, and on mountaintops. Along a lengthy straightaway, a marshy pond on the left, known as Berkshire Pond, is filled shore to shore in late summer with both of Massachusetts's native lilies: the aforementioned bullhead and the exquisite fragrant white waterlily. Picnic tables and benches overlook the lily pond.

As you move away from the water, shift your attention to nonflowering plants, including lush sensitive and interrupted ferns—and the green stalks of horsetails. Both of these plant groups have existed virtually unchanged on Earth for hundreds of millions of years. Pass a few homes, and watch out for a patch of poison ivy on the right before the next crossing at Old State Road (1.6 miles from the trailhead), where you'll walk around green metal gates. (Quite handily, trail distances are stenciled on the pavement.)

Perhaps the last remaining artifacts of the rail line, other than the railroad bed itself, are concrete whistle posts. A large white *W* adorns the top of each one. The posts let the engineer know when to sound his locomotive's whistle. They're situated at 0.25-mile intervals on either side of a road crossing. The first whistle post appears near the Cheshire town boundary marker on your right, roughly 2 miles from the Berkshire Mall Road trailhead.

At this point, it's obvious that you're traveling on a former railroad track bed because it drops off steeply to either side. Walk under utility lines supported by tall, paired wooden poles that cut a swath over the hills to either side. The next road crossing, right after a miniature duck pond with domestic fowl, is the intriguingly named Nobody's Road. The origin of the name is anybody's guess. A panoramic vista of North Mountain lies to the east, beyond Route 8. After passing some willows, cross clear Gore Brook, which nourishes an alder and red maple swamp. Ahead and to the west, Savage Hill, at 1,924 feet above sea level, represents the height-of-land along this segment.

The view becomes expansive moments later as you gain the southern end of the Cheshire Reservoir basin. While cattails and lilies provide habitat and food for aquatic mammals and birds, to the north the surface is more open. Two series of benches and picnic tables face the lake at this especially scenic location. Check out a little pool on the right where bluegills are often visible. Camp Mohawk's beach lies on the opposite shore.

As you reenter refreshing woodland shade, note the quaking (or trembling) aspens, the favorite food of beavers. They may all have sprouted from the same rootstock—clones, if you will—something aspens are apt to do. Their heart-shaped leaves are attached to twigs by means of long, laterally flattened stems, which makes them flex and rustle (quake) with the wind. Maples, ashes, and oaks are more dominant here, and some of the oaks are quite large. After another whistle post, young and middle-aged white ashes and giant cottonwoods dominate the scene. The latter are fast-growing relatives of aspens and produce truckloads of minute seeds, each seed attached to a mass of cottony fluff that enables it to fly on the air currents. Wind carries the seeds far from the parent trees, and in summer, they pile up in windrows.

Arrive at Farnams Road between familiar green metal gates. A restroom building sits to your left along the shore of Cheshire Reservoir's upper basin. This is a favorite shore-fishing location. Benches and picnic tables make it a welcoming spot for a relaxing break before you retrace your steps 3.7 miles to the parking area at Berkshire Mall Road.

DID YOU KNOW?

The name Ashuwillticook is derived from the American Indian word for the south branch of the Hoosic River. It means "at the in-between pleasant river," or "the pleasant river between the hills," those hills being the Greylock Range to the west and the Hoosac Range to the east.

MORE INFORMATION

Open dawn to dusk, year-round. Access is free. Dogs must be leashed; owners must clean up after their pets. Skiing is allowed. Motorized vehicles (except electric-powered vehicles used by people with disabilities), horses, alcoholic beverages, fires, hunting, trapping, feeding of wildlife, and removal of park resources are prohibited. Accessible restrooms are available at the Berkshire Mall Road parking area in Lanesborough and at Farnams Road at the turnaround point in Cheshire. For information about the Massachusetts Department of Conservation and Recreation's Universal Access Program, see mass.gov/orgs/universal-access-program.

NEARBY

If you're looking for a takeout meal, cold drink, or cider and doughnuts (in season) after your hike, try Whitney's Farm Market & Garden Center, a local favorite, at 1775 South State Road (MA 8) in Cheshire; open daily 9 A.M. to 6 P.M. (413-442-4749, whitneysfarm.com).

19 PITTSFIELD STATE FOREST: LULU CASCADE, BERRY POND, TILDEN SWAMP

This triangular loop boasts a trifecta of water attractions: lovely cascades along Lulu Brook and two of the state's highest natural water bodies—scenic Berry Pond and Tilden Swamp, a former bog turned into a beaver pond.

FEATURES

Location Pittsfield, Lanesborough, and Hancock, MA
Rating Moderate
Distance 5.8-mile loop
Elevation Gain 1,000 feet
Estimated Time 3 to 3.5 hours
Maps USGS Pittsfield West and USGS Hancock; Massachusetts Department of Conservation and Recreation map: mass.gov/doc/pittsfield-sf-trail-map/download
GPS Coordinates 42° 29.576' N, 73° 17.927' W
Contact Massachusetts Department of Conservation and Recreation, 413-442-8992, mass.gov/locations/pittsfield-state-forest

DIRECTIONS

From the intersection of US 7 and MA 9 at Park Square in the center of Pittsfield, turn west onto West Street and travel 0.5 mile. Turn left to continue on West Street. Drive an additional 2.2 miles to Churchill Street on the right. Follow Churchill Street for 1.7 miles and then turn left onto Cascade Street and drive 0.7 mile to the Pittsfield State Forest contact station (trail maps available). From there, continue another 0.7 mile to Lulu Brook Day Use Area and a spacious gravel parking lot on the left. The trailhead is across paved Berry Pond Circuit Road at an iron gate.

TRAIL DESCRIPTION

Walk to the far (north) end of the parking lot and cross paved Berry Pond Circuit Road diagonally. At a brown gate and trail sign near where Lulu Brook flows under the road, begin on Lulu Brook Trail, marked with occasional blue blazes (use caution in icy conditions).

In about 0.1 mile, arrive at Lulu Cascade, an enchanting small waterfall where the brook plunges 8 feet into a crystal-clear pool surrounded by mossy boulders. Continue to follow Lulu Brook Trail along a schist ledge above the brook. Over the next mile or

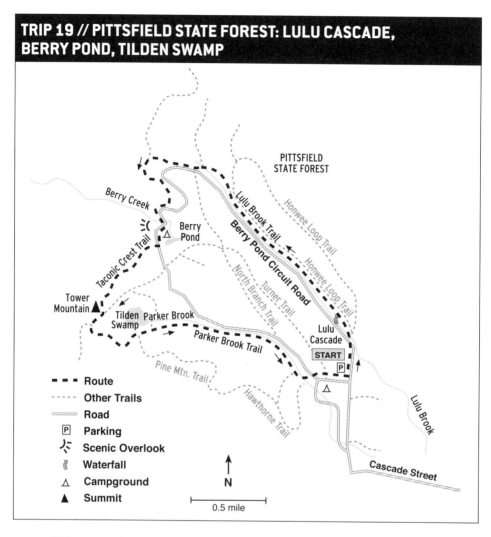

so, you'll be treated to additional smaller cascades. A big, egg-shaped milky quartz boulder, resistant to erosion and flecked with moss, will likely catch your eye. Walk upstream on an undulating path through a ravine cut by the brook under a canopy of hardwoods—oak, ash, maple, birch, and beech—joined by hemlock. Striped maple and hobblebush fill out the understory. Tall meadow rue—spindly stalks with thumbnail-sized leaves topped by starry white flowers—enlivens the banks in summer.

Lulu Brook Trail alternately climbs along the leafy slope and dips to brook level. Watch for partridgeberry and ground-hugging trailing arbutus (mayflower), the Massachusetts state flower, along the upper level. At one point along the stream, a tilted schist ledge with flat slabs juts out. On humid summer days, fog may hang above the cold flow. The abundant moisture makes this a verdant place. Continue uphill, closely paralleling Honwee Loop Trail (which offers slightly easier walking) on the right. After traversing several wooden spans across minor drainages, arrive at a stone wall composed largely of milky quartz. Tall white pines rise up and create a needle-cushioned path that levels out farther from the brook. Pass through a plantation of red pines with ramrod-straight, pinkish trunks, and arrive at a T intersection with an old woods road at Lulu Brook Trail's upper end. Turn left onto the woods road, walk a short distance to a rocky ATV track, and then turn left again and cross a bridge over the brook. At approximately 1.6 miles, turn right onto the paved circuit road and walk 150 feet to a blue-blazed path on the right that connects to Taconic Crest Trail. Turn right onto the path and soon bear left on a narrower path under birches, maples, and beeches. Below these trees are shiny-leafed clusters of the northern wildflower called goldthread.

At an unmarked intersection, bear left and amble easily along the slope for a few hundred feet, reaching Taconic Crest Trail (marked with white diamonds on blue squares) at a T intersection. Turn left onto Taconic Crest Trail and climb past plush patches of shining club moss. The trail levels out under oaks and beeches, and a luxuriant growth of hay-scented fern blankets the ridgeline forest's floor. (This forest is stunted due to the thin soil and a harsh microclimate.) Pass a trail register box on the left. When you arrive at Berry Pond Circuit Road again, turn right and stroll 150 feet to a white-on-blue blaze for Taconic Crest Trail on the right, at a sign for Azalea Fields. Turn right and follow the path along the edge of a field where raspberry canes proliferate. Mountain azalea shrubs bloom pink in late May and offer a fragrant aroma.

Enter young woodland with Canada mayflower and ferns and soon arrive at a level clearing—just feet from the summit of Berry Mountain—and a T intersection. Shad trees, red maple, mountain ash, and several species of shrubs—arrowwood, bilberry, meadowsweet, lowbush blueberry, and azalea—thrive atop the bedrock. Descend through a tunnel of vegetation to the paved circuit road, where a vista at a gravel pullout at 2.4 miles offers a wonderful westerly view into New York all the way to the Catskills.

After taking in the scenery, walk downhill along the paved circuit road's grassy shoulder to the state's highest natural water body—Berry Pond (2,150 feet) at 2.6 miles. Showy blossoms of fragrant white waterlilies dot its surface in summer. Close to shore, look for pumpkinseed sunfish fanning their tails to create circular depressions in which the female deposits her eggs for the male to guard. Continue along the shoreline and follow the gravel driveway past campsites.

Rejoin the paved circuit road and bear right on Taconic Crest Trail, which branches off the circuit road here and continues up the far side into beech, maple, and oak woodland. As the path levels out among the hardwoods, notice that some red oaks have twin trunks—the probable result of stump sprouting following logging. Begin an easy descent. Small light gaps are now filled with hay-scented fern and raspberries. Delicate maidenhair fern may attract your attention just before some eye-catching milky quartz ledge outcroppings softened by emerald-green mosses. Flutelike voices of hermit thrushes are often heard under this leafy canopy.

Climb moderately along the slope's flank, taking advantage of a few switchbacks, to reach a shrubby clearing on the summit of Tower Mountain (2,193 feet), approximately 1 mile from Berry Pond (3.6 miles overall). Regenerating woody vegetation has obscured this former vista. Abundant lowbush blueberry patches start producing ripe fruit by the end of June—a tasty consolation. No doubt black bears visit here as well. Taconic Crest Trail bears right at this Y intersection, but bear left instead to begin the descent to the

Colorful blooms of wild azaleas make for a striking sight near Berry Mountain's summit in June.

trailhead on the upper portion of blue-blazed Pine Mountain Trail, a narrow path that leads down through a shrubby growth of wild raisin and raspberry. Descend through fern growth from which young trees—especially black cherry, shad, and red maple—rise.

Pass a couple of informal trails on the right and arrive at the intersection with a portion of Taconic Skyline Trail, a rutted gravel ATV road, under a mix of hardwoods and white pines. Turn right and follow the track a few hundred feet to the left to continue on Pine Mountain Trail, which heads toward Tilden Swamp. Follow it through a mostly deciduous forest with a fairly dense understory. A few American chestnuts have managed to reach 4 or 5 inches in diameter. These root sprouts are a sad reminder that this species dominated the forest community before the onset of the chestnut blight in the 1920s. Pass a trail that joins on the right and continue easily down the slope. The water's surface is visible through the trees, which are mostly beech, oak, birch, and white pine.

At the junction with Parker Brook Trail on the right, make a quick detour straight ahead to a view of Tilden Swamp, which was originally a bog until beaver activity turned it into a pond during the 1990s. At the pond's southeastern end, you can inspect the tall, arched dam constructed by the world's second-largest rodent. Yellow bullhead lilies protrude from the water in summer; this peaceful spot is home to dragonflies, damselflies, pickerel frogs, and bullfrogs. Beaver ponds are part of a natural cycle, and one day Tilden Swamp may transition back to a bog. Parker Brook is the outflow from the pond.

Retrace your steps to the intersection and turn left onto Parker Brook Trail (Pine Mountain Trail branches north to a wooden footbridge over Parker Brook). Descend along Parker Brook's southern banks through beech, maple, birch, and oak. The narrow, water-cut gorge is quite deep, and the pliable branches of hobblebush are bountiful on its steep side slopes. Colorful woodland warblers are a treat for the eyes as they search for leaf-munching caterpillars and other insects in the foliage from late spring through summer. One such species found here is the lovely Canada warbler, which sports a necklace of black on its citron-yellow breast.

Continue a steady descent along a hillside graced with ferns and a cover of hardwood trees. Hemlocks increase in number before you reach an intersection with a trail on the right. Stay straight to continue on Parker Brook Trail at the junction with a multiuse path that runs up to Hawthorne Trail. Pass clumps of wintergreen and partridgeberry, whose red fruits are eaten by grouse. Head to a four-way intersection and turn left to cross Parker Brook on a wooden ATV span. Before turning, check out the angular schist outcroppings along the stream under an umbrella of hemlocks.

Continue to follow Parker Brook Trail past two paths that appear almost immediately beyond the brook—one on the left under oaks and then another on the right. Walk past campsites and more chestnut sprouts to the one-way paved circuit road, where rows of Depression-era Norway spruces stand. Bear right on the circuit road, walk 50 feet, and turn left onto wide gravel Crossover Road, heading moderately uphill past a modern, seasonally open restroom building. Pass several side paths, including unsigned Turner Trail on the left. Mature oak trees tower on the right. After you pass a metal forest gate, reach the paved road and turn left, following it several hundred feet straight back to Lulu Brook Day Use Area and your vehicle.

DID YOU KNOW?

Characteristic bog species, including the carnivorous pitcher plant, round-leafed sundew, and leatherleaf, once grew profusely in the damp, acidic soil of Tilden Swamp. Since the beaver flooding, however, only a few remnants of bog denizens currently survive along the largely inundated shoreline.

MORE INFORMATION

Open sunrise to sunset, year-round. A day-use parking fee ($5 Massachusetts residents, $20 out of state) is charged from mid-May to Labor Day. Restrooms, open seasonally, are available at Lulu Brook Day Use Area. Skiing, mountain biking, dogs, and hunting in season are allowed. Camping is available at Berry Mountain (13 sites), Parker Brook Campground (19 sites), and Bishop Field (6 sites, groups up to 20 people), and Lulu Brook (groups up to 50 people). Picnicking is permitted, but alcoholic beverages are prohibited on all state lands.

NEARBY

The Berkshire Museum, at 39 South Street (US 7) in Pittsfield, offers an array of art, history, and natural science exhibitions, activities, and attractions. An aquarium of native and exotic creatures is a favorite. The museum is open Monday through Saturday, 10 A.M. to 5 P.M., and Sunday, noon to 5 P.M. Call 413-443-7171 or visit berkshiremuseum.org for fees and other visiting information.

20 WARNER HILL

This enjoyable hike on the Appalachian Trail leads through northern hardwoods interspersed with evergreens. Warner Hill's partially cleared summit yields a pleasing view of Mount Greylock.

FEATURES

Location Dalton and Hinsdale, MA
Rating Moderate
Distance 6.3 miles round trip
Elevation Gain 430 feet
Estimated Time 3 to 3.5 hours
Maps USGS Pittsfield East; Appalachian Trail Conservancy online map: appalachiantrail.org/explore/hike-the-a-t/interactive-map
GPS Coordinates 42° 27.391' N, 73° 09.711' W
Contact AMC Western Massachusetts Chapter Massachusetts AT Committee, amc-wma.org/appalachian-trail-management-committee
Appalachian Trail Conservancy (New England Regional Office), 802-281-5894, appalachiantrail.org/explore/explore-by-state/massachusetts

DIRECTIONS
From the intersection of MA 9 and East Street in Pittsfield (1.25 miles east of the junction of MA 9 and US 7 at Park Square), follow East Street east for 3.0 miles to Division Road at the Dalton town line. East Street becomes South Street in Dalton. Drive north on South Street for 0.85 mile to Grange Hall Road on the right. Follow Grange Hall Road for 1.1 miles and park on the wide gravel shoulder on the left. Parking in winter along Grange Hall Road may not be possible because the road shoulder is not plowed.

TRAIL DESCRIPTION
This hike follows the white-blazed Appalachian Trail (AT), with a short side trip to Kay Wood Shelter. Cross to the south side of Grange Hall Road (watch for traffic speeding downhill around the curve) and ascend the rather steep slope on the AT, which is lined with white ash, red maple, black cherry, and American beech. Note the interesting steplike gneiss rock outcropping studded with quartz crystals. As the path levels out, prince's pine and cedar club moss—ancient nonflowering plants—add a fairyland quality to the forest floor. On the right stands a fine yellow birch, one of the classic indicators of northern hardwood forest.

TRIP 20 // WARNER HILL

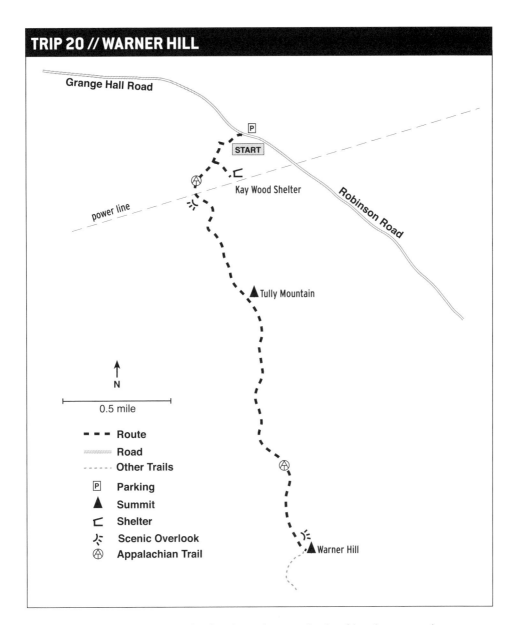

After passing the remains of a fireplace chimney built of local stone and mortar on the left, the path descends into a shallow gully. Planted non-native Norway spruces also indicate past human presence. After a moderate climb up the far side of the gully, reach a blue-blazed trail on the left at 0.3 mile that leads to Kay Wood Shelter, which has a privy and a picnic table. A metal box near the structure is designed to keep hikers' food safe from black bears. The shelter's picturesque setting on a moss-and-lichen-covered gneiss outcropping makes the 0.3-mile round trip worthwhile. You'll also pass a massive sugar maple on the left en route.

Periodic clearing by volunteers keeps the summit of Warner Hill open, making it a fine spot for a rest break.

Return to the AT, turn left back onto it, and climb moderately along the slope. Screened views of the Taconic Range's rounded summits to the west are possible after leaf fall. Note the wind-thrown black cherry on the left whose root ball tenaciously grasps stones. Negotiate small boulder fields, their stones cleverly used in construction of this section of the trail. The hilltop appears grassy, but it's actually thickly vegetated with sedges, which are similar to grasses but bear triangular stems rather than round ones.

Cross a power-line gash about 0.3 mile beyond the Kay Wood Shelter side trail, filled with blackberry brambles and meadowsweet shrubs. Its elevation of 1,981 feet makes a pleasant view of Lenox Mountain possible. The path beyond the right of way is straddled by emerald clumps of club mosses and spinulose wood fern, both of which remain green year-round. Walk a gently undulating route under a leafy canopy and through a shallow bowl. A dark green hemlock grove to your left contrasts with the comparatively light green shades of maples, cherries, and beeches. Past a tiny drainage rill, you'll come across an expansive growth of shining club moss, which in late autumn emits a smoky cloud of microscopic spores if you brush against it. (The highly flammable spores once provided the flash for early flash photography.)

Traverse damp areas on several series of plank bridges. Gray-barked shad (juneberry) shares the damp earth with yellow birch. Be alert for well-camouflaged ruffed grouse that you might encounter as you begin a gradual climb to the 2,085-foot summit of Tully Mountain, reached at 1.5 miles. (Unfortunately, this wooded peak does not offer long views.) Twin yellow birches stand trailside on the left. As you stride over an exposed chunk of gneiss bedrock, note the 6-inch-thick milky quartz intrusion that filled a fracture when the bedrock was buried deep underground hundreds of millions of years ago.

Along this high-elevation stretch are pockets of boreal evergreens—red spruce, specifically. In a damp swale, goldthread and wintergreen bloom in spring and summer, respectively. Both display white blossoms. Goldthread's are star shaped, and wintergreen's resemble tiny bells.

Follow along a ledge outcropping, the slope dropping off to the left, and descend into a hobblebush stand. The shrub's big, heart-shaped leaves are among the first to reveal their multiple hues in autumn. Conifers become more common now, interspersed with hardwoods. Cross two small streams about 60 feet apart and then walk through a bowl hemmed in by dramatic gneiss ledges—a sort of miniature canyon that provides ideal den habitat for porcupines and other wildlife. Climb out at the far end, bearing left around a low outcropping, and pass an old woods road, where the trail levels out.

More screened views of forested ridges are to the right. Black birches are suddenly common as you descend into a col and then amble up and cross another woods road. The trail bears right and descends gently to a ledge on the right that juts out like a ship's prow. Wild strawberries, whose small fruits are relished by many creatures, have gained a foothold in pockets of soil atop the rock. Following the AT all the while, continue left, then right, and pass a number of fallen stone walls before entering a scruffy woodland of gnarly old apple trees and viburnum shrubs. Cross an unmarked path and begin a gradual climb amid more apple trees and 6- to 8-inch-diameter shad trees.

Hay-scented ferns fill the slope just below the summit of Warner Hill. Their light green fronds wither and fade to an amber hue after frost ends their growing season. A sign on a tree tells you that you've finally reached your objective: the 2,050-foot summit of Warner Hill at 3.3 miles. Make a short scramble up to the high point, where sprouting gray birch and highbush blueberry spring from pockets of soil amid rust-stained gneiss bedrock. This modest growth still permits fine views north 16 miles to the Greylock Range (the first perspective of Mount Greylock for northbound long-distance AT hikers) and west to the Housatonic Valley. The rotating white blades of wind turbines are visible on ridges to the north and northwest. Periodic clearing of brush by AT volunteers keeps the outlook open. The Trust for Public Land purchased 370 acres east of the summit in 2017 and subsequently sold the land to the National Park Service, thus permanently protecting it as part of the Appalachian National Scenic Trail corridor.

The AT turns right at this point and continues south (reaching Blotz Road in 0.9 mile), but retrace your steps northward 3.0 miles to your vehicle at Grange Hall Road to complete this hike.

DID YOU KNOW?
Kay Wood Shelter is named for Dalton resident Kay Wood ("Grandma Kay"), who hiked the entire AT from 1988 to 1990, completing it at age 71. She welcomed so many hikers into her home over the years that it became a recognized stop along the trail.

MORE INFORMATION
Open year-round; access is free. Motorized vehicles, mountain bikes, horses, and hunting are not permitted on or along the AT. Camping is allowed at Kay Wood Shelter only. The AT in Massachusetts is maintained by volunteers of the Appalachian Mountain Club Western Massachusetts Chapter's Massachusetts AT Committee. For more information on the Trust for Public Land's involvement with Warner Hill, see the trust's website (tpl.org/our-work/warner-hill).

NEARBY
Mass Audubon's Canoe Meadows Wildlife Sanctuary in Pittsfield has 3.0 miles of walking trails along the Housatonic River and its associated wetlands. From the intersection of Dalton Division Road and East Street, follow Dalton Division Road south 1.6 miles. Turn right onto Williams Street and continue for 2.0 miles to Holmes Road. Turn left and drive 0.3 mile to the sanctuary entrance on the left. Admission is free, but donations are appreciated. The sanctuary is open 7 A.M. to dusk, year-round (413-637-0320, massaudubon.org/get-outdoors/wildlife-sanctuaries/canoe-meadows).

TRAIL TRIBULATIONS

The Appalachian National Scenic Trail (the AT) is one of the most extensive continuous footpaths in North America. Its 6-inch-high-by-2-inch-wide white blazes are iconic. The first of several such continental trails, it was the brainchild of Massachusetts native Benton MacKaye. Although MacKaye conceived the idea in 1921, his dream was not fully realized until 1937. Stretching for 2,192 miles from Springer Mountain in northern Georgia to the craggy summit of 5,267-foot Katahdin in Maine's Baxter State Park, the AT is walked by hundreds of thousands of hikers annually. But only a few hundred hardy souls, known as thru-hikers, complete the roughly five- to six-month journey in a single year. Numerous others complete state or regional segments or spend short intervals of time on the trail every year until they have traversed its entire length.

Along the AT's 2,000-plus-mile route, shelters provide respite for long-distance hikers. In summer, you're likely to encounter at least a few of these thru-hikers on their way north or south. Many adopt an emblematic moniker or "trail name" that you'll find at the bottom of journal entries in trail registers along the AT. The majority set out from Georgia in March, before winter has fully retreated. Their goal is to reach Katahdin in late summer or early fall, before winter reasserts itself. Therefore, most pass through the Berkshires around June, some pausing to enjoy the relative luxury of Bascom Lodge atop Mount Greylock, Massachusetts's tallest peak, where hot showers and warm meals are a welcome change from their daily routines. If you can get a thru-hiker to stop long enough to chat, you'll almost certainly enjoy the experience.

Although the AT is under the jurisdiction of the National Park Service, which designated it a National Scenic Trail in 1968, in Massachusetts a cadre of dedicated, hardworking volunteers from the Appalachian Mountain Club's Western Massachusetts Chapter maintains the AT for all of us. They deserve our considerable gratitude.

In Massachusetts, the AT passes over some of the most scenic ridgelines in the Berkshires, from the Vermont border to the Connecticut line—about 90 miles. Many of the original segments have been relocated farther from roads and onto acquired conservation land. Changes and improvements continue.

The following hikes in this guide include portions of the AT: Pine Cobble and East Mountain (Trip 3), Greylock Range Traverse (Trip 5), Hopper Trail to Mount Greylock Summit (Trip 6), Mount Greylock and Ragged Mountain via Bellows Pipe Trail (Trip 8), Saddle Ball Mountain (Trip 14), Mount Greylock State Reservation: East Side (Trip 15), Cheshire Cobbles and Gore Pond (Trip 17), Warner Hill (Trip 20), October Mountain State Forest: Finerty Pond (Trip 29), Upper Goose Pond (Trip 30), Tyringham Cobble Reservation (Trip 35), Benedict Pond and the Ledges (Trip 37), East Mountain and Ice Gulch (Trip 41), Race Brook Falls and Mount Race (Trip 44), Guilder Pond and Mount Everett (Trip 45), and Sages Ravine and Bear Mountain (Trip 49).

21 OLD MILL TRAIL

This out-and-back trail is steeped in the area's industrial history. It is also an enjoyable hike to take with children.

FEATURES

Location Hinsdale and Dalton, MA
Rating Easy
Distance 3 miles round trip
Elevation Gain 155 feet
Estimated Time 1.5 to 2 hours
Maps USGS Pittsfield East; Berkshire Natural Resources Council map: bnrc.org/fileadmin/files/Maps/BNRC_ Old_Mill_Trail_2023_FINAL.pdf
GPS Coordinates 42° 26.877′ N, 73° 07.831′ W
Contact Berkshire Natural Resources Council, 413-499-0596, bnrc.org/reserves/old-mill-trail

DIRECTIONS

From the north: From the intersection of MA 8, MA 8A, and MA 9 in Dalton, drive south on MA 8, entering the town of Hinsdale after 2.5 miles. Continue for another 0.4 mile to Old Dalton Road on the left (no sign). Follow Old Dalton Road for approximately 100 feet and turn left into the Old Mill Trail parking area, which has space for eight to ten vehicles.

From the south: From the intersection of MA 8 and MA 143 in Hinsdale, proceed north on MA 8 for 0.7 mile to Old Dalton Road on the right (no sign). Follow Old Dalton Road to the parking area.

TRAIL DESCRIPTION

The parking area and the first 0.7 mile of the trail, which is ideal for wheelchairs, mobility devices, and strollers, were renovated in 2024 to meet full U.S. Forest Service standards for accessibility. Begin at a kiosk where maps and a detailed interpretive guide that relates the interesting industrial history of the area are available. The East Branch of the Housatonic River—a narrow stream here—borders the majority of Old Mill Trail, which is well blazed. Stroll beneath sugar maples and white ashes with distinctive crosshatched bark (now threatened by the emerald ash borer) and past the 2-foot-tall, leafless green stems of scouring rush. Ostrich ferns, which produce edible fiddleheads when young, also thrive in the moist soil. A couple of flowering dogwood trees—more

TRIP 21 // OLD MILL TRAIL

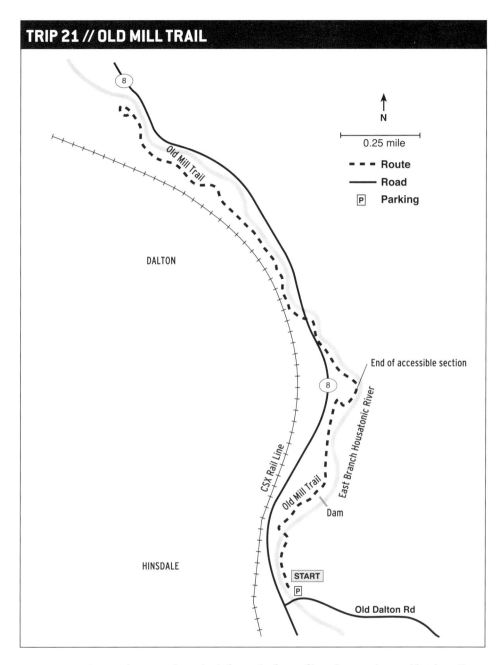

common to the south—stand on the left just before a fiberglass-and-wood bridge. Cross the bridge to follow the river downstream along its opposite bank.

Water-thirsty cottonwoods line the banks, while wild grapevines provide tasty meals for wildlife in late summer and early fall. In quick succession, cross two short bridges, one flanked by a dense stand of spotted joe pye weed. Nearby, goldenrods and asters provide nectar and pollen for insects. After reentering the maple woodland, notice a rusting automobile just beyond a quartzite boulder on the left. Three stones mark a short side path that leads 100 feet to the right to the ruins of a breached dam upstream of the old Plunkett Brothers Mill, which produced textiles in the mid-nineteenth century. As you continue on Old Mill Trail, homes come into view through the forest. For much of way, the route follows river terraces, alternating between segments near the water's edge and higher up on the banks.

Enter a dense streamside hemlock stand, where a cooler microclimate is quite noticeable and gives rise to northern hardwood species, such as yellow birch. Here, the wide path follows the route of the original penstock, a channel that carried water from the dam down to the Renfrew Cotton Mill, where it powered the machinery. For a stretch, the trail is tunneled into the earth, but then it turns right and heads down an easy hairpin turn to the river. The forest floor is almost devoid of vegetation beneath the dense evergreen shade. Red maples soon join the hemlocks, and a few patches of hobblebush pop up here and there. Continue on, passing several massive glacial boulders between the river and the highway. Patches of shining club moss poke up from the leaf litter. The gravel accessible section ends at a small turnaround and rest area with two benches.

The path narrows and soon leads over the top of a concrete penstock that once housed a large steel water pipe, the remains of which are soon visible. Walk over a small bridge and carefully cross MA 8 at 0.7 mile. Enter the northern section of Old Mill Trail at the far end of the guardrail, where the route parallels the road for a bit and then reenters forest. Follow along the base of the slope where boulders protrude. This is arguably the most picturesque portion of the hike. The treadway has been expertly fashioned from

The northern end of Old Mill Trail passes by remains of infrastructures that formerly conveyed water to nearby factories.

native stones into well-placed steps. (Watch your footing in icy conditions.) In contrast to this tranquil scene, an active CSX railroad line runs atop the slope on your left.

The trail climbs easily and moves temporarily away from the Housatonic River, crosses through a bramble-filled power-line cut, and reenters mixed forest of birch, beech, maple, and hemlock before returning to the river. Cross one final bridge over a feeder stream and continue to walk above the river. In spots, Christmas fern provides welcome color year-round. An imposing black cherry tree on the right is virtually hollow at the base. Yellow birches—with fine-peeling, brassy bark—become more numerous, and some are quite large. Note the clumps of plantain-leafed sedge, with evergreen leaves about 1 inch wide.

Follow the trail down to the river again and cross quartzite boulders in the narrow floodplain. Invasive Japanese knotweed has established a foothold here. A patch of native shrub called leatherwood is also present. Its bark is so strong that American Indians once used it as rope and for bowstrings. Ahead in the river are concrete structures that once supported the penstock's 4-foot-diameter steel pipe. The trail passes between more concrete supports that lead to what remains of the exposed penstock pipe on the left and ends here, among large hemlocks. The land bordering is posted private, no trespassing. When you're ready to leave, retrace your steps upstream 1.5 miles back to your vehicle.

DID YOU KNOW?
The East Branch of the Housatonic River originates at Muddy Pond in the towns of Washington and Hinsdale, flows through the Hinsdale Flats Wildlife Management Area, and continues through downtown Dalton. It is one of three headwater tributaries that join in Pittsfield to form the main stem of the Housatonic.

MORE INFORMATION
Open during daylight hours year-round. Access is free. Skiing, mountain biking, and leashed dogs are allowed. Motorized vehicles, fires, camping, littering, and cutting or removing vegetation are prohibited. Hunting, fishing, and trapping are permitted in season. Housatonic Valley Association (hvatoday.org) built Old Mill Trail in 2010. Crane and Company donated the land to Berkshire Natural Resources Council in 2016. The Massachusetts Division of Fisheries and Wildlife (413-684-1646, mass.gov/locations/masswildlife-western-district-office) holds the conservation restriction on the property.

NEARBY
Ashmere Lake, a 287-acre impoundment of Bennett Brook, lies just east of Hinsdale center. At the lake's southern end, Ashmere Lake State Park includes a public boat launch on Hickingbotham Road. Seven-acre Ashmere Island, a Berkshire Natural Resources Council property, may be reached by canoe or kayak (bnrc.org/trails-and-maps/ashmere-island).

As of 2024, a small grocery store was scheduled to open at the former location of Hinsdale Trading Company (371 Old Dalton Road), across from the Old Mill Trail parking area.

22 WINDSOR STATE FOREST AND NOTCHVIEW

From the rugged, densely wooded ravine of Steep Bank Brook to open hilltop fields at Notchview Reservation, this hike traverses diverse settings in the remote uplands of Windsor.

FEATURES
Location Windsor, MA
Rating Moderate to Strenuous
Distance 4.7 miles round trip
Elevation Gain 1,000 feet
Estimated Time 3.75 hours
Maps USGS Windsor; The Trustees of Reservations Notchview map: thetrustees.org/wp-content/uploads/2023/10/notchview-trail-map.pdf Massachusetts Department of Conservation and Recreation Windsor State Forest map: mass.gov/doc/windsor-state-forest-trail-map/download
GPS Coordinates 42° 31.407' N, 73° 00.365' W
Contact The Trustees of Reservations, 413-684-0148, thetrustees.org/place/notchview
Massachusetts Department of Conservation and Recreation, 413-663-8469, mass.gov/locations/windsor-state-forest

DIRECTIONS
From the intersection of MA 9 and West Main Street in West Cummington (just east of the Windsor town line), follow West Main Street along the north side of the Westfield River for 0.8 mile. Turn right onto Savoy Road, which becomes River Road in Windsor, and continue 2.8 miles to the Windsor State Forest main entrance at the intersection with Windsor Jambs Road (marked as Lower Road on some maps). Turn left and cross a bridge over the Westfield River to enter the parking area. If the entrance gate is closed, park at the intersection with Windsor Jambs Road.

TRAIL DESCRIPTION
This hike links Windsor State Forest and Notchview (a Trustees of Reservations property), which cumulatively protect nearly 5,000 acres in the wooded hills of Windsor. From the state forest contact station, bear right and follow a gravel path past an interpretive sign that details the efforts of the Civilian Conservation Corps, which built picnic areas, the road bridge at the entrance, a log dam with four stone piers on

TRIP 22 // WINDSOR STATE FOREST AND NOTCHVIEW

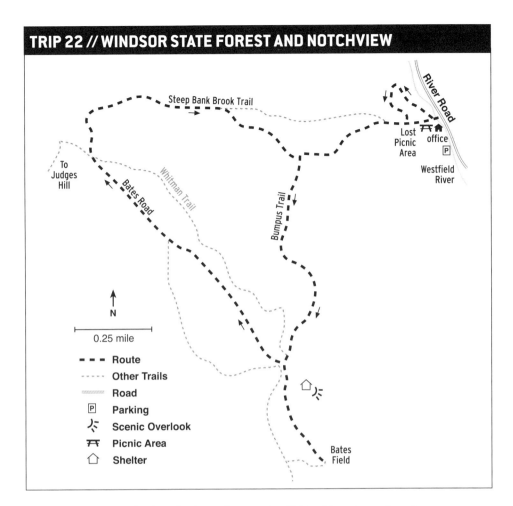

Westfield River, and other facilities during the 1930s. Pass through a day-use area on the banks of Westfield River, a designated National Wild and Scenic River and significant tributary of the Connecticut River.

At a pavilion at the field edge, enter the woods on blue-blazed Lost Picnic Area Trail, so named because it traverses an abandoned picnic grove. After about 200 feet, make the first crossing of Steep Bank Brook (to bypass the crossing when water levels are high, start the hike on Steep Bank Brook Trail, which begins at a signed trailhead next to the restrooms). Continue along the ravine, where evergreen red spruces, indicators of the high elevations, and hemlock trees shade the valley slope. Bear left past several large old white pines, including a giant multitrunked specimen. During years with food shortages in their native boreal forest regions, red crossbills and other finches travel long distances to New England to feed on the seeds of coniferous trees, such as those at Windsor State Forest. Descend to the second crossing of Steep Bank Brook, where wooden steps lead to the base of the channel. Scramble up the opposite bank and continue to the nearby junction (unsigned) with Steep Bank Brook Trail at 0.3 mile.

Black bears, which have recovered from historical population declines, are common in the hills of Windsor and the surrounding eastern Berkshire hills.

Turn right onto Steep Bank Brook Trail, marked with periodic blue blazes, and ascend at a steep grade on a woods road. (*Note*: This hike bypasses a portion of Steep Bank Brook Trail along the brook's edge in Windsor State Forest, which, as of this writing, had not been recently maintained and had eroded spots, blowdowns, and indistinct markings.) Another giant pine towers to the right. Yellow birch, a familiar species of northern hardwood forests, displays vivid golden foliage in autumn. Adaptable trout lilies grow in diverse settings in midspring throughout this route, including wooded slopes and open fields. Other ephemeral wildflowers include red trillium, yellow violet, and wild oat. At the upper end of the steep section, pass a small tributary brook. When leaves are down, glimpse surrounding uplands to the north. Near the state forest boundary, the grade levels as the path bends right along the wooded slope, past more trout lily colonies and a sign for Notchview.

At 0.8 mile, reach the intersection (unsigned) with white-blazed Bumpus Trail, part of Notchview's trail network. Follow the left branch of Bumpus Trail south on a much gentler ascent through hardwood forest interspersed with a few spruce, heading away from Steep Bank Brook's ravine. Familiar calls of migratory songbirds, such as the *see-see-see-su-zee* refrain of black-throated green warblers and the loud *teacher-teacher-teacher* of ovenbirds, are most evident from late April to mid-July. Woodland butterflies include red admirals, which have a long flight season that extends from May to October. Old stone walls and a portion of an abandoned road stand as evidence that these densely forested uplands were cleared for agriculture by early European settlers. Bear left, cross a brook, and traverse seasonally wet areas where colonies of false hellebore and spring beauty, a characteristic wildflower of rich Berkshire soils, thrive in spring.

Ascend to the northern end of Bates Field, an expansive meadow on the site of a former farm that closed in 1957. Several trails in this portion of Notchview, including Bumpus Trail at Bates Field, are groomed for cross-country skiing in winter. Snowshoeing is allowed next to ski tracks; please avoid walking on groomed tracks and be alert for skiers. The Bates family, for whom the field is named, owned a 200-acre homestead on the grounds. Bumpus Trail leads south along the west side of the field to the height-of-land (approximately 2,065 feet), where views extend to the hills and ridges of the upper Westfield River watershed at the Berkshires' eastern edge. Pierce Shelter, near an apple tree and nest box, houses a shaded picnic table.

South of the shelter, Bumpus Trail and grass paths lead past old foundations and a row of sugar maples that makes for a classic New England scene, especially during the peak of fall foliage in early to mid-October. Watch for pileated and red-bellied woodpeckers hunting in trees along the forest edge. At the field's southern end near Shaw Road, approximately 2 miles from the trailhead, return to the height-of-land near the shelter. Here, you can retrace your steps to return directly to the trailhead (continue straight at the intersection with Lost Picnic Area Trail for a 3.8-mile round trip) or make a loop that includes some rugged terrain along Steep Bank Brook (4.7-mile round trip), as described here.

To continue the circuit, from a signed intersection and trail map at the field edge on the west side of the shelter, follow Bates Road (groomed for skiing in winter) northwest along a wide, mostly level woods road. Pass a trail junction and posted map at 0.5 mile from the field (2.8 miles overall). Continue on Bates Road past stone foundations, old sugar maples, and a spreading yellow birch tree.

At 3.3 miles, reach the intersection with white-blazed Steep Bank Brook Trail on the right, just after the junction with Whitman Trail. (To extend the hike with an out-and-back detour to Judges Hill, continue on Bates Road for 0.1 mile and then turn left and ascend for 0.3 mile to the 2,297-foot summit, Notchview's highest elevation.) Turn right and descend along Steep Bank Brook's upper reaches. For the next 0.6 mile, the route crosses the brook numerous times; use caution when water levels are high and watch your footing on rocks. Along the way, pass more false hellebore colonies and a grove of eastern hemlock, which thrives in rugged ravines. Winter wrens, easily identified by cheerfully warbling calls that last as long as 10 seconds, inhabit moist coniferous forests, such as those along Steep Bank Brook.

After three successive brook crossings, reach the signed intersection with white-blazed Bumpus Trail on the right at 3.9 miles. Turn right onto Bumpus Trail and make a steep but short scramble up the ravine embankment; the grade eases after about 200 feet. Continue to the aforementioned intersection at the start of the loop at 4.2 miles (watch carefully, as the junction is not marked). Bear left and retrace your steps on Steep Bank Brook Trail past the sign for Notchview and down the valley slope. At the intersection with Lost Picnic Area Trail, continue straight ahead for a few hundred feet to return to the picnic area and main entrance at Windsor State Forest.

DID YOU KNOW?

The town of Windsor, settled in 1767, initially prospered through agriculture and lumbering. Abundant timber supplied local industries such as sawmills, tanneries, woodworking, and shingle factories. However, by 1850, depleted forests and lack of railroads caused Windsor and other nearby towns to rapidly decline.

MORE INFORMATION

Open sunrise to sunset year-round. Access is free for this hike (a seasonal fee is charged at Notchview's main entrance during winter for skiing and snowshoeing). At Windsor State Forest, leashed dogs, skiing, mountain biking, horseback riding, and hunting are allowed. Restrooms and a picnic area are available at the main entrance.

At Notchview, dogs must be leashed at Bates Field from April 1 to August 15 to protect nesting grassland birds. Dogs are not allowed on trails north of MA 9 during ski season. Please keep to the side of groomed ski trails in winter. Mountain biking is allowed only on town gravel roads. Hunting is allowed in season north of Bates Road.

NEARBY

Windsor Jambs, a scenic gorge and 100-foot waterfall, lies in the southwestern portion of Windsor State Forest. A 0.2-mile path leads to views of the falls and a rocky ravine. The most direct access is via a parking area on Schoolhouse Road, 0.1 mile from the intersection with Windsor Jambs Road (also known as Lower Road). Jambs Trail, which begins at the campground near the main entrance, offers a round trip of approximately 2.1 miles.

23 SHAKER MOUNTAIN

From a trailhead near the beautifully maintained Hancock Shaker Village, this loop leads to historical and religious sites in the neighboring hills of Pittsfield State Forest.

FEATURES

Location Hancock, MA
Rating Moderate
Distance 5.5-mile loop
Elevation Gain 1,500 feet
Estimated Time 3 to 4 hours
Maps USGS Pittsfield West; Massachusetts Department of Conservation and Recreation map and guide: mass.gov/files/documents/2016/08/nd/shaker.pdf
GPS Coordinates 42° 25.808′ N, 73° 20.429′ W
Contact Hancock Shaker Village, 413-443-0188, hancockshakervillage.org Pittsfield State Forest, 413-442-8992, mass.gov/locations/pittsfield-state-forest

DIRECTIONS
From the intersection of US 7 and US 20 in the center of Pittsfield, follow US 20 west (West Housatonic Street) for 6.0 miles to the trailhead parking area on the right (north) side of the road, opposite Hancock Shaker Village.

TRAIL DESCRIPTION
This outing begins on Hancock Shaker Village land and then enters Pittsfield State Forest. You may want to tour the village's many historical buildings now or upon your return, but be sure to leave sufficient time to complete the hike. From the trailhead on US 20, pass a gate and follow Shaker Trail, blazed with a white circle in a green triangle, north up to 1-acre Shaker Reservoir, constructed in 1818 to supply water to the village. Look back to the south for a partial view of the village, including the iconic round barn, as you ascend away from US 20. Enter deciduous woodland where sugar maples display colorful foliage in October. Pass a trail intersection on the right and continue along Shaker Trail beneath a canopy of oak, maple, hickory, black cherry, and black birch on Shaker Brook's west side. A low stone wall, the first of many, is on the left.

Pass the foundations of a bridge that once led over the stream to the North Family Dwelling site. A patch of native bloodroot blooms white in early spring on this side of the brook. A bit farther up, arrive at Lower Dam, which supplied water power to the

TRIP 23 // SHAKER MOUNTAIN

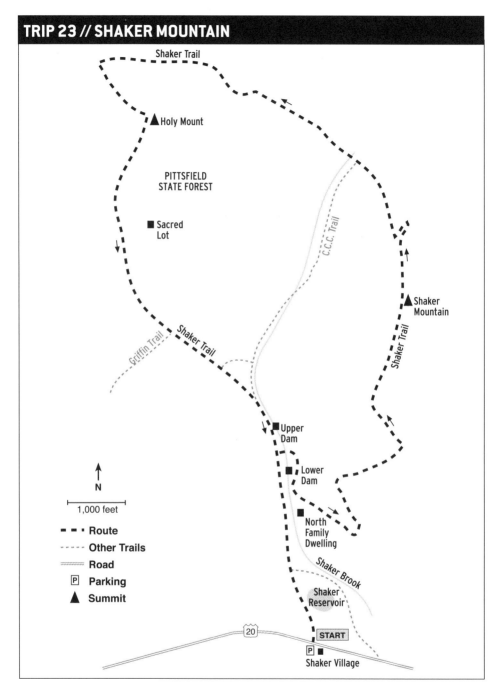

village. A slope rises to the left, and yellow birch becomes evident as the road begins a gradual ascent.

At 0.6 mile, reach the start of the Shaker Trail loop (be aware of potentially fallen trees and intermittent blazes in some places). Turn right and cross a wooden footbridge over Shaker Brook to begin a counterclockwise circuit (blazes are more visible in this direction). Walk a short distance downstream on a dirt road past Shaker Mill site foundations to the North Family Dwelling site, which dates to 1821. The site is named for the geographic location of this communal dwelling, which housed 20 to 40 or more people. An extensive carpet of shiny green periwinkle (*Vinca minor*) marks the location of a former garden. Follow contours and switchbacks to ascend the moderately steep slope, where you'll encounter white pines—some large—and hemlocks mixed with oaks and beeches. In late spring, look for the yellowish pinecone-like form of American cancerroot (also known as bear corn)—a parasite on oak roots. At a branch in the road, turn left. When you arrive at a four-way intersection with a steep woods road that leads to an airplane beacon near the summit, cross this rocky road and bear left; arrive at a second, higher intersection with the same road. Cross the road again and continue steadily up Shaker Trail toward the Hancock Shaker community's Holy Ground on Shaker Mountain, marked by an interpretive sign. In spring and fall, special religious services were held here. This brushy area has four sections of white picket fence demarcating the four corners of the site. American chestnut sprouts are numerous within, as are bracken ferns.

Continue uphill on an easy grade, passing young white pines and hemlocks. The predominant trees are oak, black cherry, American beech, and white birch. Cross the wooded summit at approximately 1.8 miles and descend past dense hobblebush patches into hemlock woods on the contouring woods road. After a sharper descent, the path levels out through thick hay-scented ferns and reaches a four-way intersection with the multiuse CCC Trail, which often shows heavy ATV travel (off-road vehicles are allowed in Pittsfield State Forest). Turn left and then immediately right (do not go straight ahead) to stay on blazed Shaker Trail toward the Shakers' Holy Mount. Continuing left leads down the ravine between the two promontories—the most direct route back to the village. Smooth gray schist bedrock protrudes from the path as you make your way across the head of the valley. Stately oaks rise where the stone walls on your right once bordered open pastures.

Reach an intermittent Shaker Brook tributary and cross it on stones; a stand of young hemlocks rises to your right. Hardwoods—white ash, sugar maple, and black cherry—thrive on the slope. After frost has killed other ferns, a luxuriant growth of spinulose wood fern has the forest floor to itself. (*Note*: Erosion by ATVs may cause water to flow down the path during wet seasons as you head uphill.)

At the next intersection, turn left to continue on Shaker Trail. Many of the rocks in the adjacent stone wall contain white quartz, visible through the mossy covering. Beech trees become more common now among the oaks, and below them is a miniature "forest" of club mosses. These attractive nonflowering plants reproduce by spores as well as by runners (stemlike growths) and are indicators of once-pastured ground. On the left, beyond the rock wall, hay-scented fern grows profusely.

After you start climbing again, amid lowbush blueberries, turn right and pass through a gap in the stone wall (wide enough to permit a team of oxen to pass in historical times), entering a flat area wooded with red maple, oak, cherry, and beech. The Holy Mount of the Shaker community of New Lebanon, New York, used this land for about ten years in the mid-nineteenth century. Extensive stone walls demarcate a site of several fern-filled acres. Follow the stone wall to a side path on the left that leads 100 feet to the best example of the wall builder's craft on this hike. This summit (3.5 miles from the trailhead), like others in the area, was once denuded of timber and long views were possible, but the trees have grown back enough to obscure those views.

Return to Shaker Trail and bear left. The path, which leads downhill, is needle-cushioned beneath a stand of young white pines. Encounter more stone walls with wide gaps as you descend moderately under oak and beech to the Sacred Gap, a natural amphitheater where the Shakers gathered for prayer and reflection. A small rock dam impounded water from a spring. Turn left on the woodland path to head up through hardwood forest and then down, arriving at a fire road (open to motorized vehicles) that soon parallels Shaker Brook. Turn left and follow the rocky double track. An impressive black oak on the right bears the long scar of a lightning strike. A little farther, at the base of a white ash on the left, sharp-lobed hepatica offers delicate lilac-hued blossoms in early spring.

At 4.1 miles, reach the intersection with Griffin Trail. Turn left and follow combined Shaker Trail and Griffin Trail for the next 0.4 mile. At the next intersection, turn right to continue the main Shaker Trail loop (for an optional short detour, turn left, make a short climb, and then descend under pines and mixed hardwoods to an intersection near Shaker Brook. Turn right to return to Shaker Trail). Follow Shaker Trail downstream to the site of Upper Dam, where an overgrown wooden staircase leads down to the brook. Dry masonry walls are visible on the opposite bank. The flow once powered a waterwheel built in 1810 (it was destroyed by flooding in 1976). A little more walking brings you back to the footbridge over Shaker Brook to close the

From a trailhead near Hancock Shaker Village and its iconic round barn, the Shaker Trail circuit leads to an old dam and other historical sites on Shaker Mountain.

loop at 4.9 miles. Continue straight to retrace your steps down West Road to the trailhead near the village.

DID YOU KNOW?

During the early nineteenth century, the celibate religious sect known as the Shakers built a thriving community of 350 people at this site in Hancock, which they called City of Peace. Residents of a nearby Shaker community in New Lebanon, New York, are said to have called to their fellow Shakers across the 1-mile-wide valley between Holy Ground and Holy Mount.

MORE INFORMATION

Open year-round; access is free for hikers. Leashed dogs are allowed. Motorized vehicles, firearms, hunting, and fishing are not permitted. Off-road vehicles and seasonal hunting are allowed in Pittsfield State Forest. Hancock Shaker Village is open from April to October and for seasonal events; see hancockshakervillage.org for dates, admission fees, and other information. Restrooms and a café are on village grounds.

NEARBY

The Shaker Museum preserves an extensive collection of Shaker artifacts, books, and archival items. The grounds and trails at the Historic Mount Lebanon Site, at 202 Shaker Road in New Lebanon, New York (off US 20, 4.2 miles west of Hancock Shaker Village and Shaker Trail), are open to the public year-round. A new state-of-the-art, four-floor museum is under construction in Chatham, New York, as of 2024. See the Shaker Museum website (shakermuseum.us) or call 518-794-9100 for information and updates.

24 MAHANNA COBBLE

Starting from Bousquet Mountain Ski Area, a relatively short ascent on Mahanna Cobble Trail leads to a rocky lookout and bench atop Lenox Mountain's north summit, where vistas to Monument Mountain and Mount Everett await.

FEATURES

Location Pittsfield and Lenox, MA
Rating Moderate
Distance 3 miles round trip
Elevation Gain 790 feet
Estimated Time 2 hours
Maps USGS Pittsfield West, Berkshire Natural Resources Council map: bnrc.org/fileadmin/files/Maps/BNRC_Mahanna_Cobble_2023_FINAL.pdf
GPS Coordinates 42.25.153 N, 73.16.570 W
Contact Berkshire Natural Resources Council, 413-499-0596, bnrc.org/reserves/mahanna-cobble

DIRECTIONS

From Pittsfield center, at the intersection of US 7 and MA 9, follow US 7 south for 2.6 miles. Turn right (west) onto Dan Fox Drive and continue 1.0 mile to the Bousquet Mountain Ski Area entrance at 101 Dan Fox Drive. Bear left to enter the hiker parking area at an information sign.

TRAIL DESCRIPTION

At the northern end of Lenox Mountain's ridge, Mahanna Cobble, an exposed rock outcropping, provides views across the central Berkshires. Mahanna Cobble Trail, recently established by Berkshire Natural Resources Council (BNRC) in conjunction with Bousquet Mountain Ski Area, links a trailhead at the ski facility with a 222-acre BNRC tract that abuts Mass Audubon's Pleasant Valley Wildlife Sanctuary on the upper slopes. The trail forms the northern section of the High Road, a long-distance route that connects conservation areas, trails, and communities (see "Taking the High Road" on page 136).

The first section of Mahanna Cobble Trail traverses a portion of Bousquet Mountain Ski Area. A minor relocation of the trail is being finalized as of late 2024. (Future

TRIP 24 // MAHANNA COBBLE

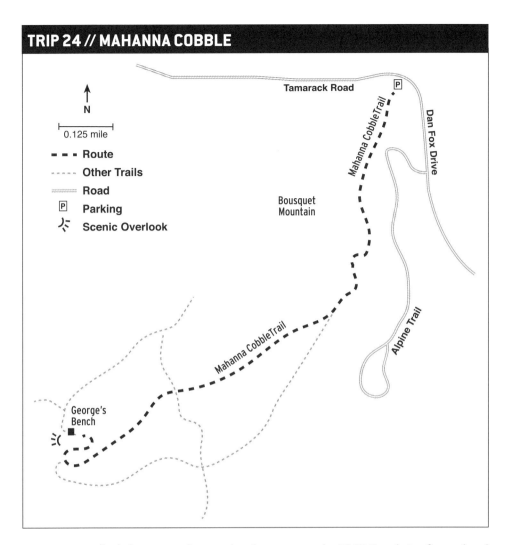

winter access for hikers is unclear at the ski area; see the BNRC website for updated information. Please respect the property and be alert for potential changes.) The trail route, clearly delineated with signs, blue blazes, and High Road markers, follows the Drifter ski run on a moderately steep ascent parallel to the property's eastern boundary. Wildflowers such as bluets, common blue violets, and wild strawberry grow along the sunlit slopes and open areas in spring; red trilliums and white violets bloom in adjacent strips of forest. Red-eyed vireos, migratory songbirds that favor mature deciduous forests, sing almost continually throughout spring and early summer days. Look back to the northeast for a view of Mount Greylock, which rises in the distance beyond a housing development.

At approximately 0.5 mile, Mahanna Cobble Trail levels and bears left off the ski run to the BNRC property boundary. Continue on Mahanna Cobble Trail, now a footpath marked with blue blazes, through a more natural setting of oak-hardwood forests. Supplied with nutrients from Lenox Mountain's bedrock, rich soils sustain wildflowers such as foamflower (appropriately named for small white flower clusters), bloodroot, and trout lily. Resume ascending at mostly easy grades through hemlock groves where shady evergreen cover limits plant growth on the forest floor.

Apart from a few short switchback turns, Mahanna Cobble Trail traces a mostly straight course along the southeastern side of Lenox Mountain's ridge. Pass two seasonal brooks and a rocky section with a growth of younger forest. Year-round resident birds of these woods include diminutive golden-crowned kinglets, which nest in mixed and coniferous forests in the Berkshire Hills and northern New England. Their faint, high-pitched *bee-bee-bee* call can be difficult to hear. Northern flickers often forage for insects on the forest floor. Eastern chipmunks make dens under old stumps, decaying trees, and rock piles. During summer and early fall, they actively gather food, such as nuts, acorns, and seeds, for winter storage.

As you gain elevation, notice that trees become shorter on the drier, rocky upper slopes. Eastern starflower, a familiar woodland wildflower that thrives in a variety of habitats and soils, blooms in mid to late spring. Glimpse surrounding hills to the south through trees, especially from November to early May. This segment of Mahanna Cobble Trail, which was designed to minimize impact on the surrounding environment, features several well-crafted stone steps and reinforced trail edges.

Bear right near the property boundary with Pleasant Valley Wildlife Sanctuary and continue to the nearby base of Mahanna Cobble. Cross exposed rock, turn left, and make a final ascent past oak, hemlock, and pine trees. At 1.5 miles, reach an open ledge and a stone bench dedicated to BNRC founding director George Wislocki, who had a long and successful career conserving the region's land; he died in 2024. From the lookout, just below the cobble's 1,909-foot summit, enjoy southerly vistas across unbroken forests and hills of the central Berkshires, including nearby Kennedy Park in Lenox and the adjacent ridge of Lenox Mountain, which extends south through Pleasant Valley Wildlife Sanctuary to Olivia's Overlook at the boundary of West Stockbridge, Richmond, and Lenox. Monument Mountain, distinguished by the steep cliff on its upper east slope, rises along the Housatonic Valley corridor in Great Barrington. Farther south on the distant horizon lies Mount Everett, the highest eminence of the southern Berkshires.

Watch for birds of prey soaring on updrafts along Lenox Mountain's ridge. Northbound migrations of turkey vultures, which begin in February or March, are an early sign of spring. Black vultures, once uncommon in New England, have expanded their range north into the region in recent years.

At a trail marker near the overlook, the High Road route continues on Yokun Ridge Trail, which traverses the western end of the BNRC property and then enters Pleasant Valley Wildlife Sanctuary, a Mass Audubon property. (*Note*: Dogs and bicycles are not allowed on Mass Audubon land.) From the trail marker, retrace your steps on Mahanna Cobble Trail back to Bousquet Mountain Ski Area. Enjoy the aforementioned view of Mount Greylock as you descend to the parking lot.

DID YOU KNOW?

Bousquet Mountain Ski Area, which opened in 1935, is one of the nation's oldest ski facilities. Clarence Bousquet, who originally operated a mink farm on the grounds,

Part of the recently established High Road trail corridor, Mahanna Cobble offers vistas across the central Berkshires to Monument Mountain and Mount Everett.

installed four rope tows and floodlights for night skiing during the 1930s. He also patented and sold a device called a rope tow gripper. Mount Greylock Ski Club members helped create the trails.

MORE INFORMATION
At Bousquet Mountain Ski Area, an easement permits public access to Mahanna Cobble Trail during spring, summer, and fall; winter use is unclear as of this writing. Leashed dogs are allowed, except during the skiing season at Bousquet Mountain. Hunting is allowed on BNRC land in accordance with state laws. Hikers are welcome at Bousquet Mountain's LIFT Bistropub, a restaurant and bar on the second floor of the ski lodge; see bousquetmountain.com for hours.

NEARBY
Parsons Marsh, a BNRC property in the Undermountain Valley on the east side of Lenox Mountain, features an 1,800-foot-long accessible stone dust path and boardwalk that explores a meadow, pond, and the northern portion of Parsons Marsh. An observation platform provides opportunities to see river otters, mink, and other wildlife. The entrance is on Under Mountain Road in Lenox, 0.9 mile north of the intersection with MA 183 (West Street). Find more information at bnrc.org/reserves/parsons-marsh.

TAKING THE HIGH ROAD

Imagine hiking long distances unencumbered by heavy backpacks or camping gear, while enjoying hearty meals at restaurants, nights at an inn or a bed-and-breakfast, and diversions to cultural attractions such as Tanglewood Music Center. Inspired by community trails in Europe, the High Road, an ambitious initiative spearheaded by Berkshire Natural Resources Council (BNRC), is developing just such a network of interconnected trails with links to the region's towns and villages.

Tad Ames, a former BNRC president, originally conceived the High Road concept in 2015 to showcase the region's many natural preserves and landmarks, including mountains, ridges, forests, scenic vistas, farms, and towns. The initiative ties in with a broad conservation plan that encompasses biological diversity, wildlife habitat and travel corridors, connected landscapes, and climate change resiliency. In addition to BNRC, collaborators include organizations such as Mass Audubon, public and private landowners, and other partners.

The first High Road section, extending from Bousquet Mountain in Pittsfield to West Stockbridge Mountain in Lenox, opened in 2021. The 8.5-mile route traverses a protected greenway of more than 5,000 acres on Yokun Ridge, a section of the central Taconic Range that encompasses West Stockbridge and Lenox mountains. Connecting segments link to Lenox center, where amenities include restaurants, cafés, hotels, and shops.

From the northern trailhead at Bousquet Mountain Ski Area, the High Road follows BNRC's Mahanna Cobble Trail up the ridge to a scenic vista and stone bench at Mahanna Cobble, Lenox Mountain's north summit (Trip 24). From the BNRC property boundary, the route enters Mass Audubon's Pleasant Valley Wildlife Sanctuary and continues along Yokun Ridge Trail to Yokun Seat, a lookout with westerly views. A gentle ascent along the wooded ridge leads to Lenox Mountain's 2,146-foot true summit (Trip 25), the High Road's highest elevation, 3.7 miles from the ski area trailhead.

At Lenox Mountain's summit, a side path follows Mass Audubon's Overbrook and Bluebird trails down the ridge's steep eastern slope to Yokun Brook, where other trails explore a series of beaver ponds. From the sanctuary entrance, a short walk on Dugway Road connects to Kennedy Park, where old carriage roads and woodland paths (not marked with High Road signage) lead to the former site of an elaborate hilltop hotel, Main Street in the town of Lenox, and the Arcadian Shop on US 7.

The main High Road continues on Yokun Ridge Trail through watershed land (owned by the town of Lenox) to BNRC's Yokun Ridge South (a nature reserve). At the route's southern end, Old Baldhead Trail leads down to Monk's Pond and a trailhead at the Kripalu Center for Yoga & Health, where parking is available at the North Gate House on 35 Richmond Road. Hikers can extend the outing on Burbank Trail (Trip 26), Brothers Trail, and Charcoal Trail (Trip 27), all part of Yokun Ridge South reserve's trail network. From the Kripalu campus, a 1.5-mile road walk on MA 183 (West Street) leads past Tanglewood Music Center to central Lenox. A direct link from the Bousquet Mountain Ski Area trailhead to downtown Pittsfield, the region's hub city, is being planned.

When complete, the envisioned overall route will comprise multiple segments (each roughly 10 miles long), extending north-south across Berkshire County, with connecting paths to communities. The trail network will provide a variety of starting points and options for walkers, ranging from short, easy outings to multiday treks over mountains and hills.

In addition to benefiting hikers and attracting visitors to the region, another important goal is to increase and enhance access to trails and conservation lands for Berkshire County residents. Connections to communities with bus and railroad service, such as Pittsfield and Lenox, will reduce dependence on automobiles to reach trailheads.

Volunteer opportunities include planning, building and maintaining the route, and serving as stewards for conservation properties. For more information, including maps and updates, see bnrc.org/the-high-road.

25 PLEASANT VALLEY WILDLIFE SANCTUARY: LENOX MOUNTAIN AND BEAVER POND LOOPS

Lying in an attractive valley on the east flank of Lenox Mountain, this sanctuary's 1,300 acres and 7-mile trail system offer wonderful hiking and wildlife observation opportunities. Two loops, one a rugged ascent to a scenic vista atop Lenox Mountain and the other an easy walk to a chain of beaver wetlands, are detailed here.

FEATURES

Location Lenox, MA
Rating Strenuous (Lenox Mountain Loop); Easy (Beaver Pond Loop)
Distance 3-mile loop (Lenox Mountain Loop); 1.8-mile loop (Beaver Pond Loop)
Elevation Gain 825 feet (Lenox Mountain Loop); 115 feet (Beaver Pond Loop)
Estimated Time 2 hours (Lenox Mountain Loop); 1.25 hours (Beaver Pond Loop)
Maps USGS Pittsfield West; Mass Audubon map: massaudubon.org/places-to-explore/wildlife-sanctuaries/pleasant-valley/trails
GPS Coordinates 42° 22.959′ N, 73° 17.939′ W
Contact Mass Audubon, 413-637-0320, massaudubon.org/pleasantvalley

DIRECTIONS

From the south: From I-90 (Massachusetts Turnpike) in Lee, take Exit 10. Turn right at the end of the ramp and follow US 20 (becomes US 7/US 20 just after Cranwell Resort) west for 6.6 miles to West Dugway Road on the left (blue sanctuary sign). Follow West Dugway Road (which junctions with West Mountain Road) for 1.6 miles to the sanctuary's gravel parking area and office.

From the north: From the center of Pittsfield at Park Square, drive south on US 7 for 4.9 miles to West Dugway Road on the right and then follow the directions above.

TRAIL DESCRIPTION

Sanctuary trails are blazed blue outbound and yellow returning; intersections are signed. After registering at the office (trail maps available; check a sign for recent wildlife sightings), begin the loop on All Person's Trail, a universally accessible route that winds north and then west toward Pike's Pond. Pass a side path on the right that connects to the education center and then turn right at the intersection with Honeysuckle Lane. At the next junction, bear right to an observation area on the northeast side of Pike's Pond, constructed in 1932 to increase the sanctuary's habitat diversity. It is an

TRIP 25 // PLEASANT VALLEY WILDLIFE SANCTUARY: LENOX MOUNTAIN AND BEAVER POND LOOPS

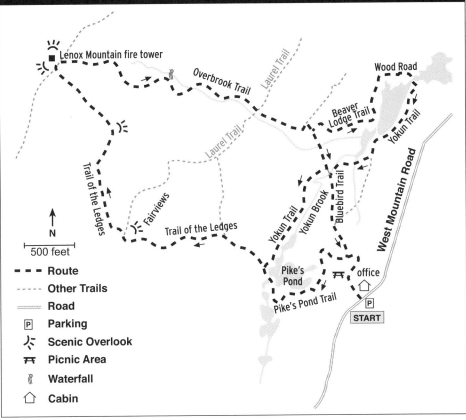

excellent vantage point for observing beavers, especially at dusk. Return to the intersection and continue on All Person's Trail around the pond's southern end. An associated boggy area hosts ferns and alders. Skunk cabbage emerges as early as February, and the yellow petals of marsh marigolds glow in May.

All Person's Trail forks into a short loop at its western end; follow either branch to a footbridge over Yokun Brook at 0.4 mile. After the crossing, bear left at the next intersection and begin ascending on Trail of the Ledges. Remnant stone walls attest to sheep grazing here as recently as 1909. Ascend 500 vertical feet in less than one-third of a mile along a steep segment leading to an 1,850-foot outlook called Fairview; some slopes approach 45 degrees. As some rock scrambling is required, hikers are advised not to use this section to descend.

A transitional forest of oak, white pine, birch, beech, and maple clothes the ridge's lower slopes. Pileated woodpeckers seek out mature trees infested with carpenter ants, while yellow-bellied sapsuckers (the only local woodpeckers that regularly migrate long distances) dine on insects and the sweet sap of birches and maples. Mountain laurel increases as you gain elevation.

At Fairview, gaze eastward to October Mountain State Forest. The remaining section to the summit, which passes several more vistas to the east and north, is not as steep. Notice that the stature of the timber decreases as you ascend, due to shallow soils and a harsher climate. (Temperatures generally decrease 1 degree for every 400 feet ascended.) Reach the grassy 2,126-foot summit at approximately 1.8 miles, where a former fire tower (off-limits to the public) now houses state police communications equipment. Here, the hike joins a portion of the High Road, a recently established long-distance trail delineated with High Road markers (see "Taking the High Road" on page 136).

A bench offers an ideal spot to admire the vistas, especially toward the nearby Taconic Range, which runs along the New York–Massachusetts border to the west. The Taconics are among the continent's oldest mountain ranges, thrust up more than 400 million years ago when what is now Africa rammed into what is now North America. Geologically speaking, Lenox Mountain is considered to be an outlier of the Taconics. On clear days, the distant Catskill Mountains are visible 40 miles to the southwest. On the westward flank, look to the right (north) for a glimpse of Mount Greylock. Richmond Pond lies at the base of the ridge. Maturing red maples obscure easterly views.

Follow signs along the fence to the upper trailhead for Overbrook Trail at a sign indicating the path to Pleasant Valley Wildlife Sanctuary. Descend through a mixed woodland; the grades are moderate with some steeper sections, but none approach the inclines of the ascent. Listen in summer for the ethereal song of the hermit thrush.

Pass a picturesque 12-foot waterfall near the first of five brook crossings. Hemlocks, not harvested due to rugged terrain, crowd the ravines. It is hard to imagine now that most of the mountain's timber was once cut for charcoal making, lumber, and firewood, and to clear land for pasture.

At the intersection with Laurel Trail, continue straight on Overbrook Trail along a stream lined with stately hemlocks. The trail bears left and widens into a dirt road. In late spring and summer, the loud *teacher-teacher-teacher* refrain of the ovenbird is ubiquitous. This species builds a roofed nest with a side entrance, resembling an old-fashioned oven. At the junction with Bluebird Trail and Old Wood Road, turn right onto Bluebird Trail and pass the junction with Beaver Lodge Trail on the left. Cross footbridges over two brooks and stroll beneath giant white pines. Some are 3½ feet in diameter and more than 100 feet tall; the tallest is a little more than 141 feet.

Arrive at Yokun Brook, home to brook trout, two-lined salamanders, and dusky salamanders. Louisiana waterthrushes are among the first warblers to return here from the tropics in mid-April; they construct their nests along the brook's banks. Continue on Bluebird Trail past more pines to a sloping field, where milkweed flowers attract a variety of butterflies in summer. From the intersection with Alexander Trail, walk about 200 yards along the field edge to the sanctuary entrance.

Beaver Pond Loop

From the sanctuary office, walk north toward a red barn on the left, where restrooms, water, and a picnic area are available. Pass the intersection with All Person's Trail (a wheelchair-accessible path that leads to Pike's Pond) and continue straight on Bluebird Trail past the education center and solar array. Tree swallows and eastern bluebirds nest in wooden boxes in the field. In July, pink milkweed flowers lure a myriad of butterflies, including hairstreaks, skippers, and monarchs. Lenox Mountain's ridge looms ahead.

Follow Bluebird Trail past a giant eastern cottonwood at the first intersection with Alexander Trail and through another field before entering a stand of tall white pines at a stone wall. Ahead is Yokun Brook, a tributary of the Housatonic River. Turn right onto signed Yokun Trail. (Both the trail and brook were named for a notable Mohican leader of the early eighteenth century.) The path winds through white ash, black cherry, and birch woods.

At a four-way intersection (where the northern end of Alexander Trail enters on the right), turn left onto a side loop that leads to beaver ponds along Yokun Brook. Signs of the rodents' presence include sizable fallen trees and scat—oval pellets of compressed "sawdust." In 1932, beavers were reintroduced at this location after an absence of almost 150 years. A bench, ideal for wildlife watching, sits near a beaver dam. At the loop's end, turn left to rejoin Yokun Trail. Pass hollows on the right where gravel was once mined. To your left is a larger pond with a beaver lodge, a conical mass of sticks and mud, at its far end. Each lodge hosts one family.

At the end of Yokun Trail, bear left onto Old Wood Road and traverse a wooden bridge at a small pond between two beaver dams. Beavers create ponds to protect themselves from predators. The upstream dam to your left is 3 to 4 feet high. Blue-purple blossoms of bottle gentians emerge in September. Beyond the bridge

While beavers are the most visible large mammals at Pleasant Valley, lucky hikers occasionally stumble upon other mammals such as this white-tailed deer fawn.

grow mountain laurels and large white pines. Japanese barberry shrubs—an invasive exotic—are abundant.

At the next intersection (0.7 mile), turn left onto Beaver Lodge Trail. Be alert in spring and summer for the sudden launch of an American woodcock—a chunky "shorebird" sporting a nearly 3-inch-long bill with a flexible tip to pull earthworms from the moist soil. Winterberry grows in a beaver-dug channel on the left, beyond the winding boardwalk. During warm seasons, a multitude of ferns (mostly New York fern) carpet the sunny openings. Pass the first beaver pond you reached, but from the opposite side. Here, the path curves right onto a low mound above another small pond, where vegetation partially obscures a beaver lodge.

Continue on Beaver Lodge Trail around the swamp and into a stand of pines and hemlocks, where golden-crowned kinglets shelter during the cold months. At a signed junction, turn left and follow Bluebird Trail across another boardwalk. Now at Lenox Mountain's base, cross a span over a brook. More tall pines rise 100 feet above the needle-cushioned forest floor. At an intersection at Yokun Brook, turn right onto Yokun Trail's southern section at 1.1 miles and amble under pines to a point above the brook where the soothing sound of flowing water is omnipresent.

Traverse mixed woodland that now includes red oak and yellow birch. The green leaves of false hellebore pushing up through the floodplain soil are a welcome sight in April. Emerge into sunlight at another beaver pond.

At the intersection with Trail of the Ledges, turn left, cross a footbridge, and follow universally accessible All Person's Trail along Pike's Pond's southern end. Trailing arbutus (mayflower), the Massachusetts state flower, blooms from late April to early May. Its sandpaper-like leaves and delicate pink blossoms hug the ground in sunny openings. Eastern chipmunks utter a fluty whistle and scamper for their burrows when danger threatens. They harvest acorns, beechnuts, and hazelnuts for winter dining. Fragrant mountain azalea shrubs display tubular pink flowers in late May. Mountain laurel's white-and-pink blossoms are an impressive sight in late spring or early summer.

All Person's Trail bears left to continue around Pike's Pond, best viewed as the path climbs a few feet to higher ground at two large sugar maples. Hooded mergansers and wood ducks nest in wooden boxes fastened to trees. Walk beneath planted Depression-era red pines, where high-strung red squirrels chatter. The trail curves left and follows a boardwalk through a shrub swamp bordered by alders and larches. Interrupted ferns grow high on drier ground, while royal and cinnamon ferns (the latter with cinnamon-hued, fertile fronds) crowd the decking. Detour left at the next intersection to an observation area on the northeast shore of Pike's Pond. From the intersection, complete the hike by following All Person's Trail past Honeysuckle Lane to the trailhead near the sanctuary office.

DID YOU KNOW?

The Lenox Fire Tower, built in 1970, was a Berkshire landmark until it burned in March 1995. Although the popular observation tower afforded 360-degree vistas, the 70-foot steel structure had not been staffed and used as a fire lookout since 1988. The tower's old frame now supports emergency communications equipment.

MORE INFORMATION

Trails are open dawn to dusk, year-round. Hours for the sanctuary office are 9 A.M. to 4 P.M. daily from June to October; 10 A.M. to 4 P.M. Tuesday to Sunday from November to May. Fees: $5 for adults; $3 for children 2 to 12 and senior citizens 65 or older. Access is free for Mass Audubon members and Lenox residents. Restrooms and water are available at the office. Pets, mountain bikes, horses, hunting, trapping, fishing, and collecting are not permitted.

NEARBY

Tanglewood Music Center has been the world-renowned summer home of the Boston Symphony Orchestra since 1937. Each summer, hundreds of thousands of visitors flock to the Berkshires to enjoy concerts. The main entrance is at 297 West Street in Lenox, about 2 miles from the sanctuary; visit bso.org or call 888-266-1200 for ticket information.

BRINGING BACK THE BEAVER

Beavers, herbivorous furbearers with legendary persistence and ingenuity, are adept at constructing engineering marvels that, in their own way, rival those of humans. Beaver wetlands are a crucial part of the ecology of the Berkshires and other regions. Although beavers are common in western Massachusetts now, such was not the case as recently as the early twentieth century.

From the time of European settlement, beavers were killed for their splendid pelts. Long, glossy guard hairs protrude above a dense, luxuriant underfur that insulates the animal against damp and cold—just the right attire for a creature that doesn't hibernate and spends a good portion of its waking hours submerged in chilly water. Beavers constituted the bread and butter of the fur trade that provided impetus for the exploration of much of North America. By the late eighteenth century, though, beavers had been eliminated from Massachusetts.

In the late 1920s and early 1930s, some people sought to repatriate the former native after an absence of almost 150 years. They felt it was time to recalibrate the balance of nature. Thus, in 1932, S. Morris Pell, warden of Pleasant Valley Bird and Wildflower Sanctuary, acquired—after considerable effort—one adult female and two adult males from the Blue Mountain Lake region of New York. Pell and his helpers constructed a sturdy fenced enclosure around 1½ acres of willows and alders bordering Yokun Brook. The trio was introduced to their new quarters at 5 P.M. on October 8; by dawn the next morning, they had constructed their first dam and pond.

Beavers build ponds to safeguard themselves from land-bound predators. Although certainly not defenseless on terra firma, the pudgy beaver transforms into a study in grace in its watery realm. An enlarged liver enables it to remain submerged for up to 15 minutes. And just like humans, beavers use the water's buoyancy to float cargo, be it tree branches that serve as construction material for dams and their homes (called lodges) or food, in the form of leafy twigs.

For some people, the mere mention of beavers engenders disdain. But why? The answer seems clear enough: North America's largest rodents sometimes compete with humans for waterfront territory, and their dams can cause property damage and flooded roads.

Beaver wetlands have many virtues. They absorb storm runoff like the proverbial sponge and release it slowly, minimizing flooding. Wetlands provide natural purification for runoff entering groundwater aquifers. And beaver ponds provide homes for a litany of other creatures, from mosquito-eating dragonflies to fish, wood ducks and other waterfowl, and moose. If frogs could vote, beavers would win the popularity contest hands down.

26 LENOX MOUNTAIN: BURBANK TRAIL

This enjoyable loop takes you through diverse woodland to a pleasing lookout on the southern slope of Lenox Mountain. A historical homesite and a former estate's reservoir add interest.

FEATURES

Location Richmond and Lenox, MA
Rating Easy to Moderate
Distance 3.2-mile loop
Elevation Gain 540 feet
Estimated Time 1.5 to 2 hours
Maps USGS Stockbridge; Berkshire Natural Resources Council map: bnrc.org/fileadmin/files/Maps/BNRC_Yokun_Ridge_South_2023_FINAL.pdf
GPS Coordinates 42° 21.109′ N, 73° 20.259′ W
Contact Berkshire Natural Resources Council, 413-499-0596, bnrc.org/reserves/olivias-overlook-at-yokun-ridge-south

DIRECTIONS

From I-90 (Massachusetts Turnpike), take Exit 10 in Lee. Bear right at the end of the ramp and follow US 20 west for 4.1 miles. (US 20 joins US 7 just after Cranwell Resort; the route then becomes combined US 7 and US 20.) Turn left at the traffic light onto MA 183 South (Walker Street). Drive for 1.1 miles to the intersection with MA 183 in Lenox center. Continue straight on MA 183 South for another 1.5 miles (past the entrance to Tanglewood Music Center). Bear right onto Richmond Mountain Road and follow it uphill for 1.4 miles to a circular gravel parking area on the left at Olivia's Overlook. (*Note*: The parking area may fill to capacity on pleasant summer and fall weekends.)

TRAIL DESCRIPTION

This excursion's best view is from the parking area at Olivia's Overlook and takes in Stockbridge Bowl (also known as Lake Mahkeenac) and the verdant ridges beyond. The lookout is named for Olivia Stokes Hatch, whose family donated the land to the Berkshire County Land Trust and Conservation Fund.

Carefully cross Lenox Road and enter the woods at the trailhead on the north side of the road. A kiosk, complete with a large trail map (and often a supply of printed maps), is about 50 feet into the forest. Walk up into diverse woodland of eastern hemlock, oak,

TRIP 26 // LENOX MOUNTAIN: BURBANK TRAIL

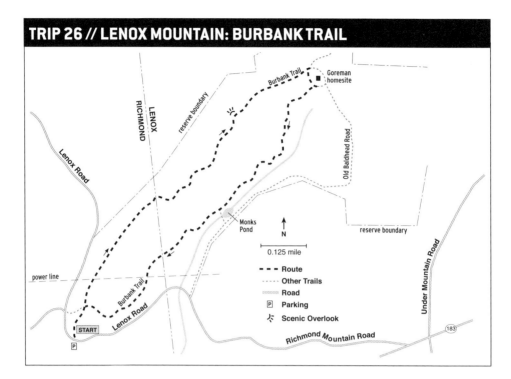

ash, and red maple. Note the gray schist outcroppings veined with milky quartz. This erosion-resistant rock type forms the spine of the Lenox–Stockbridge Mountain ridge. Enter a darker forest in which hemlock predominates, joined by yellow, black, and gray birches as well as shade-tolerant American beeches and sun-loving oaks. In spring, a wet depression to the right is filled with a profusion of purple violets.

Follow the blue-blazed path and arrive at a signed four-way intersection. (*Note*: All Berkshire Natural Resources Council trails on Yokun Ridge are marked with blue blazes.) Continue straight ahead on Burbank Trail. Begin a moderate climb past schist outcroppings and emerge into sunlight as you reach a power-line cut. Wintergreen on the left bears coral-red fruits in late summer and during fall. This sunny, dry, linear landscape also provides suitable growing conditions for pale corydalis, which bears tubular pink-and-yellow flowers in May. Eastern towhees are among the bird species that nest in such artificial shrublands. Listen for their *chewink* calls and *drink-your-tea* songs.

Back in the moister forest, the trail undulates under oaks, hemlocks, and mountain laurels. Woodland wildflowers here include *Clintonia* (blue-bead lily), cucumber root, and sessile-leafed bellwort (wild oat), which all produce yellow blossoms. In time, the path climbs, gently at first and then more steeply, paved in spots with bedrock. Witch hazel, a spreading shrub, blooms here in autumn. Striped maples, small trees with greenish bark, produce green flowers in May.

After a few more undulations through oaks and hop hornbeams, Burbank Trail arrives at a short side path that leads left to an outlook at 1.0 mile. The view to the northwest through a gap in the forest is limited but worth a look. A nearby plaque indicates that the trail was named for Kelton (Kim) Burbank, a local attorney and conservationist. Lowbush blueberries thrive in the acidic soil beneath the pines and oaks. Return to Burbank Trail and turn left. Striped maple, red maple, and witch hazel abound beneath the oaks. Gaudy scarlet tanager males sing their burry refrains from high in the oaks in late spring and early summer. In contrast, their yellow-green mates blend in with the foliage. When you reach a signed path, turn right to continue the loop on Burbank Trail, heading toward Old Baldhead Road.

The route descends through a forest of white ash, big-tooth aspen, black birch and gray birch, red maple, and red oak. At 1.4 miles, reach a cellar hole on the left—all that remains of the Gorman homesite, occupied by that family from 1852 to 1892, although dates on a concrete marker indicate occupation from 1838 to 1898. The Gormans farmed this 44-acre hardscrabble lot until they sold it to the Wall Street financier Anson Phelps Stokes to become part of his Shadowbrook estate. Philanthropist Andrew Carnegie later owned the property.

Blue-blazed Burbank Trail briefly joins Old Baldhead Road (part of the long-distance High Road route) and bears right. Soon reach an intersection and turn right to remain on Burbank Trail. Morrow's honeysuckle, an introduced exotic ornamental, outcompetes native shrubs here.

Opalescent Monks Pond once supplied water to Anson Phelps Stokes's Shadowbrook estate, which was later owned by Andrew Carnegie.

After traversing a series of bog bridges, bear left to continue a gradual descent to a stone wall composed of small pieces of schist. Reach a hemlock stand and drop into a shallow gorge through which a small brook spills. Some towering hemlock specimens border the brook. Gray birches, which preceded the conifers, have succumbed to the hemlocks' shade, but yellow birches thrive in the cool shadows. The wide path passes a sofa-sized boulder on the right.

Turn right at a log bench by the brook and amble under hemlocks and hardwoods. Cross a bridge and bear left. The path changes to a wider old cart road and leads down to an opalescent pond in a serene setting on the left. This was the Shadowbrook estate's reservoir. During the twentieth century, it took on the name Monks Pond; a Jesuit order owned the property at the time. (The Kripalu Center for Yoga & Health, below Olivia's Overlook, now occupies the former monastery.) Reach a signed intersection at the far right end of the reservoir and bear right to remain on Burbank Trail, following it past the earthen dam's concrete spillway. The trail stays high above the flow, and ledge outcroppings make the scene picturesque. Listen for the call of the 21-inch-tall barred owl: *who cooks for you, who cooks for you all*. The path rises moderately along this steep hillside; the slope was reinforced with rock during construction, making for excellent footing. Cross the power-line corridor again, where tall mountain laurels bloom profusely in late June.

The trail undulates easily under hemlocks and then through deciduous woodland of birch, beech, maple, and oak before reentering evergreens. Before long, you are back at the first intersection. Turn left and retrace your steps across Lenox Road to your vehicle.

DID YOU KNOW?

During the eighteenth century, virtually the entire Lenox–Stockbridge Mountain ridge was denuded of timber. Much of the wood was reduced to charcoal to feed local iron furnaces—iron production was a thriving early Berkshire industry—until almost all the nearby timber had been harvested. As a result, coal became a cheaper source of fuel for the furnaces.

MORE INFORMATION

Open dawn to dusk, year-round. Access is free. Hiking, skiing, mountain biking, horseback riding, leashed dogs, and hunting in season are permitted. Motorized vehicles, fires, camping, littering, and cutting or removing trees or plants are prohibited.

NEARBY

Chill out at Stockbridge's Kripalu Center for Yoga & Health, visible below Olivia's Overlook. The center offers presentations, training, and workshops related to yoga and healthy living. From the intersection of MA 183 and Richmond Mountain Road, follow MA 183 west for 1.6 miles to the entrance on the right. See kripalu.org for more information.

27 WEST STOCKBRIDGE MOUNTAIN: CHARCOAL TRAIL

West Stockbridge Mountain is the main attraction of Yokun Ridge South, a reserve in the southern portion of Yokun Ridge. This enjoyable loop trail leads through mature woodlands and features a couple of pleasing vistas.

FEATURES

Location Stockbridge, West Stockbridge, and Richmond, MA

Rating Moderate

Distance 1.6-mile loop

Elevation Gain 530 feet

Estimated Time 1 to 1.5 hours

Maps USGS Stockbridge; Berkshire Natural Resources Council map: bnrc.org/fileadmin/files/Maps/BNRC_Yokun_Ridge_South_2023_FINAL.pdf

GPS Coordinates 42° 21.109′ N, 73° 20.259′ W

Contact Berkshire Natural Resources Council, 413-499-0596, bnrc.org/reserves/olivias-overlook-at-yokun-ridge-south

DIRECTIONS

From the center of Lenox, at the intersection of Walker Street, MA 183, and US 7A (Main Street), follow MA 183 (West Street) for a little more than 1.5 miles. Then turn right onto Richmond Mountain Road and drive 0.4 mile to a gravel parking area on the left at Olivia's Overlook. (*Note*: The parking area may fill to capacity on pleasant summer and fall weekends.)

TRAIL DESCRIPTION

This hike starts at Olivia's Overlook, at the same parking area as for Burbank Trail (Trip 26). After enjoying the scenic view over Stockbridge Bowl, begin on the west side of the parking area by following blue-blazed Charcoal Trail across a gas pipeline corridor flush with grasses, goldenrod, catchfly, and other forbs in summer. Look for bright blue indigo buntings, which favor brushy growths and forest edges, in late spring and summer. Traverse a short wooden span to a map kiosk at the edge of a shady forest, where the Charcoal Trail loop begins. Turn left and follow blue blazes along a wide old woods road under hemlocks and oaks. The path descends gently along a ravine for the first portion of the route.

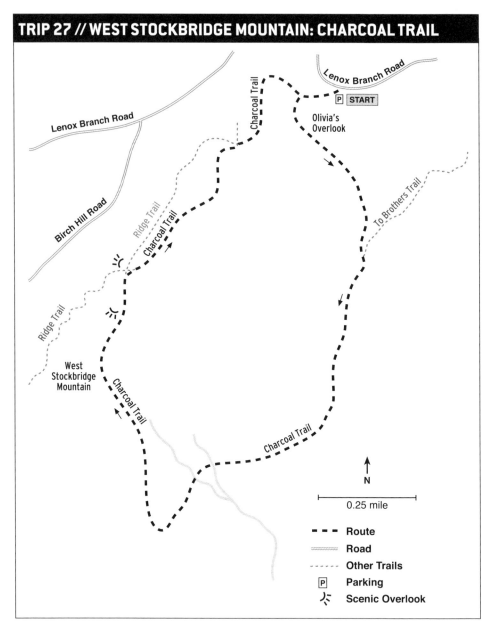

White oak, whose leaves have rounded lobes, joins the deciduous woodland mix, while witch hazel and American chestnut sprouts form a trailside understory. Stride across stretches of schist bedrock as you continue an easy descent through abundant mountain laurel that blooms in mid-June to early July. Pass the signed intersection for Brothers Trail on the left and continue straight. Brothers Trail leads for 0.9 mile to Richmond Road and Old Baldhead Road (part of the long-distance High Road; see "Taking the High Road" on page 136).

150   SECTION 2 // CENTRAL BERKSHIRES

At the BNRC property boundary, Charcoal Trail turns right (roughly halfway through the 1.6-mile loop). Listen for the deeply resonant drumming or loud laughing call—sometimes described as maniacal—of the pileated woodpecker and the mellow tremolo of the wood thrush. Shade-tolerant black birches become common, while evergreen Christmas ferns enliven the woodland year-round.

Begin an easy climb through mixed deciduous and coniferous woods—a variety of oak, black birch, and hemlock. The deep shade and acidic soil prohibit the growth of virtually any other plant life. Traverse several drainage streams, which have dissected the slopes and carved small ravines of varying depths, on well-crafted rockwork. White ashes, sugar maples, and mature oaks in this vicinity are impressively tall and straight. Stride up a stone staircase amid fallen hemlocks and reach an angular boulder where the path levels out briefly and then climbs gently. Cross a trickling drainage and pass remnant stone walls to your right. A few massive white pines escaped the lumberman's ax here. Wend along the base of an outcropping studded with mosses and ferns, including hay-scented fern, spinulose wood fern, and rock-loving common polypody.

Higher up the slope, the trees—American beech and red maple—are of much smaller stature due to the thin soil. Stone steps lead to a fern glade near the height-of-land, and lowbush blueberry and Canada mayflower grace the forest floor. The hoarse, singsong voice of the bright red male scarlet tanager fills the late spring and early summer air, but the bird itself is seldom seen.

At about 1.1 miles from the trailhead, reach the first of two scenic vistas at a rocky bald where a bench offers a view south to Monument Mountain and the Butternut ski area beyond. Note that the schist bedrock is tilted vertically. Continue on Charcoal Trail to a signed intersection just north of the summit. Turn left to reach a rocky perch with a bench, where you can take in a gorgeous scene west across a wooded valley. The outlook is part of Ridge Trail, which runs roughly parallel to Charcoal Trail along the reservation boundary, entering private land just south of the summit. A few small sassafras saplings, with mitten-shaped leaves, grow here. When you're ready, return to Charcoal Trail, or continue north on Ridge Trail, marked with periodic red blazes. Descend through oak, hemlock, and laurel. Blueberries and Canada mayflowers thrive in the acidic soil, while common polypody ferns cap some boulders. At times, the downward angle increases. Bush honeysuckle and *Clintonia*, a native lily, bloom yellow in spring, while the small shrub maple-leaf viburnum adds its umbels of whitish-pink blossoms.

From the lower junction of Ridge Trail and Charcoal Trail (marked with signs for Charcoal Trail only), continue on Charcoal Trail. Drop down easily and pass more angular outcroppings on the left under an oak canopy. A few additional twists and turns lead you back to the map kiosk and the trailhead at Olivia's Overlook.

If you have time for another short hike, check out nearby Stevens Glen, also a BNRC property. A 1.2-mile trail leads to an observation platform at a rocky chasm and picturesque cascades on Lenox Mountain Brook. To reach the trailhead from Olivia's Overlook, drive north on Richmond Mountain Road for approximately 0.1 mile to the intersection with Lenox Branch Road. Turn left onto Lenox Branch Road and continue 0.6 mile to the signed trailhead on the right. Additional parking is available 100 yards farther ahead, opposite the intersection with Deer Hill Road.

Beneath Olivia's Overlook at the trailhead for Burbank and Charcoal Trails lies 398-acre Stockbridge Bowl, also known as Lake Mahkeenac.

DID YOU KNOW?
Olivia's Overlook is named for Olivia Stokes Hatch, who, with her husband, John D. Hatch Jr., and her brothers, Anson Phelps Stokes Jr. and Isaac N. P. Stokes, donated the land. Tenneco Inc. of Houston funded the construction of the overlook.

MORE INFORMATION
Open dawn to dusk, year-round. Access is free. Hiking, skiing, mountain biking, horseback riding, leashed dogs, and hunting in season are permitted.

NEARBY
The Mount, at 2 Plunkett Street in Lenox, is the former home and 113-acre estate of Pulitzer Prize–winning novelist and short story writer Edith Wharton (1862–1937), best known for her ghostly tales. The grounds are open daily from dawn to dusk; see the website for seasonal dates and hours, admission fees, and other information (413-551-5111, edithwharton.org). The Terrace Café is available seasonally for dining. The property sometimes closes early for events and programs.

ALIEN INVADERS

They're green; they've arrived from far, far away; and they are threatening to take over. Little green beings from Mars? No, invasive exotic plants! Ask most land managers what their biggest concern is regarding species diversity, and it's a good bet they'll answer, "invasive species." Continent-wide, invasive exotics are second only to habitat loss on the list of threats to biological diversity.

Well-known invaders include purple loosestrife, Eurasian watermilfoil, Japanese barberry, round-leafed bittersweet (also known as Asian bittersweet), and garlic mustard. What makes a plant (or an animal for that matter) perfectly respectable in one part of the globe but such a menace in another? Plants translocated from their native haunts to foreign soil have no insect or mammal herbivores, fungi, or diseases to keep them in check. In their homelands, species face a long-evolving system of checks and balances to prevent rampant growth. When a species is transported (either by accident or on purpose) outside its range, the possibility exists that in its new home, sans controls, it will outcompete the local natives.

In Pleasant Valley Wildlife Sanctuary, Kennedy Park in Lenox, Burbank Park in Pittsfield, and a few other locations, a recently recognized threat has the potential to do serious damage to our forests. That threat is hardy kiwi (*Actenidia arguta*). If you've never heard of it, you're not alone. So recent is this realization that the species has yet to be added to the official state registry of invasive exotic plants.

Hardy kiwi hails from Southeast Asia, a region from which a variety of other troublesome plants, including round-leafed bittersweet, arrived. Both round-leafed bittersweet and hardy kiwi have found the soils and climate of Massachusetts to be welcoming because they mimic those of their homeland. Like bittersweet, hardy kiwi (related to the popular kiwi fruit available in grocery stores) is a climbing vine, but it is even more aggressive. And that says a lot! Kiwi spreads mostly by runners, but it also produces tasty, grape-sized, seed-filled green fruits that are distributed by birds and mammals looking for a treat. Although it doesn't constrict the trunks of trees the way round-leafed bittersweet does, it grows so prolifically as to completely engulf woody natives and rob them of sunlight. Kiwi-filled light gaps are a frightening vision of complete alien dominance, and native species have little chance against these invaders.

Although currently restricted in its range, hardy kiwi is potentially a major threat to deciduous forests in the Berkshires. Berkshire Environmental Action Team volunteers have been working to remove hardy kiwi growths since 2012. Mass Audubon, the Massachusetts Division of Fisheries and Wildlife, and town agencies are collaborating on control measures at Kennedy Park.

28 SCHERMERHORN GORGE TRAIL

From the still waters of wildlife-rich Woods Pond to the cascading flow of Schermerhorn Brook, flanked by massive trees, this hike provides dramatic contrasts.

FEATURES

Location Lenox, Lee, and Washington, MA
Rating Moderate to Strenuous
Distance 3.7 miles round trip
Elevation Gain 620 feet
Estimated Time 2 to 2.5 hours
Maps USGS East Lee; Massachusetts Department of Conservation and Recreation map: mass.gov/doc/october-mountain-state-forest-trail-map/download
GPS Coordinates 42° 20.985' N, 73° 14.638' W
Contact October Mountain State Forest, 413-243-1778, mass.gov/locations/october-mountain-state-forest

DIRECTIONS

From I-90 (Massachusetts Turnpike), take Exit 10 in Lee. Bear right at the end of the ramp and follow US 20 west through Lee (US 20 joins US 7 just after Cranwell Resort) for 4.6 miles to Housatonic Street in Lenox. Turn right onto Housatonic Street and drive 1.3 miles to where the paved road turns sharply right. Leave the pavement and continue straight ahead on gravel, parking on the right between the railroad tracks and the pedestrian bridge. (*Note*: Parking space is available for approximately four vehicles. Do not block the driveway to the private residence on the left, and do not obstruct access to the canoe landing on the pond edge to the right.) Parking is also available outside the railroad tracks, on the right, but be aware that this is an active rail line.

TRAIL DESCRIPTION

Cross the arched steel-and-wood pedestrian bridge at the south end of Woods Pond and admire the sight of October Mountain. The reflection off the pond is especially eye-catching during fall foliage season in early to mid-October. The Housatonic River plunges over Woods Pond Dam—which backs up the river's flow to create the 100-acre pond—about 200 yards to the right (south). Exotic Morrow's honeysuckle lines the gravel roadway beyond the bridge.

TRIP 28 // SCHERMERHORN GORGE TRAIL

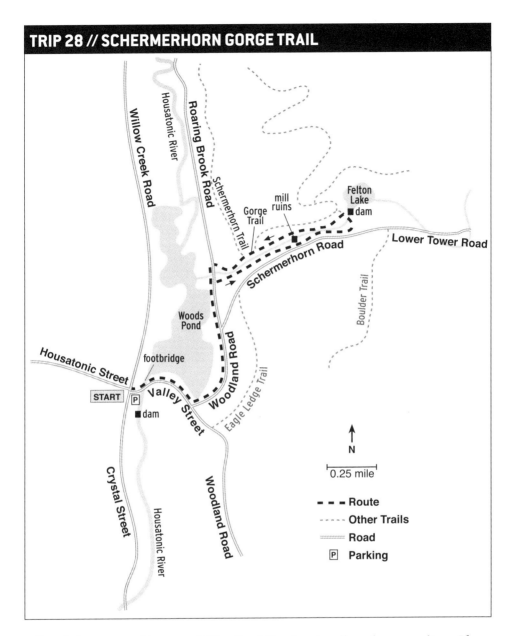

Bear left upon reaching gravel Woodland Road and walk under power lines. If you visit from May to early July, you'll be impressed by the exuberance of birdlife. Yellow warblers and a myriad of other avian life-forms abound in and around the pond, including belted kingfisher, Canada goose, wood duck, mallard, and warbling vireo.

The road hugs the pond shore, affording views of the water and surrounding hills. The bucolic scene disguises the fact that Woods Pond holds the highest concentrations of carcinogenic polychlorinated biphenyls (PCBs) in the Housatonic River system, caused by twentieth-century industrial pollution upstream in Pittsfield. (A cleanup

Schermerhorn Brook cascades down a rocky slope in October Mountain State Forest, Massachusetts's largest state forest.

proposal is being debated as of this writing.) Bear left at another gravel road to continue around the pond. Primarily young woodland of white ash, sugar maple, and gray, black, and yellow birch stands above the water body. A few massive white pines tower in stark contrast to the younger deciduous growth. Walk past a huge red oak on the right and then encounter more impressive trees.

Pass two woods roads on the right separated by a modest high-gradient stream flowing down the hillside into Woods Pond. Reach the state forest boundary to your right shortly before the intersection with paved Schermerhorn Road, also to the right. Continue straight on Woodland Road, paralleling the boundary of the George Darey Wildlife Management Area along the Housatonic on the left. Giant oak trees grow in the valley's nutrient-rich soil.

The sound of Schermerhorn Brook heralds your arrival at the intersection with blue-blazed Gorge Trail, 1.1 miles from where you parked. Turn right at a small wooden sign to begin a moderate climb under sugar maples, ashes, and oaks. The brook to your left gushes over and around boulders of gneiss and quartzite. American yew—a low evergreen shrub—thrives in the shade near the water.

Follow Gorge Trail as it turns right, continues to climb, and then bears left to ascend above the flow; watch your footing here. A two-step waterfall is soon visible below. The rugged slopes of the gorge hold some impressive old oaks and hemlocks. One hemlock trunk is 3 feet across. The trail briefly moves farther from the water as the incline eases and then eventually levels out and rejoins the brook, roughly 30 feet above it. Mountain maple, a small understory tree similar in size to striped maple but with brown bark and smaller, toothier leaves, grows in the gorge along the flowage.

Tread up stone steps and past a jumble of big gneiss boulders in the rocky streambed. After a bit, reach the partial stone foundation of what was probably a millhouse long ago. Along the way, note the characteristic alternating dark and light bands of the gneiss. In spring and early summer, the loud, ringing notes of the bobbing, striped Louisiana waterthrush can be heard even above the roar of the water; these warblers winter in the tropics and nest along fast-flowing upland streams. On the right, a hemlock grows from a rock crevice, inexorably breaking apart the rock. Schermerhorn Brook soon splits in two, forming a narrow floodplain.

Emerge briefly into a brighter patch of maples near Schermerhorn Road on the right. After reentering shady hemlock forest, pass a 100-year-old fallen tree cut years ago to accommodate the trail. White pines and a mammoth oak stand on the left a few feet farther along. The steepness of these slopes made timber harvesting here less economical, resulting in some truly impressive specimen trees remaining today. The reverberating drumming of the crow-sized pileated woodpecker is an increasingly common percussion in such mature Berkshire woodlands. Even if you don't hear or see one of these memorable birds, you will likely come across the deep, rectangular cavities they excavate to reach carpenter ant colonies.

The gorge deepens again, and soon Gorge Trail approaches close to the brook. After the brook negotiates a 90-degree bend to the left, the well-blazed trail follows it up to a gravel road. A keystone arch bridge built of native stone lies ahead, beneath which flows Schermerhorn Brook, at the outlet from Felton Lake. Turn left to cross the bridge at 2.0 miles. An earthen dam to your right impounds the water body. Three-inch-long bullfrog tadpoles sometimes swim in the concrete spillway.

After the bridge crossing, begin the return segment at a trail sign under planted Norway spruces. Turn left and follow blue-blazed Gorge Trail along the north side of Schermerhorn Brook, past a small, derelict shack some 100 feet to your right. The gorge seems deeper from this side, and the descent is moderately steep. Hobblebush, maple-leaf viburnum, and bush honeysuckle shrubs fill sunlit gaps in the forest. Patches of young American beech appear as the trail again closely approaches the brook. The aforementioned stone millhouse ruins are more easily observed from this side. Walk under a mixed canopy of hemlocks, oaks, and northern hardwoods; cross an intermittent tributary stream on large, flat stones; and continue downward along Schermerhorn Brook.

The woodland is more predominately deciduous in this area—especially rich in oaks. Hobblebush shrubs bloom here in early May. Both Solomon's seal—with greenish flowers hanging down from each leaf node—and false Solomon's seal—with white blossoms at the tip of the stalk—thrive on the forest floor. The brook tumbles over moss-cushioned boulders, and its roaring intensifies with the gradient. A few stone steps take you down to the water's edge again.

The yellow trumpets of bush honeysuckle are numerous. Blue cohosh, which has oddly purple-green leaves, blooms in spring in a sunny canopy gap. The descent steepens as the gorge narrows markedly and the brook drops precipitously. As you proceed downward, the cascades become more dramatic. One four-step section is particularly impressive. Finally, bear right, away from the brook. Amble down more stone steps and negotiate a series of short switchbacks down the slope. Reach the brook again, pass a huge oak on the right, and arrive back at Woodland Road. Turn left and retrace your steps to Woods Pond (bearing right at the intersections), the pedestrian bridge, and the parking area.

DID YOU KNOW?
The George Darey Wildlife Management Area and the adjoining western slopes of October Mountain State Forest constitute a significant portion of the 12,280-acre Upper Housatonic Area of Critical Environmental Concern designated by the commonwealth in 2009. It is home to 32 state-listed endangered or threatened species and dozens of vernal pools.

MORE INFORMATION
Open sunrise to 30 minutes after sunset, year-round. Access is free. Leashed dogs, mountain bikes, skiing, and hunting in season are allowed. Motorized vehicles are not permitted on Gorge Trail. The campground includes 44 sites and 3 yurts.

NEARBY
Railroad buffs will enjoy the Berkshire Scenic Railway Museum, at 10 Willow Creek Road in Lenox (near the parking area for this hike; cross the railroad tracks, turn right onto Willow Creek Road, and walk 100 yards to the museum on the right). The restored 1903 Lenox Station once welcomed Gilded Age "cottagers" to their Berkshire summer homes. The museum is open Saturdays, 10 A.M. to 2 P.M., Memorial Day weekend to Labor Day. Hoosac Valley train rides on the historical Adams Branch are offered weekends and holidays from Memorial Day weekend to late October, departing from Adams Visitor Center, 3 Hoosac Street, Adams (413-637-2210, berkshiretrains.org).

29 OCTOBER MOUNTAIN STATE FOREST: FINERTY POND

From the historical Jacob's Ladder Trail Scenic Byway, this route follows the Appalachian Trail over a couple of wooded promontories to a serene pond ringed by mountain laurel in Massachusetts's most expansive state forest.

FEATURES

Location Becket and Washington, MA
Rating Moderate
Distance 6 miles round trip
Elevation Gain 870 feet
Estimated Time 3.5 hours
Maps USGS East Lee; Massachusetts Department of Conservation and Recreation map: mass.gov/doc/october-mountain-state-forest-trail-map/download
GPS Coordinates 42° 17.577' N, 73° 09.684' W
Contact October Mountain State Forest, 413-243-1778, mass.gov/locations/october-mountain-state-forest

DIRECTIONS

From the west: From I-90 (Massachusetts Turnpike), take Exit 10 in Lee. Turn left at the traffic light at the end of the ramp and follow US 20 (Jacob's Ladder Scenic Byway) east for 4.2 miles to a paved pullout on the right and the Appalachian Trail parking area at the Lee–Becket town line. The gravel lot accommodates seven cars.

From the east: From MA 8 North/US 20 in Becket, follow US 20 west for 7.8 miles to the paved pullout and Appalachian Trail parking area on the left.

TRAIL DESCRIPTION

This hike starts at the same parking area and trailhead as the Upper Goose Pond hike (Trip 30). From the kiosk, which displays maps of the Appalachian Trail (AT) route, walk east to the pedestrian crossing sign on the left. (Do not walk along US 20 to the AT crossing; this is very hazardous because some spots have no shoulder.) Use caution crossing the highway. On the north side of US 20, follow a narrow, blue-blazed access trail into a forest of American beech, eastern hemlock, and white pine. The tiny and fuzzy paired white blossoms of partridgeberry bloom in ground-hugging mats here in early summer.

TRIP 29 // OCTOBER MOUNTAIN STATE FOREST: FINERTY POND

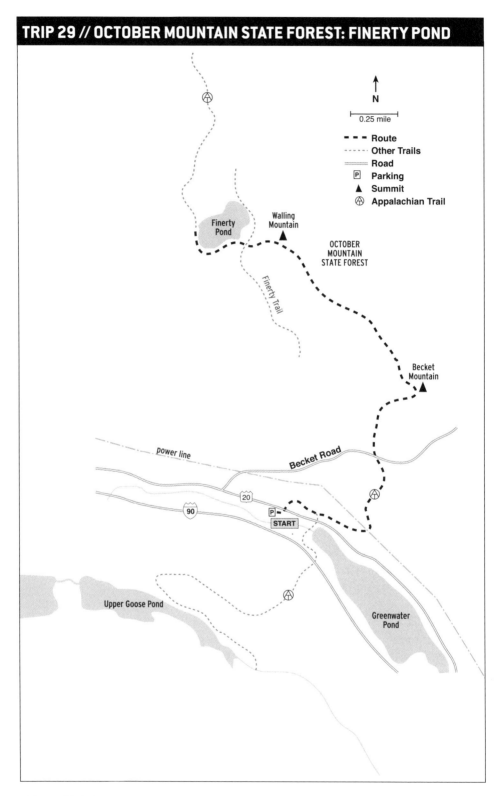

160 SECTION 2 // CENTRAL BERKSHIRES

The route parallels US 20 for about 100 yards. Bits of rusted barbed wire embedded in tree trunks on the left are evidence of former livestock pasturing. At a Y intersection, turn left and follow the white-blazed AT northbound, uphill, under red and sugar maples; bear left at an especially large sugar maple. Cross a damp area filled with light green sensitive fern, a species characteristic of wetlands. A sign attached to a tree gives distances to various landmarks along the route. A depression a bit farther on the right probably holds a vernal pool. Climb stone steps, then log steps, up a slope covered with maple, hemlock, birch, and oak. A mammoth twin white pine commands attention on the left. Canada mayflowers bloom in spring beneath the pines. Abundant beech saplings, often sprouting in clones from the same rootstock, populate the understory.

Traverse the first of several boulder fields. The gneiss rocks are banded alternately light and dark. A moderate climb leads to a level woods road where the route turns right. The sound of flowing water should be evident as you cross two wide snowmobile trails in rapid succession near their junction. Continue to follow the white blazes as the AT skirts a dark hemlock ravine cut by a brook. The trail soon bears left, away from the woods road, and enters a power-line right of way. Various ferns and yellow loosestrife flourish in the sunny depression. Rejoin the brook under a canopy of hemlocks and cross it on moss-covered stones. The soothing sound of running water replaces the mechanized din of vehicles on US 20 and the Massachusetts Turnpike.

The trail climbs gradually through rock-strewn mixed woodland. Mingling with the dominant beeches are multitrunked oaks, which indicate that the species may have been selectively logged here a century ago, because multiple stems sprout from cut oak stumps. Logging near the trail has created diverse habitats for wildlife. Cross a shallow brook on stones and follow the level path up to paved Becket (Tyne) Road at 1.1 miles. Cross the road and climb easily under hardwoods that edge a boulder field on the slope to your right.

For a bit the AT parallels an old skid road over which logs were once hauled out. Next to a dead beech on the left, a gray gneiss boulder has weathered into tiers. Unfortunately, the vast majority of the American beech trees in this forest are diseased and dying. Beech scale insects make tiny incisions to get at the tree's sap. *Nectria* fungus invades the tree through the holes and wreaks havoc on its circulatory system. An outward symptom is rough, broken black bark all over instead of smooth, gray bark.

Bear right and stride over a knoll with some big, non-native Norway spruces. The narrow trail leads through young beech woods and ferns, traversing striated bedrock in spots. High winds have snapped many of the beech trunks.

A short climb takes you to the top of Becket Mountain (elevation 2,178 feet), where the path levels out in a hay-scented fern glade at 1.5 miles. Concrete footings are all that remain of a tower that stood here when the summit was fully open. A trail register hangs from a tree. Turn left, remaining on the AT, and pass a cluster of gneiss boulders to begin an easy descent through a beech, birch, and maple woodland. A rectangular, flat-topped boulder on the right is capped by wild oats (lilies, not grasses) that flower pale yellow in spring.

Continue over gently rolling terrain past another jumble of rocks. In early summer, red-berried elder shrubs sport crimson fruits. Zigzag up another slope and amble

A short side trail leads to a pond access point where in late June and early July mountain laurel puts on a fine show.

through a hay-scented fern glade under broad-leafed trees. The trail begins another easy descent and levels out among hobblebushes in rocky woods. The large, heart-shaped leaves of the hobblebushes shade black-throated blue warbler nests. Soon the character of the forest changes markedly. Scattered maple trees on this flat ridgeline permit enough light to reach the forest floor for a dense layer of raspberry, ferns, elderberry, and climbing false buckwheat to thrive.

The trail climbs again and levels out on top of Walling Mountain at approximately 2.5 miles. It might be difficult to tell that you're at 2,200 feet above sea level, given the minor elevation change since the last bump along the ridge. Pass car-sized hunks of gneiss and look for woodland wildflowers such as *Clintonia* (blue-bead lily) and cucumber root. The latter has modest but beautiful flowers, with curved yellow petals hanging from a second tier of whorled leaves.

From here, the descent gets a bit rougher. Patches of shining club moss, a nonflowering fern relative, form a green carpet on the forest floor. Wood frogs and red efts wander in search of invertebrate prey as the path switchbacks down.

Shortly before reaching Finerty Pond, cross Finerty Trail, a woods road used by all-terrain vehicles. Continue to follow the AT, which widens and leads down to a mountain laurel bush on the right and then turns left to follow near the shore at 2.9 miles. If you pass this way in late June or early July, you'll be treated to a fantastic laurel flower show. About 100 feet past the laurel, a short side path leads to the best shoreline access point. Look for evidence of beaver activity, such as fallen or cut trees and lodges, along and near the water's edge.

In summer, bullfrogs bellow and green frogs announce your arrival with a little *eek* as they flee. An impressive old yellow birch stands on the left just before you follow a cushioned path past an angular boulder and beneath hemlocks to a contemplative spot near the water's edge, bordered by abundant laurel shrubs. Listen for the dry, rattling call of the belted kingfisher (about 12 inches long, with a shaggy crest) from somewhere across the pond.

Here, the AT swings away from the shore. Take some time to linger and enjoy the serenity and then retrace your steps some 3 miles back to the parking area. Near the end of the hike, be sure to bear right on the blue-blazed path rather than turning left to follow the AT down to US 20. Again, use caution crossing US 20 at the trailhead.

DID YOU KNOW?

October Mountain State Forest, at 16,500 acres, is the largest state forest in Massachusetts. Writer Herman Melville, whose home (called Arrowhead) in Pittsfield afforded a fine view of the mountain, reputedly coined its name. The commonwealth purchased the initial 11,000 acres of the forest from the Whitney estate in 1915. William C. Whitney served as President Grover Cleveland's secretary of the navy.

MORE INFORMATION

October Mountain State Forest is open sunrise to one half hour after sunset year-round. Access is free. Motorized vehicles, mountain bikes, and horses are prohibited on the Appalachian Trail. Camping is allowed only in designated areas. The campground includes 44 tent sites and 3 yurts. The AMC Western Massachusetts Chapter's Appalachian Trail Management Committee (amc-wma.org/at) is responsible for maintenance, management, and protection of the nearly 90 miles of the AT in Massachusetts; volunteers do this work, with assistance from the Massachusetts Department of Conservation and Recreation.

NEARBY

Jacob's Pillow, on a 220-acre former farm in Becket (358 Carter Road), is internationally renowned as a focal point for contemporary dance. A National Historic Landmark and National Medal of Arts recipient, Jacob's Pillow is home to America's longest-running dance festival, founded in 1933 by Ted Shawn. The summer season runs from mid-June to late August (413-243-9919, jacobspillow.org).

ASH UNDER SIEGE

Ash trees are a crucial component of eastern forests, providing food and cover for wildlife, material for a variety of forest products, and shade and decor for landowners and municipalities. American Indians have traditionally used the wood, leaves, and bark to make baskets, canoes, musical instruments, and medicines. Nearly 70 percent of Massachusetts's 45 million ash trees grow in the Berkshires. Sadly, all of the region's ash species (mostly white, black, and green ash) are threatened by the emerald ash borer (*Agrilus planipennis* Fairmaire), one of North America's newest and deadliest forest pests.

The emerald ash borer (EAB), named for its metallic green color, is a half-inch-long beetle native to Asia. It has relatively little impact in its home range, where trees have evolved resistance over thousands of years and there are several natural predators. Such is not the case in North America, and since being introduced to Michigan in the late twentieth century, EAB has rapidly spread across the continent, killing hundreds of millions of ash trees. EAB disperses less than 2 miles per year naturally, but humans have unwittingly conveyed it long distances by transporting infested firewood, lumber, and nursery stock.

The infestation process begins when females lay eggs on ash bark during summer. Larvae feed on the inner bark tissues, disrupting circulation of nutrients and water and killing most trees within just two to five years. Adult beetles emerge in spring and fly from May to September, searching for new host trees. EAB causes near 100 percent mortality, but a small percentage of trees have shown natural resistance. Symptoms include exposed light-colored bark caused by woodpeckers feeding on infested trees (known as "blonding"), dead upper branches, D-shaped exit holes chewed by adults, discolored leaves, and unusual root and trunk sprouts. These signs are difficult to detect in early stages, and EAB is often present for several years before being discovered.

The first confirmation of EAB in Massachusetts was in August 2012, when Massachusetts Department of Conservation and Recreation researchers discovered an adult beetle in a trap (designed to lure EAB during the summer flight season) in the town of Dalton, in the central Berkshires. EAB quickly spread throughout most of Massachusetts; nearly 220 towns reported infestations by 2023.

Eastern forests, already ravaged by pests and diseases such as hemlock woolly adelgid, gypsy moths, chestnut blight, and Dutch elm disease, stand to lose an entire genus of trees, with significant consequences for the ecosystem. According to a study published in *American Entomologist*, ash is a preferred food source for 100 invertebrate species, including several moths now potentially threatened with extinction. Wood frogs, cavity-nesting birds, and small mammals all use ash for food and cover.

From an economic standpoint, EAB has cost wood producers and land managers hundreds of millions of dollars nationwide. Massachusetts officials forecast that the loss of ash will cause overall losses of $500 million. Ash wood, coveted for its strength and elasticity, is well suited for many products, including furniture, flooring, and baseball bats. Replacing infested shade and ornamental trees is a considerable expense for municipalities and landowners.

Scientists haven't given up on ash yet, though. The United States Department of Agriculture (USDA) and state agencies are working collectively on biocontrol measures using introduced wasps that prey on EAB in its native range. Preliminary findings indicate slower infestation rates, allowing young trees to survive and produce seeds. USDA researchers have also cloned trees that have shown natural resistance. Insecticides can be used on individual trees, through treatments are expensive. You can do your part by not transporting firewood or other potentially infested materials. Report signs of EAB to local officials and the Massachusetts Introduced Pests Outreach Project (massnrc.org/pests/eabreport.htm). For information and updates about EAB in Massachusetts, see mass.gov/guides/emerald-ash-borer-in-massachusetts.

30 UPPER GOOSE POND

This out-and-back hike on the Appalachian Trail reaches one of the most scenic ponds in the Berkshires, in a serene location reminiscent of northern New England.

FEATURES

Location Becket, Lee, and Tyringham, MA
Rating Moderate
Distance 3.7 miles round trip (4.7 miles including Upper Goose Pond Cabin)
Elevation Gain 385 feet
Estimated Time 2.5 hours
Maps USGS East Lee; Appalachian Trail Conservancy online map: appalachiantrail.org/explore/hike-the-a-t/interactive-map
GPS Coordinates 42° 17.577′ N, 73° 09.684′ W
Contact AMC Western Massachusetts Chapter's Massachusetts AT Committee, amc-wma.org/appalachian-trail-management-committee
Appalachian Trail Conservancy (New England Regional Office), 802-281-5894, appalachiantrail.org/explore/explore-by-state/massachusetts

DIRECTIONS

From the west: From I-90 (Massachusetts Turnpike), take Exit 10 in Lee. Turn left at the traffic light at the end of the ramp, and follow US 20 east for 4.2 miles to the Appalachian Trail parking area on the right at the Lee–Becket town line. The gravel lot accommodates about seven cars.

From the east: From MA 8 North/US 20 in Becket, follow US 20 west for 7.9 miles to the Appalachian Trail parking area on the left.

TRAIL DESCRIPTION

This is the same parking area and trailhead as the October Mountain State Forest hike (Trip 29). From the kiosk with a display map, walk east a short distance to the pedestrian crossing sign at US 20. Do not walk along US 20; this is very hazardous because some spots have no shoulder. Use caution crossing the highway. A narrow, blue-blazed access trail on the north side of the highway leads through a forest of American beech, eastern hemlock, and white pine. It parallels US 20 for about 100 yards and then joins the Appalachian Trail (AT). Turn right and follow the white-blazed AT southbound down to the highway.

TRIP 30 // UPPER GOOSE POND

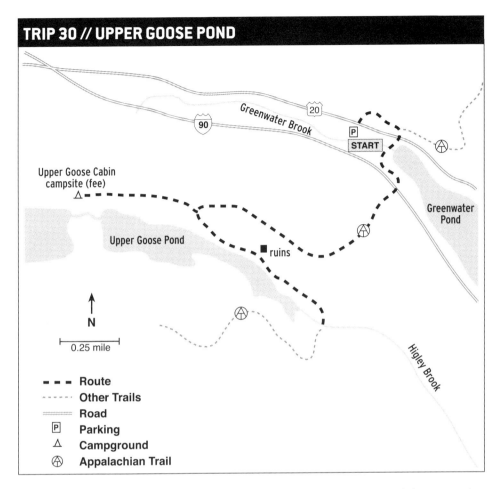

Cross US 20 again, pass through a gap in the guardrail, and proceed down wooden steps. Old orchard trees litter the ground with apples in fall. A brown AT directional sign indicates that the side path to Upper Goose Pond Cabin is 1.6 miles away. Cross a wooden bridge over Greenwater Brook at a former mill site and arrive at the earthen dam that holds back the waters of Greenwater Pond. Turn right and follow the AT toward a pedestrian bridge over the Massachusetts Turnpike. Bear left and circle up and around to cross above the westbound lanes of I-90 and then traverse a second concrete span above the eastbound lanes. The bridges accommodate snowmobiles in winter (one of the few places on the AT where motorized use is permitted) and also serve as a wildlife crossing over the busy highway. October Mountain's plateau looms to the north.

Reenter woodland at 0.6 mile. At a trail split, continue to follow the white-blazed AT by taking the left fork (the right fork is a snowmobile corridor). Ascend fairly steeply under a canopy of sugar and red maples, white ash, yellow birch, and red oak. A metamorphic rock ledge (gneiss) pops up on the left. Bear left around the ledge and ascend stone steps, passing more outcroppings amid the steady roar from the interstate. Ferns and green-trunked striped maple saplings, hobblebush shrubs, and beech sprouts shade

TRIP 30 // **UPPER GOOSE POND** 167

evergreen club mosses. Higher up, red oak becomes more common. After the trail levels out briefly, watch for an impressive white ash more than 2½ feet in diameter on the left, which bears an AT blaze. Ashes provide the sturdy lumber required for ax handles and baseball bats. Unfortunately, many are succumbing to the emerald ash borer, which arrived in the area in 2012 (see "Ash Under Siege" on page 164).

As you begin climbing once again, young, shade-tolerant beech trees cover the north-facing slope along with birches, maples, and oaks. At the boundary of the Upper Goose Pond Natural Area, the height-of-land, find an AT trail register. You may want to peruse the register for interesting insight into the exploits of AT thru-hikers and other trail users. From here, descend gradually through small patches of hobblebush, identifiable by its big, paired, heart-shaped leaves. It features clusters of small white flowers in spring, red fruits in summer, multihued foliage in autumn, and large, straw-colored buds in winter. As the din of the highway fades away, you'll feel you're in a different world.

As you head to the right, an impressive gray ledge—uptilted at 30 degrees—juts out to your right. The woodland now includes mountain laurel and its tiny relative wintergreen. Both retain their leaves through winter, adding color to the woods. This south-facing slope encourages a dominance of oaks, through which a screened view of a ridgeline is possible. Follow the slope contour and then descend more steeply and follow an impressive 250-foot exposed gneiss ledge. Brown-and-black rock tripes (lichens) cling to its vertical face, turning green only after absorbing moisture. Descend again and soon reach a signed junction at 1.7 miles indicating that Upper Goose Pond Cabin is 0.5 mile down the blue-blazed side path. If you have time, it's worth a visit. The cabin, which offers overnight accommodation for AT backpackers, is on a laurel-studded slope above the lake. Privies are available at the cabin and at two designated camping areas.

Back on the white-blazed AT, continue straight on what is now an old woods road through beech, oak, black birch, and mountain laurel. Turn right, off the road, where the AT's white blazes lead down toward the pond. Reach Upper Goose Pond and turn left to follow the trail as it hugs the shoreline on its way toward Higley Brook at the pond's eastern end. Stunning views of the 45-acre pond (elevation 1,465 feet) abound through gaps in the vegetation. Arrive at the site of a former sportsmen's lodge—the Mohhekennuck Club—constructed in the first decade of the twentieth century. A fallen chimney and a few foundation stones are all that remains. A short path leads to a tiny gravel beach popular as a canoe landing. Continue on the southbound AT along the shoreline through mountain laurel, which blooms pinkish-white in late June.

A thick growth of shining club moss carpets the forest floor at one spot on the right. White ghost pipes—parasitic on oak roots—bloom here in summer. The hardwood forest is also home in spring and summer to many species of colorful wood warblers, vireos, and thrushes. The path moves away from the water before arriving at Higley Brook, which is spanned by a modest wooden bridge. Canada lilies bloom in early July along this permanent water source for the pond. Goose Pond Road is 1.9 miles farther, but this is the end point for your hike. Retrace your steps approximately 0.5 mile to the lodge ruins and then 100 yards beyond to where the AT bears right, up the slope. Pay attention, as this intersection can be easily missed. Rejoin the AT and follow it back to the beginning of the hike.

DID YOU KNOW?
The Mohhekennuck Club, a gathering of sportsmen, was incorporated in 1909 and operated for 72 years. In 1981, the club conveyed its lands along Upper Goose Pond, one of the largest undeveloped ponds in Massachusetts, to the National Park Service to become part of the Appalachian Trail corridor and to serve as a wilderness preserve in perpetuity.

MORE INFORMATION
Upper Goose Pond Cabin, while open to all AT visitors, is managed primarily for long-distance hikers (see amc-wma.org/files/at_committee/UGPC_FAQ.pdf for details). Volunteer caretakers are present mid-May through mid-October. Camping is allowed at two designated campsites near the cabin. Mountain biking is not allowed. The AMC Western Massachusetts Chapter's Appalachian Trail Management Committee is responsible for operation of the cabin and for maintenance, management, and protection of the nearly 90 miles of the AT in Massachusetts. Volunteers do this work, with assistance from the Massachusetts Department of Conservation and Recreation.

NEARBY
Camping is available from mid-May to mid-October at nearby October Mountain State Forest in Lee. This primitive camping area has 47 nonelectric tent and RV/trailer sites on three levels and includes 3 yurts. For more information, call 413-243-1778 or visit mass.gov/locations/october-mountain-state-forest.

So close to the Massachusetts Turnpike, yet appearing to belong in northern New England, Upper Goose Pond is a gem.

3 // SOUTHERN BERKSHIRES

The southern Berkshires remain the most agricultural part of the Berkshires. Hayfields and dairy barns dot the landscape of the broad Housatonic River valley, and the valley's marble bedrock fosters lime-loving plants. The southern Berkshires feature quaint towns and villages, pastures dotted with cattle, forests in which mountain laurel puts on a dazzling show, and summits and ridgelines that offer endless views. Some consider this area to be the most scenic in the region.

The excursions in this section include steep climbs, pastoral settings, impressive waterfalls, and even some old-growth giants. For instance, magical Ice Glen (Trip 31) offers a cool respite from summer heat and shelters old trees; Guilder Pond and Mount Everett, the region's highest summit (Trip 45), offer outstanding mountain laurel blooms; Alander Mountain (Trip 46) boasts one of the most expansive vistas in the Berkshires; and the quartzite peak of Monument Mountain (Trip 32) is a beloved destination for many. Highlights of less traveled southeastern uplands include pastoral Appalachian Trail views from Tyringham Cobble (Trip 35), wildflower and wildlife habitats at Bob's Way (Trip 38), and the remote wooded valley of Clam River (Trip 39).

The southern Berkshires are also renowned for waterfalls. Bash Bish Falls (Trip 43) is arguably the commonwealth's most spectacular, but Race Brook Falls (Trip 44), Campbell Falls (Trip 40), and Sages Ravine (Trip 49) are evocative in their own right.

In the southeastern Taconic Mountains, the summits of Round Mountain, Mount Frissell, and Brace Mountain (Trip 50) offer a wealth of vistas at the boundaries with New York and Connecticut, and Alford Springs (Trip 34) encompasses wooded ridges in a scenic valley. For an easier ramble, try universally accessible Riverfront Trail and Housatonic River Walk (Trip 33) near downtown Great Barrington, lovely Lime Kiln Farm (Trip 47), or the botanically renowned Bartholomew's Cobble Reservation (Trip 48), which includes an outstanding perspective of the region from an open hilltop. Whatever your preference of scenery or level of difficulty, the southern Berkshires have it all.

Facing page: On a ridge above Bash Bish Falls, South Taconic Trail leads to an overlook with views of wooded hills and fields.

31 ICE GLEN AND LAURA'S TOWER

Three interconnected trails explore a trifecta of diverse natural attractions: Ice Glen, a primordial, rocky cleft, studded with mammoth hemlocks and pines, that holds pockets of ice into summer; Laurel Hill's summit, where an observation tower provides pleasing views; and the Housatonic River.

FEATURES

Location Stockbridge, MA
Rating Moderate
Distance 3.7 miles round trip
Elevation Gain 610 feet
Estimated Time 2.25 hours
Maps USGS Stockbridge; Laurel Hill Association map: laurelhillassociation.org/sites/default/files/laurel-hill-trail-map.pdf
GPS Coordinates 42° 16.255′ N, 73° 18.674′ W
Contact Laurel Hill Association, 413-298-2888, laurelhillassociation.org

DIRECTIONS

From I-90 (Massachusetts Turnpike), take Exit 10 in Lee. Turn left at the exit ramp traffic light and then take the first right onto MA 102. Proceed west on MA 102 for 4.6 miles to the intersection with US 7 at The Red Lion Inn in Stockbridge. Turn left and follow US 7 south approximately 0.4 mile to Ice Glen Road on the left (immediately after crossing the Housatonic River and the railroad overpass). Drive up Ice Glen Road for 0.5 mile to a small pull-off parking area on the left, adjacent to a gravel driveway and a sign for Ice Glen. Do not block this private driveway! Parking is limited to four vehicles. Alternate parking is available at a trailhead at the end of Park Street off US 7 (take the second left at the Mobil gas station following the left turn at The Red Lion Inn).

TRAIL DESCRIPTION

Walk about 250 yards up the private gravel driveway, lined by white pines; the driveway soon turns to asphalt as the grade increases. Where the asphalt turns right, bear left onto white-blazed Ice Glen Trail, a woodland path leading toward the mouth of Ice Glen, home to one of Massachusetts's most accessible old-growth forests. If you visit in

TRIP 31 // ICE GLEN AND LAURA'S TOWER

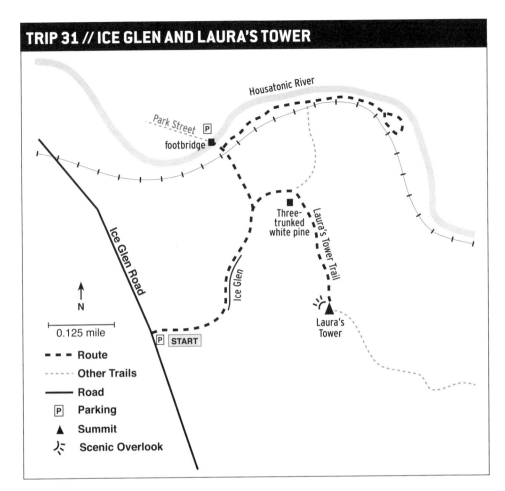

summer, you'll notice a refreshing drop in temperature as you reach the trail. A jumble of large boulders and the twin pillars of a white pine on the left and an eastern hemlock on the right serve as a kind of portal to the glen. The oldest hemlocks here are more than 300 years old. Truck- and cabin-sized boulders are green with moss and topped by ferns. Mosquitoes are often plentiful in this area, so be prepared.

Native stone steps, artfully placed and expertly arranged by the nationally renowned trail builder Peter Jensen, lead into the defile. The slopes that create the glen rise abruptly on both sides, inspiring a sense of awe. The cool microclimate in this north-to-south-trending cleft, shaded by towering evergreens and insulated by massive quartzite boulders, is quite amazing. On a sultry summer afternoon, the air temperature in the glen's cold pockets may be 20 to 25 degrees Fahrenheit cooler than the surrounding areas. If you gaze down into the crevices between the boulders, don't be surprised to see remnant ice there, even in summer. In fact, it is so cool that atmospheric moisture condenses in the ravine to form an eerie ground fog.

Although the glen is less than 0.25 mile long, don't rush through this haven of tranquility, with its narrow crevices and twists and turns. Watch your footing—the rocks often are wet and a bit slippery in spots. Still, this is not a dangerous place to walk if you have the proper footwear and use caution.

According to geologists, the final act of the glen's creation began some 15,000 years ago during the last ice age. The meltwater from a receding glacier just north of here, as well as the effects of freezing and thawing over a multitude of years, loosened chunks of quartzite from the opposing hillsides. The rocks subsequently tumbled down into the cleft between the hillsides.

Birdsong adds to the atmosphere here in late spring and early summer; listen to the vocalizations of hermit and wood thrushes (characterized by flutelike phrases), the trill of dark-eyed juncos, the effervescent tune of the tiny winter wren, and a multitude of other songs from warblers and vireos. The massive, straight-trunked trees include four of the state's tallest white pines—one is 151 feet high! The oldest are between 170 and 200 years of age.

Some trunks of fallen trees, covered in moss, serve as "nurseries" for tree seedlings that have taken root in their decaying wood. Low spots collect pools of tannin-stained water. Shoulder past one massive boulder on the left that is decorated with rock tripes (lichens), which are leafy and green when wet but platy and brown when dry.

The trail levels out and emerges into a bowl. Some 30 feet to the left, an inscription on the moss-covered rock face commemorates David Dudley Field's donation of the property to the town of Stockbridge in 1891. Birches, maples, and ashes (some massive) merge with the evergreens here. Begin a gradual descent and soon arrive at a signed intersection with orange-blazed Laura's Tower Trail at a gigantic, triple-stemmed

Pockets of ice often persist into June within the crevices formed by the massive boulders of Ice Glen.

white pine at 0.5 mile. Years ago, a violent windstorm snapped off numerous mature pines, as evidenced by dead snags. Young deciduous trees compete for light under the remaining pines.

Turn right onto Laura's Tower Trail (going straight takes you down to the Housatonic River) and begin a gradual 0.4-mile ascent of Laurel Hill. Large maples and ashes (and a few oaks) thrive here. The grade increases as the trail winds past cabin-sized boulders. Big-tooth aspens, with their straight, furrowed trunks, are members of this woodland, which also includes red oaks, birches, red maples, beeches, and far more undergrowth (mostly mountain laurels and sapling striped maples) than is found beneath the shade of pines and hemlocks. Climb the slope on a few moderate switchbacks.

At 0.9 mile, reach a sturdy observation tower at Laurel Hill's summit, 1,465 feet above sea level. The 30-foot tower, designed by local engineer Joseph Franz, was named for David Dudley Field's daughter-in-law, Laura. Climb the steel staircase to a viewing platform just about even with a low canopy of oak, red maple, cherry, birch, and ash. A 360-degree panorama was once visible, but tree growth on adjoining property has obscured much of the view to the south. A horizontally mounted brass locator disk indicates the names of promontories, their elevations, and the airline distances to them. The most prominent feature to the northwest is West Stockbridge Mountain, 4.5 miles away. Mount Greylock lies 25.5 miles to the north.

A yellow-blazed trail opposite the path you ascended leads to Beartown State Forest, several miles distant, but retrace your steps to the signed Y intersection. Turn right to follow combined Laura's Tower and Ice Glen trails down to the Housatonic River. Cross a footbridge and descend easily through a stand of monolithic white pines. Listen for the high-pitched, cheerful whistle of brown creepers, which nest behind slabs of loose bark. The sound of traffic becomes more evident as you reach a power-line right of way filled with raspberry bushes.

Cross the Housatonic Railroad line (this is an active line—use caution!) to a stone arch–and–steel suspension bridge built in 1936 by the aforementioned Joseph Franz, 0.8 mile from Laura's Tower (1.7 miles overall). Walk across the wooden decking to enjoy a fine view of the Housatonic River. A brass plaque announces that this bridge replaced the original one given to Stockbridge in 1895 by Mary Hopkins Goodrich, founder of the Laurel Hill Association. A parking area and an accessible trailhead are on the north side of the river at the Park Street cul-de-sac.

On the south side of the bridge, begin the final out-and-back segment on Mary Flynn Trail, a wheelchair-accessible, yellow-blazed path. The route, which includes several benches, follows a former trolley line east between the Housatonic River and the railroad tracks for 0.6 mile. A stand of maidenhair fern delights the eye near a short loop at the trail's eastern end.

Retrace your steps to the bridge and then turn left and follow combined Laura's Tower and Ice Glen trails back to the signed Y intersection (3.2 miles). Turn right on Ice Glen Trail to return to the Ice Glen Road trailhead.

DID YOU KNOW?

The Laurel Hill Association, the oldest existing village beautification society in America, was founded in 1853 by Mary Hopkins Goodrich, the great-granddaughter of Stockbridge missionary founder John Sergeant. The association, which has acquired almost 500 acres in town over the years, seeks to improve the quality of life and the environment in Stockbridge.

The engineer Joseph Franz had many talents. In addition to designing the Shed at Tanglewood Music Center and the Ted Shawn Theatre at Jacob's Pillow, he figured out how to transmit electricity through buried power lines in downtown Stockbridge, built one of the earliest hydroelectric generating plants in the world (in West Stockbridge), and supervised construction of many other buildings and electrical systems throughout the United States.

MORE INFORMATION

Trails are open sunrise to sunset, year-round. Access is free. The trailheads have no restroom facilities. Vehicles, horses, camping, and fires are prohibited. The Laurel Hill Association maintains Ice Glen Trail, Laura's Tower Trail, and Mary Flynn Trail; the town of Stockbridge (413-298-4170, stockbridge-ma.gov) owns Ice Glen.

NEARBY

The Red Lion Inn, an iconic Berkshire landmark, is one of only a few continually operating inns from the eighteenth century. Established in 1773, the inn was rebuilt in 1897. It has 125 rooms and offers formal and informal dining and live entertainment. The inn is at 30 Main Street in Stockbridge (413-298-5545; redlioninn.com).

Naumkeag, a 48-acre property of The Trustees of Reservations, is at 5 Prospect Hill Road in Stockbridge and features a historical home and gardens with scenic views. Seasonal events include a spring tulip and daffodil show and an elaborate light display during the holiday season. Visit thetrustees.org/place/naumkeag for hours, fees, and other information.

32 MONUMENT MOUNTAIN RESERVATION

It would be difficult to name another hike as steeped in history as this one on Monument Mountain. Some 20,000 hikers annually enjoy a pilgrimage to the fabulously picturesque summit of jagged quartzite boulders capped by pitch pines.

FEATURES

Location Great Barrington, MA

Rating Moderate

Distance 2.7-mile loop

Elevation Gain 765 feet

Estimated Time 2 hours

Maps USGS Great Barrington, USGS Stockbridge; The Trustees of Reservations map: thetrustees.org/wp-content/uploads/2022/02/monument-mountain-trail-map.pdf

GPS Coordinates 42° 14.598′ N, 73° 20.121′ W

Contact The Trustees of Reservations, 413-298-3239, thetrustees.org/place/monument-mountain

DIRECTIONS

From the east: From I-90 (Massachusetts Turnpike), take Exit 10 in Lee. Turn left at the traffic light at the end of the ramp and then take the first right onto MA 102. Continue 4.6 miles to the intersection with US 7 at The Red Lion Inn in Stockbridge. Turn left and drive south on US 7 for 3.0 miles to the reservation entrance and a large gravel parking area on the right.

From the south: At the junction of US 7 and MA 23 in Great Barrington, proceed north on US 7 for 5.9 miles to the reservation on the left.

TRAIL DESCRIPTION

Begin at the map kiosk shaded by Depression-era red pines. Turn right and head north on yellow-blazed Hickey Trail. White pines, black cherry trees, red maples, red oaks, and white ashes tower above sapling American beeches, witch hazel, and striped maples with smooth, greenish trunks. Given that Monument Mountain Reservation was established in 1899, the forest here has had more than 120 years to regenerate. As a result, many white pines and oaks are of impressive proportions. However, many of the

TRIP 32 // MONUMENT MOUNTAIN RESERVATION

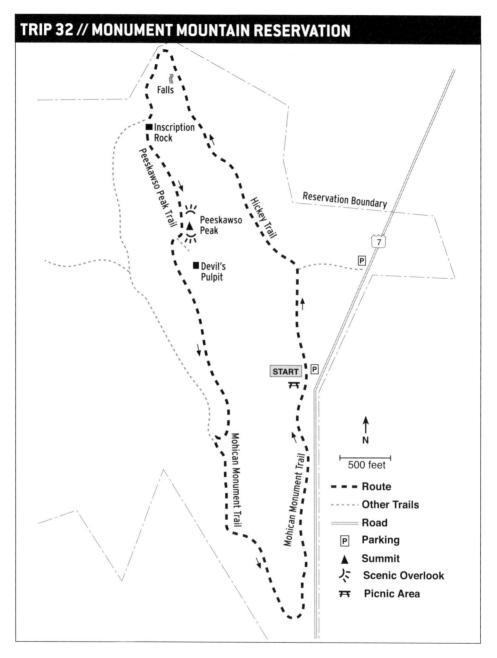

shade-intolerant pioneering gray birches have died. The well-trodden trail initially parallels the contour of the slope and passes a twin white oak near a quartzite boulder. White oaks produce sweet acorns relished by wild turkey and deer.

The trail soon bears left to begin a moderately steep climb. Pass a white-blazed path on the right and continue uphill. Note a massive red oak, fully 3 feet in diameter, on your right. Red oak acorns are bitter with tannic acid, unlike white oak acorns. Enter the year-round shade cast by eastern hemlocks at the junction with a wider woods road;

bear right here. The grade becomes gentler. Gray, angular quartzite boulders are more numerous, and a cabin-sized boulder hems in the trail. Crusty lichens and little polypody ferns have colonized the rock's rough, erosion-resistant surface.

A talus slope, created by repeated freezing and thawing over eons, is visible to the left after leaf fall. This jumble of massive quartzite boulders reposes at the foot of the mountain. Talus (meaning "toe" in Greek) slopes like this are rare in the region. The hard, gray rock is actually 600-million-year-old beach sand compacted under tremendous heat and pressure deep underground. A verdant mat of ferns caps some slabs.

Follow Hickey Trail right, then left, under columnar hemlocks and pines, to continue the moderate climb. Mature white pines produce thousands of winged seeds relished by birds and small mammals. At a point where the trail turns left and ascends more steeply, the flowing water of a small, crystal-clear brook has carved an attractive hemlock ravine. The trail levels out at the top of the ravine and traverses a log bridge over the brook. A short spur path on the left leads to a close-up view of a modest seasonal waterfall. In winter, water frozen mid-flow makes mammoth icicles that drape the outcropping. On your right, the tall, straight tree reaching skyward is a tulip tree, a southern species near its northern range limit here.

Return to Hickey Trail and climb more steeply now. Hemlocks, red maples, and oaks mix as you push up the ravine. The trail narrows and ascends to the reservation's northern boundary on the right. Turn left at the big outcropping; the trail levels out among mountain laurel shrubs. After negotiating another log bridge, head up through boulders decorated with flaky brown rock tripes; these lichens turn green after rains.

At Hickey Trail's upper end at 0.8 mile, reach a signed three-way intersection with blue-blazed Mohican Monument Trail and red-blazed Peeskawso Peak Trail near Inscription Rock, which commemorates Virginia Butler's donation of the property in October 1899, in memory of her sister Rosalie. Continue straight on Peeskawso Peak Trail, which winds up and over quartzite staircases and among boulders to the summit at 1,642 feet. Gnarly pitch pines, white pines, and mountain laurels dominate these craggy heights.

Watch your footing, especially in winter, as you wend your way among the quartzite blocks. Several excellent viewpoints invite visitors to relax and enjoy the scenery. To the north is the bluish double hump of Mount Greylock, almost 30 miles distant. Much closer, at the foot of Monument Mountain, sprawl the vegetated waters of Agawam Marsh. The Housatonic Valley, lined with erodible marble, spreads out below to the south, and Mount Everett looms in the southwest. These landmarks are not all visible from the same perch, so move about (carefully) to get the full effect. When you reach a signed intersection with a short side path leading to the Devil's Pulpit overlook, turn left and follow a rock staircase to a vista of the Devil's Pulpit (a striking columnar formation and favorite haunt of turkey vultures) and a portion of the Housatonic Valley to the south. The summit ridge can be a fine place to witness the spring hawk migration up the valley in late April.

When you're ready to resume the hike, continue on Peeskawso Peak Trail as it descends moderately, climbing over rocks on the west flank of the mountain. In early summer, listen for the sweet trill of yellow-and-olive pine warblers that nest among the

From Monument Mountain's popular summit, views extend north along the Housatonic Valley to Mount Greylock.

pine boughs. The male's song is similar to that of the dark-eyed junco, another breeder here. The path levels out as you reach a signed intersection at 1.5 miles. Turn left here on blue-blazed Mohican Monument Trail and stroll under towering white pines, hemlocks, large oaks, red maples, beeches, and black birches. This old woods road has a gentle grade, and many hikers use this longer route in reverse to reach Inscription Rock and the summit.

The trail turns left to parallel US 7 and undulates over rocks and beneath hemlocks as it travels along the eastern talus slopes at the foot of the mountain. A triple-trunked chestnut oak stands on the left, recognizable by its rough, platy bark and wavy-edged leaves. Evergreen wood fern and the smaller polypody thrive among the boulders. Some slabs have impressive dimensions and rusty faces where oxidation has revealed the iron content of the rock.

When you arrive back at the picnic area under the red pines where you began, look for pileated woodpecker excavations (foraging holes) on the tree trunks.

DID YOU KNOW?

On August 5, 1850, writers Nathaniel Hawthorne and Herman Melville made a now-storied picnic excursion on Monument Mountain. A thunderstorm forced them to take shelter in a boulder cave. It is said that Melville's conversations with his friend Hawthorne that day inspired his seafaring novel *Moby-Dick*.

MORE INFORMATION

Open sunrise to sunset year-round. No fee for Trustees members (parking code required); $6 parking fee at a self-serve kiosk for nonmembers. Picnic tables are available, but no restrooms are on-site. Skiing is allowed. Dogs must be leashed. Motorized vehicles, mountain bikes, rock climbing, and fires are prohibited. Hunting is allowed in season.

NEARBY

Taft Farms, specializing in pesticide-free, sustainable agriculture since 1961, has a produce retail store, greenhouse, and deli at 119 Park Street in Great Barrington. Taft Farms is open daily, 8 A.M. to 6 P.M. (413-528-1515; taftfarmsgb.com).

WRITTEN IN STONE

The great natural beauty of the Berkshires has drawn creative minds to these hills and valleys for centuries. Look no further than Tanglewood Music Center as proof. Whether in music, art, or literature, "the purple hills," as the geographer and author Roderick Peattie called them, have inspired many writers and artists, including nineteenth-century authors Nathaniel Hawthorne, Herman Melville, William Cullen Bryant, and Henry David Thoreau.

No doubt the single most chronicled meeting of literary minds ever to occur in the Berkshires took place on August 5, 1850, when Nathaniel Hawthorne and Herman Melville hiked Monument Mountain. There, it is said, they became fast friends. As the story goes, Hawthorne, who had a home in Lenox, gave Melville inspiration for *Moby-Dick*, his most famous work, while they huddled together in a cave during an electrical storm. Perhaps the bedrock ledge, over which a falls drops during the wet months, was their shelter. Each year on August 5, a group of aficionados re-creates the hike of these literary giants.

Melville wrote his masterpiece while residing at Arrowhead (which now houses the Berkshire Historical Society), his home on Holmes Road in Pittsfield. Literary lore has it that the sight of Mount Greylock, or Saddleback Mountain as it was known then, dusted with snow, inspired the idea of the giant white sperm whale.

Influential nature writers have tromped Berkshire paths, Henry David Thoreau foremost among them. Thoreau hiked to Mount Greylock's summit on the present Bellows Pipe Trail (Trip 8) and wrote about it in *A Week on the Concord and Merrimack Rivers*. William Cullen Bryant, who spent ten years in Great Barrington, wrote about Monument Mountain in his poem by the same name in 1824. He penned many other works with natural history themes at his home in nearby Cummington. Closer to the present day, Hal Borland, a longtime resident of Connecticut's Litchfield Hills, wrote evocatively about the bucolic landscape he so loved. A trail at Bartholomew's Cobble Reservation (Trip 48) is named in memory of Borland, who passed away in 1978.

A quote from Thoreau seems like a fitting motto for the hiker: "An early morning walk is a blessing for the whole day." Perhaps hiking the Berkshires will inspire you as well.

33 RIVERFRONT TRAIL AND HOUSATONIC RIVER WALK

On the banks of the Housatonic River, two connected greenway trails provide opportunities for people of all abilities to enjoy river views, meadows, bird-watching, historical sites, and wildflowers, as well as downtown Great Barrington's numerous attractions.

FEATURES

Location Great Barrington, MA

Rating Easy

Distance 2.3 miles round trip

Elevation Gain Minimal

Estimated Time 1.5 hours

Maps USGS Great Barrington; Great Barrington Land Conservancy map: gbland.org/sites/default/files/inline-images/Riverfront%20Trail.jpg

GPS Coordinates 42° 11.130′ N, 73° 21.675′ W

Contact Great Barrington Land Conservancy, gbland.org/riverfront-trail and gbriverwalk.org

DIRECTIONS

For Riverfront Trail's main entrance (the starting point for this hike), from downtown Great Barrington follow US 7/MA 23/MA 41 south to a traffic circle where MA 23/MA 41 branches right. Continue on US 7 south for 0.2 mile and then turn left at a sign for Olympian Meadows (an athletic field complex) and follow the driveway to parking areas at the sports fields.

To reach Riverfront Trail's southern section, from Olympian Meadows drive south on US 7 for 0.7 mile. Turn left on Brookside Road, pass the Bostick Gardens apartment complex, and turn left to enter the parking area, which has space for two cars.

TRAIL DESCRIPTION

Riverfront Trail and Housatonic River Walk, both projects of Great Barrington Land Conservancy (GBLC), form a nearly contiguous recreational route along the western banks of the Housatonic River. Completed in 2020 after several decades of planning, universally accessible Riverfront Trail comprises a 0.6-mile section that runs between the Olympian Meadows athletic fields to Bridge Street and a 0.15-mile section that extends north of Brookside Road. (The long-term plan is to eventually connect both via

TRIP 33 // RIVERFRONT TRAIL AND HOUSATONIC RIVER WALK

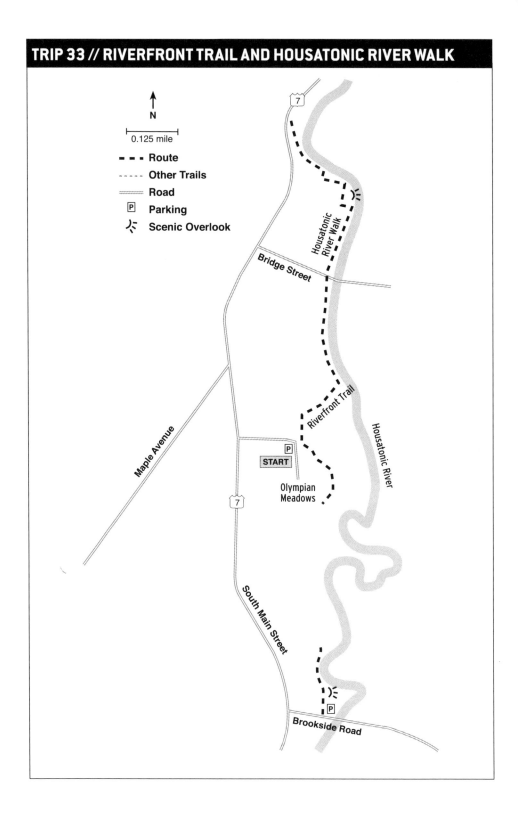

184   SECTION 3 // SOUTHERN BERKSHIRES

Great Barrington Fairgrounds.) Interpretive signs describe native and planted trees along the route.

Housatonic River Walk (0.5 mile one way) has two short segments, known as the downstream and upstream sections, between Bridge Street and US 7 (Main Street) in downtown Great Barrington. The downstream section is universally accessible.

At Olympian Meadows, Riverfront Trail's northern section begins at a GBLC sign behind the softball field. Adaptable American crows, known for their intelligence, often feed around the fields. Bear left to head north along the Housatonic River's west banks (a segment of the trail on the right leads along the back of the athletic fields; GBLC is working to develop a short loop). The first tree identification sign marks a box elder, a species that grows in floodplains and forest edges.

Cross a wooden footbridge and pass a Norway maple tree. On the right, a seasonally flooded oxbow bend in the Housatonic River provides habitat for woodpeckers, nuthatches, and brown creepers, as well as waterfowl such as wood ducks and hooded mergansers. A large, multitrunked silver maple, another characteristic floodplain species, towers above the path to the left.

Amble through sunlit meadows that host a variety of birds, including eastern bluebirds, goldfinches, song sparrows, juncos, and cardinals, plus migratory northern orioles, scarlet tanagers, common yellowthroats, and chestnut-sided warblers. Visible across the shrubby field on the left is Searle's Castle, one of Great Barrington's distinctive historical landmarks. Built in 1883, the structure, now privately owned, has been used as a girls' boarding school, a training and conference center, and a country club. To the right, one of the Housatonic Valley's high rolling hills rises above the river's east banks. Colorful meadow flowers carpet the fields from spring through early autumn.

Reenter woods at signed honey locust and burr oak trees, with the river nearby on the right. The valley's moist soils provide ideal growing conditions for American basswood trees, identified by large, heart-shaped leaves. A colony of wild geranium, also known as cranesbill, blooms along the trail in mid and late spring. Maroon foliage distinguishes a striking European beech on the left.

Continue past a stone bridge and a grove of katsura trees (native to Asia) to an information sign with maps and brochures for local trails. At 0.6 mile, reach Riverfront Trail's northern end at Bridge Street, near Memorial Field and Railroad Street Youth Project facilities on the left and a road bridge over the Housatonic River to the right. Downtown Great Barrington is a quick 0.2-mile walk to the left via Bridge Street.

On the north side of Bridge Street, enter the downstream (southern) section of Housatonic River Walk, which continues along the Housatonic River. After about 200 feet, a short nature trail branches to the right. Enter W.E.B. Du Bois River Memorial Park, named in honor of the prominent civil rights leader who advocated for protection of the Housatonic and other rivers. The park, formerly a rubbish dump, features planted wildflowers and a rain garden where native plants and soils benefit the floodplain by absorbing water and nutrients. Parking is available at the entrance at the intersection of Church and River streets.

At 0.2 mile from Bridge Street, Housatonic River Walk's downstream section ends at River Street next to the Berkshire Corporation parking lot. To reach the upstream section, turn right and walk along River Street to its end and then turn left on Dresser Avenue, and continue for another 300 feet to the entrance on the right at the St. Peter's church parking lot. At a T intersection, bear right to make a short out-and-back diversion to an overlook named for the electrical inventor William H. Stanley. Return to the junction and continue past a marble bench and boardwalk to Housatonic River Walk's northern end at Main Street (US 7), next to a Dollar General store. Here, you can visit downtown Great Barrington before retracing your steps back to the Olympian Meadows trailhead.

Riverfront Trail's short southern section features a panoramic view of the Housatonic River and opportunities to see a variety of wildlife. From the posted map at the Brookside Road entrance, follow the stone dust path north past sugar maples and an American elm. Eastern cottontail rabbits often feed along the edge early and late in the day. After roughly 500 feet, reach an open vista on the banks of the Housatonic River, looking east across a shallow oxbow bend. A bench provides a pleasant spot to pause and watch for birds, including ducks, Canada geese, and migratory songbirds. You may also glimpse a raccoon in brushy cover or feeding along the river's edge.

Walk past shrubby growths of honeysuckle and azalea to the path's northern end at a bench and fence at the edge of a field on the south side of the Great Barrington Fairgrounds. The mixed habitats offer opportunities to see hawks, white-tailed deer, and songbirds.

The southern segment of Riverfront Trail features an open view of the Housatonic River and opportunities to see waterfowl, raccoons, and other wildlife.

DID YOU KNOW?
Great Barrington originally formed as a settlement in 1726 on a travel corridor from Springfield, Massachusetts, to Albany, New York. The advent of railroads prompted the town's development as a resort destination during the nineteenth century. Searle's Castle was originally part of the estate of a wealthy family.

MORE INFORMATION
Riverfront Trail is open dawn to dusk year-round. Bicycles and horses are not allowed. Leashed dogs, skiing, and snowshoeing are permitted. Cartop boat access to the Housatonic River is available on Brookside Road at a small parking area just east of Riverfront Trail's southern section trailhead (parking for boaters only).

Housatonic River Walk is open for walking and nature viewing during spring, summer, and fall. Please stay on the designated trail and do not climb on riverbank slopes. Bicycles are not permitted.

NEARBY
Another universally accessible trail recently opened in Great Barrington at Thomas and Palmer Brook Reserve, a Berkshire Natural Resources Council property that protects 267 acres of wetlands, meadows, and wooded uplands. Meadow Loop, a 0.5-mile packed stone dust path, leads through old fields, a former orchard, and a wildlife habitat restoration area. Woodland Trail and Whale Rock Trail (neither is universally accessible) provide a 0.9-mile out-and-back ascent to Whale Rock, a wooded outcropping atop nearby Three Mile Hill. The entrance is on MA 23 (State Road), 0.7 mile east of the intersection with US 7. See bnrc.org/trails-and-maps/thomas-and-palmer-brook for details.

34 ALFORD SPRINGS

This less traveled segment of the Taconic Mountains features wooded ridges with outstanding wildlife habitat. An upland forest management area and several lookouts provide scenic views of the Alford Brook valley and Mount Greylock from multiple angles.

FEATURES

Location Alford, MA

Rating Moderate

Distance 5.1 miles round trip

Elevation Gain 940 feet

Estimated Time 2.5 to 3 hours

Maps USGS State Line MA/NY, USGS Alford; Berkshire Natural Resources Council map: bnrc.org/fileadmin/files/Maps/BNRC_Alford_Springs_2023_FINAL__1_.pdf

GPS Coordinates 42° 14.877' N, 73° 26.721' W

Contact Berkshire Natural Resources Council, 413-499-0596, bnrc.org/reserves/alford-springs

DIRECTIONS

From Exit 10 on the Massachusetts Turnpike, drive west on MA 102 for 4.6 miles to the intersection with US 7 in Stockbridge. Turn left onto US 7 and travel south 3.9 miles to Great Barrington. After passing Monument Mountain, turn right and follow West Stockbridge Road for 0.5 mile. Turn right (north) onto MA 183 and then take the next left on Division Street and continue for 3.0 miles. Turn right onto Seekonk Road and drive 3.1 miles to the intersection with Mountain Road. Turn right onto Mountain Road, bear left past a driveway on the right, and proceed 0.7 mile to the Alford Springs Father Loop parking area at the junction with Old Village Road.

TRAIL DESCRIPTION

Alford Springs encompasses 900 acres of ridges and streams in the picturesque Taconic highlands. Most of the land was slated to become a housing development in the late twentieth century, but the project never happened after the market slowed. Berkshire Natural Resources Council (BNRC) and MassWildlife (Massachusetts Division of Fisheries and Wildlife) acquired the various parcels between 2002 and 2018.

TRIP 34 // ALFORD SPRINGS

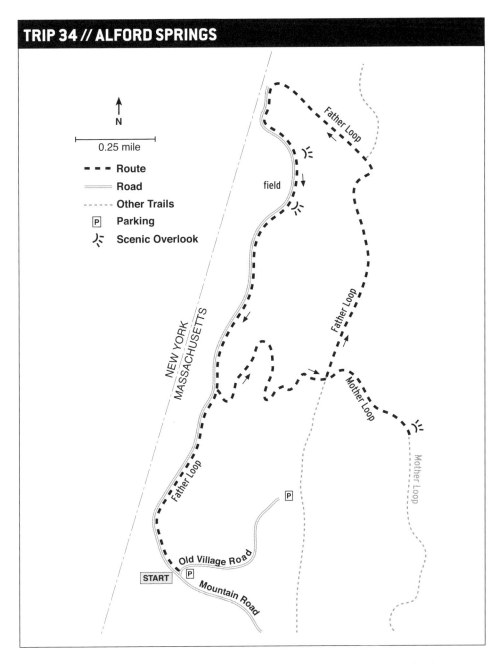

This outing combines Father Loop, a 4.3-mile circuit leading to the highest point and best view, with a short detour to a vista on Mother Loop, a 2.4-mile circuit in the reserve's southeastern portion. The well-graded woods roads and trails are ideal for snowshoeing and for intermediate to experienced cross-country skiers comfortable with moderate grades. Trails are blazed blue; maps are posted at the trailhead and at junctions.

From the Mountain Road trailhead, follow Father Loop along a woods road past the first of many stream and brook crossings (all via culverts). These waterways, draining into Alford Brook on the east side of the ridge and into the Green River to the south, are the source of the property's name, though no true springs exist. In late spring and summer, you'll likely be greeted by the *pee-a-wee* call of eastern wood peewees, flycatchers that breed near forest openings, such as the trailhead. A large, four-trunked sugar maple rises above the path on the right. Basswood trees, with large, heart-shaped leaves, thrive in moist upland valley forests like the one this hike explores.

At 0.2 mile, reach an open area at a former log landing near the New York state line. Clusters of tiny bluet wildflowers, also known as little bluets, azure bluets, or Quaker ladies, bloom amid the rocks in spring. From the right-hand side of the clearing, continue on Father Loop past another brook crossing. Begin an easy to moderate ascent of the west side of the ridge. Midspring to late spring wildflowers include golden ragwort, an aster that favors wet areas, and wild geranium, a familiar sight in open woods and along trail edges. Common dandelions, though often perceived as lawn weeds, are a food source for bees and other pollinating insects.

The circuit portion of Father Loop begins at a three-way intersection at 0.6 mile. To make a counterclockwise circuit (which avoids elevation gain on the return), turn right and traverse the crest of the wooded ridge. Spoonlike leaves of Canada mayflower color the forest floor in spring. As you begin descending, a gap in the trees affords a glimpse of Alford Brook Valley to the east, which is especially visible when the leaves are down. The trail, designed for cross-country skiing, winds down the east slope at an easy to moderate grade, passing glades of ferns and an old sugar maple on the right. A network of stone walls is evidence that early settlers once cleared these woods for pastures; the land was abandoned by the early twentieth century.

At the base of the descent, reach a four-way junction (with a posted map and wooden bench) where Father Loop intersects with the north end of Mother Loop at 1.5 miles. The reserve's Old Village Road entrance (see "More Information") is 0.3 mile from the gate on the right. Here, you have the option of adding the full Mother Loop (2.4 miles and about 1.25 hours walking time) to the hike or making a quick out-and-back detour to a vista, as described here.

Follow the left branch of blue-blazed Mother Loop past a "Horses Prohibited" sign and mossy logs; then bear right and ascend easily through hardwood forest interspersed with mountain laurels and white pines. American chestnut saplings—holdover sprouts from the blight fungus that essentially eliminated the species in the early twentieth century—are a reminder that these woods are continually stressed by introduced pests and diseases. Eastern chipmunks actively gather food during the warm months before hibernating in winter. Like other small mammals, they are affected by cyclic variations in acorn and nut crops. At 0.4 mile from the junction (1.9 miles overall), reach an outlook with a view to Tom Ball Mountain's ridge on the eastern side of Alford Valley.

Retrace your steps to the four-way junction and turn right to rejoin Father Loop, heading north and downhill along the base of the ridge. The wide, grassy path serves as edge habitat for a variety of flora and fauna, including blue violet colonies in spring. Common garter snakes bask along the sunlit opening during the warm months. Many colorful

On the east side of the Taconic Mountains, Alford Springs Reservation encompasses nearly 900 acres of wooded ridges in a picturesque valley.

dragonflies, including common whitetails and eastern meadowhawks (the last species on the wing in late October and November), are present from midspring through fall, especially near wet areas. You may surprise deer feeding at the forest edge, especially early or late in the day.

Cross a hemlock-shaded stream and descend along its ravine. The trail opening affords a glimpse of a wooded ridge to the north. More streams and creeks drain the adjacent slopes as the road reaches its lowest point. The reserve's vernal pools provide crucial breeding habitats for Jefferson's salamanders, a species of large gray salamanders found mostly in western Berkshire County and the Connecticut River valley in Massachusetts. They are listed as a species of special concern by MassWildlife because populations are threatened by habitat loss. The quack-like calls of wood frogs, often well camouflaged amid fallen leaves, are a welcome early sign of spring.

Bear left and begin the ascent to the ridgetop, following the road past stone walls, an old sugar maple, and the intersection with Saddle Trail (which leads north for approximately 1 mile to West Road at the property's northeastern boundary). Rocky areas with shrubby cover are ideal habitats for bobcats, which are fairly common in the Berkshires but highly secretive. Watch for their tracks, with four rounded toes and no claw marks, in snow and around muddy areas. Smooth-barked beech trees often display scratch marks left by black bears.

Climb along a stream valley and bear left (south) along the property boundary at the New York state line. The grade steepens on the upper slopes, but the road, originally built as part of the proposed development, provides sturdy footing. At 3.8 miles, enter a 25-acre management area, cut in 2016 to promote a healthy forest and create habitat for wildlife. Seven acres are being permanently maintained as open meadow, and the rest is gradually reverting to forest. American woodcocks, indigo buntings, common yellowthroats, ruffed grouse, pearl crescent and monarch butterflies, and white-tailed deer are among the many species benefiting from the regenerating vegetation. Common (also known as Allegheny) blackberry, which grows in disturbed areas, forest edges, and fields, is a food source for many birds and mammals, including black bears.

As you ascend through the sunlit clearing, the hike's best views unfold. Mount Greylock's distinctive profile is about 30 miles away on the northeast horizon. More prominent is Yokun Ridge, the site of several other BNRC properties, which rises above Maple Hill in West Stockbridge. A rounded, wooded peak along the adjacent Taconic ridge is on your left. From the edge of the timber harvest, continue along the paper birch–lined path to the height-of-land, where a lookout on the left offers a partial easterly glimpse across the valley.

From here, it's a fairly quick descent back to the trailhead through upland hardwood forest. Calls of black-and-white warblers, ovenbirds, red-eyed vireos, and other migratory songbirds echo from the treetops in spring and early summer. Sugar maples and birches display colorful foliage in early to mid-October; red oaks, white oaks, and chestnut oaks peak later in the month. Eastern coyotes, which arrived in western Massachusetts during the 1970s, often leave droppings along trails to mark their territories. At 0.4 mile from the ridge crest, reach the three-way intersection at the start of the loop. Retrace your steps to the Mountain Road entrance.

DID YOU KNOW?

In addition to the Alford Springs reserve, BNRC has protected 206 acres on Tom Ball Mountain's northern summit since 2018. The property abuts 200 acres of protected land in West Stockbridge.

MORE INFORMATION

Open year-round. Access is free. No restrooms are available. Skiing, mountain biking, leashed dogs, and hunting in season are allowed. The Mother Loop trailhead (not maintained in winter) is at the end of Old Village Road, 1.6 miles from the intersection with Mountain Road at the main entrance.

NEARBY

The Green River was part of a travel corridor used by American Indians and early European settlers. During the American Revolution, Colonial soldiers led by Henry Knox used the route to move artillery from Fort Ticonderoga to Boston, which precipitated the British evacuation of that city. A historical marker on MA 71 at the state line is one of 56 sites on Henry Knox Cannon Trail, a heritage trail established by the states of New York and Massachusetts in 1927.

35 TYRINGHAM COBBLE RESERVATION

This wonderful loop trail takes you through bucolic pastures to a pair of ancient, erosion-resistant promontories, known as cobbles, with splendid views of Tyringham Valley.

FEATURES

Location Tyringham, MA
Rating Easy to Moderate
Distance 2-mile loop
Elevation Gain 380 feet
Estimated Time 1.5 hours
Maps USGS Monterey; The Trustees of Reservations map: thetrustees.org/wp-content/uploads/2023/10/tyringham-cobble-trail-map.pdf
GPS Coordinates 42° 14.589' N, 73° 12.332' W
Contact The Trustees of Reservations, thetrustees.org/place/tyringham-cobble

DIRECTIONS

From I-90 (Massachusetts Turnpike), take Exit 10 in Lee. Turn left at the traffic light at the end of the ramp and then take the first right onto MA 102. After 0.1 mile, turn left onto Tyringham Road (which becomes Main Road in Tyringham) and follow it through the valley for 4.2 miles to Tyringham. Turn right onto Jerusalem Road and drive 0.2 mile to the entrance and parking area on the right.

TRAIL DESCRIPTION

After reviewing the information posted on the map kiosk, begin by following blue-blazed Cobble Loop past a photogenic red cattle barn on the right. Bear left along the edge of an expansive hayfield, where eastern bluebirds raise their young in nest boxes provided for them. A row of venerable sugar maples displays colorful fall foliage in October.

At a three-way intersection where the circuit portion of Cobble Loop begins, turn right and walk a mowed path along the lower slopes of Cobble Hill. Cleared for pasturage by Colonial farmers in the late eighteenth century, the old fields are now clothed in grasses, goldenrods, asters, crab apple trees, and white pine seedlings. Upon reaching the first of two intersections with Pavilion Trail (which leads to a metal footbridge over tumbling Hop Brook and a pavilion on Main Road, just north of the village center), turn left to continue uphill on Cobble Loop. Follow Cobble Loop as it bends left and

TRIP 35 // TYRINGHAM COBBLE RESERVATION

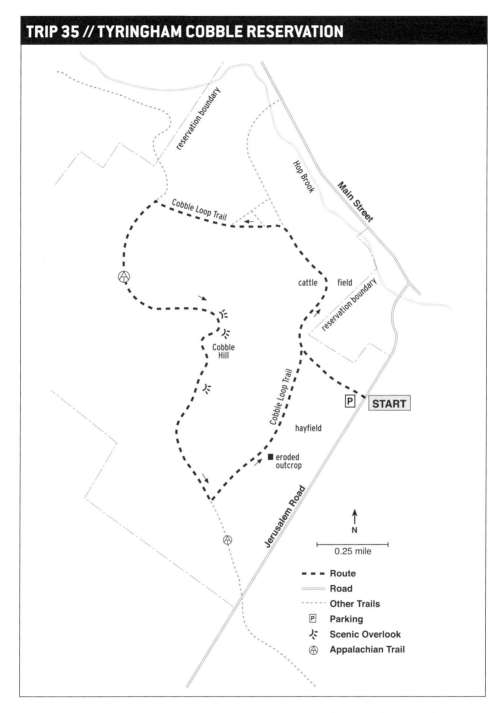

ascends steeply, swings right, and enters a white pine stand at a barbed wire fence. Pass a wooden gate and the upper intersection with Pavilion Trail and continue ascending, following blue blazes on trees that include sugar maple and black birch. Beware of poison ivy in this section.

The trail levels out after a short climb on a wide path among an all-too-thick growth of winged euonymus (an invasive exotic shrub, also known as burning bush) and Japanese barberry. Several species of woodpeckers frequent these woods, including hairy and red-bellied woodpeckers and yellow-bellied sapsuckers. (Sapsuckers forsake the north in autumn.) Omnivorous red squirrels collect and store pine seeds, gather mushrooms, and relish the occasional meal of bird's eggs or nestlings. Sadly, the large ash trees here are threatened by emerald ash borer. Walk through a gap in a stone wall and then pass an eroded and closed trail on the left under a canopy of sugar maple, black cherry, birch, and hemlock.

At a junction with the white-blazed Appalachian Trail (AT) at 0.7 mile, bear left, following the combined AT and Cobble Loop among white pines and cherry trees and fern growth. Green-barked striped maple and sapling American beech populate the forest understory layer on this easy climb, leading through a disturbed woodland characterized by more invasive shrubs and vines: winged euonymus, buckthorn, Japanese barberry, and round-leafed bittersweet. The trail steepens and enters a shady hemlock stand. Amble past a magnificent oak on the left as the path switchbacks up the slope. Turn left at a gneiss boulder and walk along a stone wall built of flat chunks of the same material. More sizable oaks appear; one on the right—more than 3 feet in girth—still has rusty barbed wire embedded in it.

Bear right at a former intersection (the other end of the discontinued trail) and pass through a wooden stile into a small meadow at the crest of the first cobble. From this

The Appalachian Trail leads to viewpoints overlooking a picturesque valley and historical village center near Tyringham Cobble.

grassy summit, enjoy fine views across the valley nearly 500 feet below. Continue over the top, negotiate another wooden stile, and enter a shallow wooded saddle between the two cobbles. A layered gneiss ledge on the left may catch your eye before you climb amid hemlocks. (The gneiss rock's stubborn resistance to erosion created these cobbles.) Turn left to continue along the second hill's contours. Watch for the large hop hornbeam with a dead limb that juts into the path on the left. At more than 20 inches in diameter, this is a giant of the species. You've now completed roughly half of the 2-mile loop.

The route crosses ledges that sport a growth of common polypody ferns—a species almost always anchored to rock. The scant soil atop Cobble Hill's true summit (elevation 1,340 feet) restricts the growth of trees, making for a windswept woodland of low-stature oak and hemlock and a prickly field form of juniper. Enjoy excellent views of the valley and Tyringham Union Church, built in 1844 and listed on the National Register of Historic Places, from atop the partially open ledge on the left.

The combined AT/Cobble Loop begins to descend, reaching a brushy field at a low bedrock outcropping littered with mica crystals. Idyllic views of the valley may convince you to linger for a bit at a picnic table. Pass through the field, where buckthorn thrives. Bear left, heading gently downhill past fuzzy stems of staghorn sumac, juniper, crab apple, raspberry, and goldenrod.

Bear left again, following the margin of the field until you reach a signed intersection where the AT and Cobble Loop part ways. Turn left on blue-blazed Cobble Loop and cross an old orchard that still holds apple and crab apple trees. Reenter the woodland, pass through a swinging wooden gate, and then turn right and amble downhill to Rabbit Rock. Over eons, the forces of wind and water have pockmarked this soft sandstone outcropping into the shape of a rabbit.

Follow the base of Cobble Hill and soon reach an unmarked junction. Turn left to continue on the loop trail, climb briefly, and then drop back down and bear left. The parking area comes into sight as you reach a fence line and parallel the upper edge of the hayfield. More Japanese barberry indicates human disturbance as you pass through a wooden gate at a barbed wire fence. Continue down a short distance to close the loop. Turn right and retrace your steps back to the parking area.

DID YOU KNOW?

Tyringham Cobble Reservation has a very intriguing geological history. The rock atop the formation is 500 million years old, older than the layers beneath it! A geologist named Daniel Clark made that discovery in 1895, surmising that a chunk of a nearby mountain had broken off and flipped upside down.

MORE INFORMATION

Open year-round, sunrise to sunset. Access is free; on-site donations from nonmembers of The Trustees of Reservations are welcome. Skiing and leashed dogs are allowed; mountain biking is prohibited. Seasonal hunting is permitted. The parking lot is not plowed during winter.

NEARBY

Ashintully Gardens (thetrustees.org/place/ashintully-gardens), also owned by The Trustees of Reservations, features award-winning plantings by the composer John McLennan and walking trails through picturesque meadows. Dogs and bikes are not allowed. The property, at the intersection of Main Road and Sodem Road in Tyringham, is open sunrise to sunset daily from April to November; access is free.

Santarella, or the Gingerbread House, is a familiar landmark in Tyringham. It was the home of English sculptor Sir Henry Hudson Kitson (1865–1947), an English sculptor who lived and worked in the United States. He created many representations of American military heroes, including the famous Minuteman statue in Lexington, Massachusetts. The house, at 75 Main Road, also once housed an art gallery. It is not currently open to the public, but a similarly charming structure called Tiny Tower is available for rent (413-243-0840; santarellagardens.com).

36 BECKET QUARRY

Becket Quarry is a place frozen in time. This hike takes you past rusting vehicles, sheds, and other abandoned artifacts of the granite quarry, used from the 1860s to the 1960s. A well-marked trail network winds through northern hardwood forest, among granite boulders, and over a small brook, leading to a panoramic vista.

FEATURES

Location Becket, MA
Rating Easy to Moderate
Distance 3.9 miles round trip
Elevation Gain 400 feet
Estimated Time 1.5 to 2 hours
Maps USGS Otis, USGS Becket; The Trustees of Reservations map: thetrustees.org/wp-content/uploads/2022/09/BecketQuarry_TrailMap_2022.pdf
GPS Coordinates 42° 15.082′ N, 73° 01.216′ W
Contact The Trustees of Reservations, thetrustees.org/place/becket-historic-quarry-forest

DIRECTIONS
From the west: From I-90 (Massachusetts Turnpike), take Exit 10 in Lee. Turn left at the traffic light at the end of the ramp and proceed east on US 20 for 12.1 miles to the intersection with Bonnie Rigg Hill Road in Becket. Turn right and follow Bonnie Rigg Hill Road uphill for 1.3 miles to the intersection with Quarry and Algerie roads. Turn left onto Quarry Road and drive 0.9 mile to the gravel parking area on the right.

From the east: From Exit 41 off I-90 (Massachusetts Turnpike) in Westfield, follow US 20 west for 12.2 miles through Westfield, Russell, Huntington, and Chester and then into Becket. In Becket, proceed to the intersection with Bonnie Rigg Hill Road on the left. From this point, see directions above.

TRAIL DESCRIPTION
Becket Quarry preserves a former granite stone quarry and surrounding forests. The Trustees of Reservations acquired the 280-acre property in 2021 from Becket Land Trust, which originally preserved the site in the 1990s. This hike combines the quarry

TRIP 36 // BECKET QUARRY

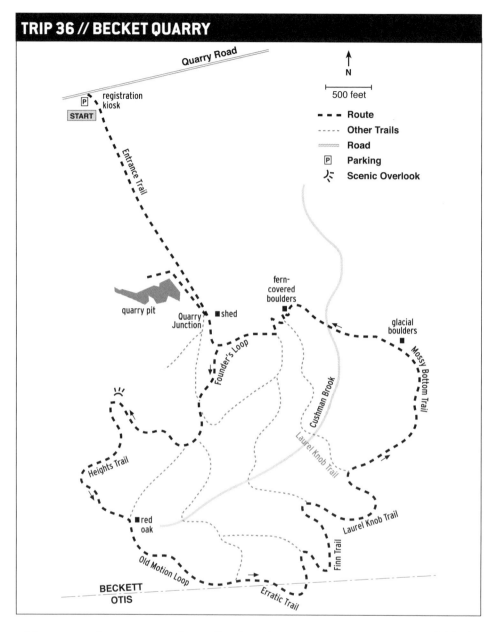

with an outer loop on several woodland trails; numerous options are available for shorter walks. Intersections are clearly signed.

A kiosk with a trail map sits at the far end of the gravel parking area. The first interpretive station features a Sullivan drill, a device that was used to drill the holes into which explosive charges were placed. The site is where granite blocks were loaded before final processing in the neighboring town of Chester. Begin by following white-blazed Entrance Trail up the old roadway beneath a canopy of oaks, maples, American beeches, yellow birches, and eastern hemlocks. In spring, a stunning wildflower display includes trout lily and red trillium. Reach a grout pile, a tall heap of granite chunks, on the right. This is the waste material from decades of quarrying. Do not climb the pile, as it can be unstable and dangerous. In summer, when warm, moist air comes in contact with the cold air flowing from the bottom of the pile, it condenses to form fog. A bit farther, on the left, is a smaller grout pile. At 0.6 mile, reach a junction of several trails that lead to the quarry and surrounding area. The skeleton of an electrical generator shed and the rusting hulks of two trucks are visible at interpretive stations. One truck hauled the granite to Chester for processing, and the other had a large tank with compressed air that powered the drills.

The upper portion of an interpretive trail, well worth the detour, leads to a restored derrick and winch and a scenic view from the top of the quarry. (Use caution in rocky areas.) You can explore the impressive water-filled quarry pit, a short distance to the right, now or when you return here later. To continue the hike, follow the leftmost road past the shed, and immediately reach an intersection at the stiff-leg derrick site. Opposite the derrick, on the right, is the rail grade to a small quarrying site where granite blocks were cut. Stay left and pass rusting artifacts of a bygone era; the quarry operated for 100 years, from the 1860s until the 1960s.

From the quarry trails junction, continue to the intersection with blue-blazed Founder's Loop, where the circuit portion of the hike begins. Follow the right fork, which leads gently uphill among granite boulders. Rocks seem more abundant than trees here! Pass a portion of the old roadway again at a wall of massive granite blocks. The rock is the same hue as the beech trunks. On the right is a rusty section of rail. When you reach a Y intersection where Founder's Loop bears left, go right on a short connecting path to red-blazed Old Motion Loop. Unfortunately, after leaf fall, the din of traffic on the Massachusetts Turnpike is audible here. Follow the right branch of Old Motion Loop for a few hundred feet to the next intersection and then turn right onto yellow-blazed The Heights Trail.

The hillside is clothed in oak and beech. A fungal disease that blackens the bark of beeches disfigures many of them here. One larger specimen among the mostly young trees displays claw marks left by a black bear that climbed this tree for its tasty nuts. After walking 0.5 mile from the Founder's Loop junction, arrive at an outlook and a granite bench—a pleasant spot to linger—at 1.2 miles overall. Tree clearing has opened up a fine view of Round Top Hill to the east.

Bear left around the bench and pass the first of several logged areas. The cutting was done in collaboration with the Massachusetts Division of Fisheries and Wildlife (MassWildlife) and the U.S. Department of Agriculture Natural Resources Conservation Service to create shrubland for species that favor brushy edge habitats, including the endangered New England cottontail rabbit.

A few young red maples show scars where a moose tore off strips of outer bark with its incisors to get at the nutritious inner bark. The fact that the bark was torn off to a height of 7 feet is a telltale sign of moose. A gentle descent leads past a gray granite outcropping on the right. A few red spruce and hemlock appear, but American beech still rules this woodland. Beech sprouts prolifically from cut stumps and by means of runners. Rejoin red-blazed Old Motion Loop. Across from you, perhaps 50 feet away, leans a massive red

The former Chester-Hudson Quarry, one of the region's most distinctive historical sites, is now part of a 300-acre preserve in the wooded hills of Becket.

oak. The giant—more than 4½ feet in diameter—is pocked with cavities where branches have rotted out, creating potential den sites for raccoons and other wildlife.

Turn right on Old Motion Loop and soon pass a large, multitrunked white pine on the left. Amble easily through beech and hemlock woodland. Granite was quarried at what is now a depression on the right where big, angular blocks are piled. Sullivan drill marks are evident on some. The depression, rimmed by winterberry shrubs, fills with water and may well serve as a vernal pool for mating salamanders in spring.

At the next intersection, bear right onto Erratic Trail and descend gradually to the hemlock-shaded junction with Finn Trail. Turn right onto Finn Trail, which follows a wide old woods road past pockets of hay-scented fern, which yellows and dies after frost. Descend briefly and turn left onto a single-track, remaining on Finn Trail. Note the hobblebush shrubs. Shining club moss and ferns carpet the ground. Follow the rocky contour of the hill and reach the junction with orange-blazed Laurel Knob Trail at a small boulder field. Turn right onto Laurel Knob Trail. A slope drops off on the left to a flat terrace. Large, rotting stumps are testimony to logging decades ago. Young beech trees and red maples now dominate.

After an old roadway joins Laurel Knob Trail on the left, reach a three-way intersection. Turn right onto Mossy Bottom Trail and soon cross a small brook. The shady woodland is home to singing hermit thrushes from spring through fall and to tiny spring peepers year-round. These little tree frogs blend in marvelously with the leaf litter. Bear right to briefly walk along the edge of a former timber harvest and then reenter woodland.

Descend through more hemlocks and cross a tote road. A cabin-sized glacial boulder protrudes from the forest floor at the edge of a small clearing, and the tall common reed stalks hint at wetlands to the right. Cross flowing Cushman Brook on flagstones. Hemlock and red maple thrive in the boggy soil.

Pass another forest management area that was logged to remove diseased beech trees and create space and sunlight to induce the growth of red and white oaks. Ascend through granite boulders—most capped by a luxuriant growth of polypody fern, spinulose wood fern, and club moss, giving this spot the feel of a temperate rainforest. The rock crevices provide den habitat for porcupines. Now walk more steeply uphill and reach a wider, unsigned roadway. Mossy Bottom Trail bears left and then away from the faint road, widens again, and rejoins Laurel Knob Trail at 2.4 miles. Turn right and head uphill on Laurel Knob Trail to the intersection with blue-blazed Founder's Loop. Turn right and follow Founder's Loop to the next intersection, at the end of the loop. Turn right and retrace your steps to Quarry Junction and the entrance.

Just past the generator shed, turn left and walk past the guy derrick site (interpretive station 6) toward the base of the quarry, lined by 65-foot-high granite walls. Watch your footing and stay back from the edge. Granite steps lead up to a terrace where you'll see granite blocks into which quarry workers cut their initials and the years 1868 and 1894. When you're ready to leave, retrace your steps 0.6 mile back to the parking area.

DID YOU KNOW?

When the Labrie Stone Products Company announced plans in 1999 to obtain the land and restart large-scale quarrying operations, hundreds of local concerned citizens donated the funds that enabled the Becket Land Trust to purchase the 300-acre property.

MORE INFORMATION

Open sunrise to sunset year-round. A $10 parking fee is charged to nonmembers of The Trustees of Reservations or Becket Land Trust between Memorial Day and Labor Day. Parking on roads adjacent to the property is prohibited. Leashed dogs are allowed. Hunting is permitted in season. Swimming and diving at the quarry, collecting or disturbing historical artifacts, and metal detecting are prohibited. See Becket Land Trust's website (becketlandtrust.org/historic-quarry) for more information about the quarry, including an exhibit in the Mullen House Education Center (open in summer by appointment) at the junction of MA 8 and Brooker Hill Road in North Becket.

NEARBY

The Becket Arts Center is a multidisciplinary community arts facility in historic Seminary Hall, Becket's first consolidated school, built in 1855. The center offers events, workshops, and exhibitions (413-623-6635; becketartscenter.org).

AMC's Noble View Outdoor Center is available for those looking to stay in the area. Ten dog-friendly campsites are available, with access to a bathhouse with hot showers, sinks, toilets, and dish washing areas. In the winter, you can book two cabins with accommodations for ten to eighteen guests. An extensive network of trails offer recreational opportunities in all seasons.

POOL PARTY

In many ways, vernal pools are oddities. They're called pools, but they usually dry up by midsummer. They're referred to as "vernal" because the breeding frenzy they host happens in early spring, sometimes while snow still coats the ground. As ephemeral as they are, vernal pools are absolutely essential to a group of creatures able to reproduce nowhere else. These include mole salamanders, wood frogs, and fairy shrimp. None can exist without these fleeting woodland water bodies.

Mole salamanders (an overall family that includes individual species such as spotted, Jefferson's, and blue-spotted salamanders) spend the bulk of their lives beneath the leaf litter. They emerge during the first early spring rains, when temperatures are about 40 degrees Fahrenheit (late March or early April in the Berkshires), and head for depressions flush with snowmelt and vernal moisture. The pools must contain leaves, sticks, and other woodland detritus that forms the basic energy source for the minute creatures that provide food for the salamander larvae.

The mating ritual of spotted and Jefferson salamanders is really something to behold as the animals writhe and twirl in love's embrace. The males drop packets of sperm that females pick up with their cloacae (short body tubes). Then the females lay a fist-sized mass of gelatinous eggs that they attach to twigs beneath the vernal pool's surface. The eggs hatch into gilled salamander larvae, which must reach sufficient size to survive on dry land before the pool disappears under the blazing summer sun.

But why rely on such undependable water sources? Because vernal pools don't contain fish, which eat salamander and wood frog eggs and larvae. Only the toxic red-spotted newt of local beaver ponds is able to coexist with the finned tribe. Many salamander species breed in brooks, bogs, or other locations out of reach of fish. So it is only the large, yellow-polka-dotted spotted salamander and the less common blue-flecked Jefferson salamander that put all their eggs in one basket, so to speak.

If you have the opportunity to get out during what biologists call "big nights," when the bulk of salamander movement to vernal pools occurs, wear your rain slicker, take a flashlight, and prepare to be amazed by the spectacle of dozens of mole salamanders and wood frogs, driven by age-old instincts, crossing highways and country lanes en route to breeding pools they may have visited each spring for ten or fifteen years. "Big nights" generally occur during the first soaking rain when the temperature is above 45 degrees in early spring. It's a sight you won't soon forget.

37 BENEDICT POND AND THE LEDGES

This hike features one of the most scenic ponds in the Berkshires, spiced up with a fine laurel bloom in late June, and a side trip on the Appalachian Trail to a splendid viewpoint from the Ledges.

FEATURES

Location Great Barrington and Monterey, MA
Rating Easy to Moderate
Distance 3 miles round trip
Elevation Gain 240 feet
Estimated Time 1.5 to 2 hours
Maps USGS Great Barrington; Massachusetts Department of Conservation and Recreation map: mass.gov/doc/beartown-state-forest-trail-map/download
GPS Coordinates 42° 12.226′ N, 73° 17.403′ W
Contact Beartown State Forest, 413-528-0904, mass.gov/locations/beartown-state-forest

DIRECTIONS

From the intersection of US 7 and Monument Valley Road (near Monument Mountain High School) in Great Barrington, follow Monument Valley Road southeast for 2.0 miles. Turn left onto Stoney Brook Road and proceed 2.7 miles. Then turn left onto Benedict Pond Road and continue for 0.5 mile to the day-use area entrance on the right. The first and larger parking area is at the boat ramp, the second at the beach.

TRAIL DESCRIPTION

From the Beartown State Forest parking area at the beach at Benedict Pond, head left past a kiosk with trail maps and walk along a wooden fence and concrete retaining wall at the pond shore to an observation deck spanning the dam's spillway. Interpretive leaflets may be available (the interpretive trail begins at the boat launch parking lot and ends here). Turn left onto blue-blazed Pond Loop Trail to begin a counterclockwise loop around the pond. Descend a few wooden steps and then turn right to follow the trail under a canopy of mixed hardwoods—especially oaks. Witch hazel, scattered mountain laurel, and striped maple dot the rocky woodland beneath the canopy; ground-hugging wintergreen is abundant. At informal trail splits, remain on the blue-blazed trail, which generally follows the pond shore past tentsites with picnic tables.

TRIP 37 // BENEDICT POND AND THE LEDGES

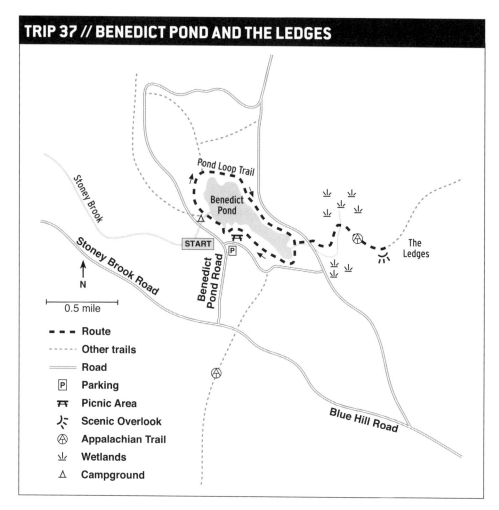

Cross a multiuse trail (open to snowmobiles in winter). Although predominately oak, the forest now includes red maple, black birch, and a few hop hornbeams. At the junction with Mount Wilcox Trail, stay straight on Pond Loop Trail and enjoy glimpses of 35-acre Benedict Pond through the trees. Pass through a couple of low, wet areas marked by cinnamon and sensitive ferns. Sensitive fern has persistent brown, bead like spore capsules. Pointed stumps, cut by beaver, are also in evidence. Witch hazel and mountain laurel border the path. Ten-foot-high arrowwood shrubs, with straight branches and blue berries, line the route as you traverse bog bridges and a small wooden span through damp ground vegetated with tall reed canary grass.

As you round the northwest end of the pond, red maples become common. Pass some white pines and a patch of trailing arbutus (the state flower) on the left that blooms delicate pink in May, hence its other moniker: mayflower. A wooden bench at the water's edge invites a pause. In winter, ice anglers seeking pickerel, largemouth bass, yellow perch, and bluegill often dot the frozen pond. Tilted gray gneiss bedrock outcroppings pop into sight on the left. Towering, straight white pines grew up in this woodland crowded by others of their kind. White ashes, black cherry trees, yellow and gray birches, and beeches join the mix, although massive oaks still rule. Camouflaged brown creepers hitch their way up the furrowed pine trunks, looking for insect eggs and larvae hidden in bark crevices.

Cross another small wooden span and continue under pines and oaks. Patches of delicate maidenhair fern soon appear. An 18-foot-high gneiss outcropping juts up 50 feet to the left. After another dampish area with a few small spruces, hobblebushes, and beaked hazelnut shrubs, arrive at a second wooden bench with a fine view. A modest clump of low-growing sheep laurel just left of the bench is easy to overlook; highbush blueberry hugs the shore. Look for a beaver lodge. The trail undulates past taller mountain laurels and enters a dense hemlock stand, where common polypody fern is anchored to a picturesque ledge. Water dripping from and through crevices in the rock creates a fantastic icicle display in winter, but watch your footing if visiting then, as this section can be very icy!

Continue to follow Pond Loop Trail on a woods road multiuse trail at 1.0 mile, bearing right as it descends gently. To your left are another tilted gneiss spine and a few white paper birches. Black birches populate the rising slope beyond. After passing a stand of spruces on the right, arrive at the Appalachian Trail (AT) intersection at 1.2 miles. Turn left to follow the white-blazed AT north toward the Ledges, about 0.75 mile (15 minutes) distant. Walk uphill easily at first, under oak, maple, and birch. As the trail levels out, observe more ledges—some dotted with leafy brown rock tripes, lichens that turn green when wet.

Bear left and ascend rocky steps tight along a rock face for the hike's first real elevation gain. The path wends through oaks and laurels above the left slope of a rocky ravine. At the head of the ravine, reach a wooden bridge over an outflow stream that originates nearby at a sizable wetlands known as Beaver Pond. (A short detour straight ahead, just before the bridge, leads to the swamp edge and the opportunity to see beavers, river otters, muskrats, and other wildlife.) Turn right to follow the AT across the bridge and then clamber up and walk along the opposite side of the 40-foot-deep defile near the verge, amid oaks and pines. After leaf fall, distant blue ridgelines become visible. Lowbush blueberry and tiny, shiny-leafed wintergreen thrive in the acidic soil beneath the trees, which are of shorter stature here on the stony ridgetop.

Watch for more trailing arbutus just before reaching a benchlike outcropping at a gap in the woody vegetation. You have arrived at the Ledges, a rocky lookout with splendid views that is an ideal spot for a snack break. Mount Everett (2,624 feet) is the high point along the third ridgeline to the southwest. In winter, the Butternut and Catamount ski areas are also visible.

When you're ready, retrace your steps on the AT to the Pond Loop Trail junction. Turn left on the combined AT and Pond Loop Trail (white and blue blazes) and cross a brook by walking over a wooden bridge set on handsome mortared stone abutments. Then turn right to continue around the southeast end of Benedict Pond. After passing a small spruce stand and a large yellow birch, negotiate the soggy ground safely via a series of bog bridges. Northern white cedar trees, or arbor vitae, between the path and the pond are unusual for this area. These flat-needled evergreens are generally bog denizens. After a minor brook crossing, the trail bears right to hug the pond shore. At 2.5 miles, reach an intersection where the AT veers left and up to the woods road; walk straight ahead to continue on Pond Loop Trail. The Benedict Pond shoreline is bordered here by a dense growth of evergreen mountain laurel that blooms luxuriantly in late June.

Although not as showy as laurel, hobblebush has conspicuous ocher buds in winter and white flower doilies in spring. The flower heads include both tiny fertile flowers and larger infertile ones that attract the attention of pollinators. Stroll through a hemlock grove and complete the loop at a picnic area and kiosk near the boat ramp. At the paved road (0.5 mile from the AT junction), turn right toward the beach parking area and your vehicle.

DID YOU KNOW?
Benedict Pond, built by the Civilian Conservation Corps in 1934, is named for Fred Benedict, a local dairy farmer who owned the surrounding land. In 1921, the commonwealth acquired the property from the lumber dealer Warren H. Davis, who had cleared much of the timber, and the former estate of Fred Pearson.

MORE INFORMATION
Open sunrise to sunset year-round. A parking fee ($8 Massachusetts residents, $30 out of state) is charged from mid-May through Labor Day weekend. Restrooms are

Amenities of picturesque Benedict Pond, built by the Civilian Conservation Corps in 1934, include a campground, swimming beach, and hiking trails.

available seasonally at the day-use area. Mountain biking is not allowed on the Appalachian Trail but is permitted on other trails. Skiing, leashed dogs, and hunting in season are allowed. The campground, which reopened in 2024 after extensive renovations, has twelve sites near Benedict Pond; amenities include new bathrooms, water sources, tables, grills, and internet connectivity. All-terrain vehicles are permitted on designated trails May through November. Snowmobiles are permitted with 4 inches minimum of hard-packed snow base.

NEARBY

Gould Farm was originally founded in 1913 as the nation's first residential therapeutic community dedicated to assisting adults with mental health challenges. The Roadside Store and Cafe at 275 Main Road in Monterey, open from 7:30 A.M. until 2:30 P.M. Wednesday to Saturday, serves breakfast and lunch. See gouldfarm.org or call 413-528-2633 for more information.

38 BOB'S WAY

A mostly easy woodland trek, ideal for families, leads to a partial view of surrounding hills and a beaver dam and lodge. Enjoy abundant wildflowers and shrubs in spring and striking foliage in October.

FEATURES

Location Monterey and Sandisfield, MA

Rating Easy

Distance 2.9 miles round trip

Elevation Gain 430 feet

Estimated Time 1.75 hours

Maps USGS Monterey; Berkshire Natural Resources Council map: bnrc.org/fileadmin/files/Maps/BNRC_Bob_s_Way_2023_FINAL.pdf

GPS Coordinates 42° 10.837 N, 73° 09.963′ W

Contact Berkshire Natural Resources Council, 413-499-0596, bnrc.org/reserves/bobs-way

DIRECTIONS

From the junction of MA 23 and MA 57/MA 183 at the Great Barrington–Monterey town line (near the Appalachian Trail crossing on MA 23), follow MA 23 east for 6.8 miles past Monterey's town center to the parking area on the right (south) side of the highway, approximately 0.2 mile west of the Monterey–Otis town line.

TRAIL DESCRIPTION

Named for the noted Berkshire conservationist N. Robert (Bob) Thieriot, Bob's Way, a 263-acre Berkshire Natural Resources Council property, preserves wooded hills, mixed upland forests, and a large beaver pond at the three-town boundary of Monterey, Sandisfield, and Otis. This hike combines a loop on the reservation's main trail (also named Bob's Way) with a detour to a lookout on two short connecting routes. Trails are signed and blue blazed.

Blue periwinkle flowers, which often indicate former garden sites, bloom around the entrance in spring. From an information sign at the trailhead, where paper maps are available, begin by following Bob's Way through mixed forests that include paper and yellow birches, hemlock, and mountain laurel. Cross a short boardwalk through wetlands at the inlet of Royal Pond, which lies just outside the reservation boundary. Characteristic wildflowers of moist forests include red trillium, which blooms at several

TRIP 38 // BOB'S WAY

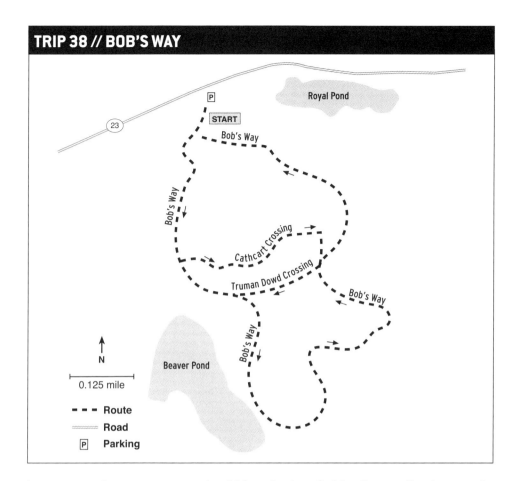

locations in the reservation, and goldthread, identified by five small, white petals. Adaptable red maples display bright red foliage in late September and early October. A dense growth of cattails, a native plant that thrives in shallow water and wetlands edges, is to the right. American Indians used cattails for medicinal purposes, food, and crafts.

Ascend through hemlocks to the start of the loop at a three-way junction on the south side of the wetlands. Follow the right branch of Bob's Way on a moderate climb through a mix of hemlock and northern and southern hardwoods, including oak, birch, and sugar maple. Pass an angular boulder as the path swings left and then right before leveling out. Spoonlike leaves of Canada mayflower carpet the forest floor in spring. Resume ascending at an easy grade past a growth of mountain laurel, an evergreen shrub that thrives in rocky woods and on mountain slopes. White or pink blooms of laurel flowers usually peak in mid to late June. Hobblebush, another familiar shrub of Berkshire woodlands, blooms earlier in the growing season, during May.

After 0.5 mile, reach a signed three-way intersection. Turn left onto Cathcart Crossing and make a short climb through sunlit hardwood forest to a stone bench, dedicated to former Monterey resident David Cathcart. Though partially screened by trees, the outlook provides a southerly view to nearby eminences on the Monterey–Sandisfield town line, including Morley Hill. Deciduous trees unfurl fresh green leaves in May, and colorful foliage peaks in early to mid-October. Large oval-shaped cavities in dead trees indicate feeding by pileated woodpeckers, which thrive in large tracts of mature forest.

A few hundred feet beyond the outlook, cross the wooded 1,765-foot hilltop, the property's highest point, and continue following Cathcart Crossing on a winding path through upland forest. Trout lilies, so named for mottled leaves that resemble body patterns of brown and brook trout, display bright yellow flowers in late April and early May. Descend to a signed four-way intersection at 0.8 mile, where the reservation's three trails converge (the eastern portion of Bob's Way, which leads back to the trailhead, branches to the left). Turn right onto Truman Dowd Crossing, a 0.2-mile connecting path named for a farmer who cultivated the land in the late eighteenth and nineteenth centuries. Pass an outcropping at the base of the hill's south slopes, where rich soils sustain white violets and red trilliums.

Rejoin the western portion of Bob's Way at a three-way intersection. Turn left, following a sign marked "wetland," and descend through rocky woods. As you approach a large pond near the reservation's southwestern boundary, an abandoned motorboat, rather out of place in the dense woods, lies just off the trail to the right. Several large birch trees grow out of the old stone foundation of a dwelling once inhabited by the Markham and Dowd families.

Descend to the southern end of the pond, which straddles the Monterey–Sandisfield town line, at 1.4 miles. A short side path leads to perspectives of a hefty beaver dam at the outlet, which holds back a considerable volume of water during spring and other wet periods. The outflow drains to Gilder Pond in the watershed of Clam River. A beaver

Red trilliums and other ephemeral wildflowers thrive in nutrient-rich soils and wetlands at Bob's Way.

lodge is visible near the dam; the best times to see the inhabitants are early or late in the day. Chestnut Hill, capped by a radio tower, rises across the water to the west. In winter, look for tracks and smooth paths, called slides, of river otters. Otters often scramble across or over beaver dams while traveling between wetlands. Great blue herons abandoned a rookery after a storm blew down nest trees at the pond in 2010.

From the pond, follow Bob's Way along an old cart road through predominantly hardwood forests with a few white pines. Black-and-white warblers, easily distinguished by calls that sound like squeaky wheels, inhabit such mixed forests near water.

Pass through dense growths of mountain laurel and descend through more hobblebush. Starflower, named for the shapes of its white flowers and leaves, blooms in May and June. Amble past hemlocks, laurels, and stone walls that indicate former farm and pasture sites. Although resident bobcats, coyotes, foxes, and wild turkeys are often elusive, tracks in snow reveal evidence of their presence and behaviors.

At 2.3 miles, return to the four-way junction with Truman Dowd Crossing and Cathcart Crossing. Turn right to continue on Bob's Way on gently rolling terrain along the east side of the hill you ascended earlier in the hike. This section of the trail is prime wildflower habitat. In addition to trilliums and trout lilies, other familiar species include blue-bead lily (*Clintonia*), which grows in cool upland forests and on mountain slopes; look for its drooping yellow flowers in May and June and blue berries during summer. Sessile bellwort, also known as wild oat, displays small, bell-shaped, creamy white flowers. Yellow violet, one of roughly 30 violet species that grow in New England, thrives in broadleaf forests. A cluster of red trilliums blooms along a small drainage in late April and early May.

At the junction at the end of the loop, turn right and retrace your steps past the wetlands to the trailhead.

DID YOU KNOW?

Bob Thieriot (1946–1998), a native Californian whose family cofounded the *San Francisco Chronicle* newspaper, protected more than 4,500 acres of land in the Berkshires. A former director of Berkshire Natural Resources Council, Thieriot also helped found land trusts in Monterey, Massachusetts, and Sonoma, California. He received the Massachusetts Governor's Award for Open Space Protection in 1998.

MORE INFORMATION

Open year-round; access is free. Skiing and dogs are allowed; hunting permitted in season. No restrooms or visitor facilities are available.

NEARBY

Lake Garfield (275 acres) lies just north of Monterey's town center and MA 23. Paddling routes lead to views of Hunger Mountain, Beartown State Forest, marshy areas, a beaver lodge, and several coves. A small public boat launch and parking area are on Tyringham Road at the lake's west end. The town beach includes parking for both resident and nonresident vehicles. Find more information at the Friends of Lake Garfield website (friendsoflakegarfield.org).

39 CLAM RIVER RESERVE

This remote, deeply wooded river valley possesses a true wilderness character. Stone foundations, wolf trees, and an old mill site offer insights into the landscape's past.

FEATURES

Location Sandisfield, MA
Rating Moderate
Distance 5.5 miles round trip
Elevation Gain 860 feet
Estimated Time 3 hours
Maps USGS Tolland Center, USGS Otis; Berkshire Natural Resources Council map: bnrc.org/fileadmin/files/Maps/BNRC_Clam_River_2023_FINAL.pdf
GPS Coordinates 42° 06.541′ N, 73° 06.791′ W
Contact Berkshire Natural Resources Council, 413-499-0596, bnrc.org/reserves/clam-river

DIRECTIONS
From Massachusetts Turnpike (I-90) Exit 10 in Stockbridge, follow MA 102 west for 0.1 mile. Turn left onto Tyringham Road (becomes Main Road in Tyringham; becomes Tyringham Road in Otis) and proceed 9.6 miles to the junction with MA 23. Continue straight to follow Town Hill Road for 4.8 miles to the intersection with MA 57 (Sandisfield Road) in Sandisfield. Turn left (east) onto MA 57 and proceed 1.5 miles to trailhead parking at the Sandisfield Town Hall Annex (66 Sandisfield Road) on the left.

TRAIL DESCRIPTION
Clam River Reserve, a 550-acre property owned by Berkshire Natural Resources Council, lies within the largely undeveloped upper Farmington River watershed in Sandisfield. The trail network comprises two loops linked by 1.2-mile Wolf Pine Trail. This trip, starting at the main entrance at the Sandisfield Town Hall Annex on MA 57, combines all three segments. The walking is mostly easy, with modest elevation gain in the northern section. Trails are marked with blue blazes; junctions have posted maps.

Begin at a trail sign on the east side of the parking lot, next to a fenced enclosure erected to keep local black bears away from the town hall's garbage cans. Wild strawberry blooms along the forest edge in mid to late spring. From the information sign (where a trail map is posted), follow Two Rivers Loop over a low knoll, where eastern

TRIP 39 // CLAM RIVER RESERVE

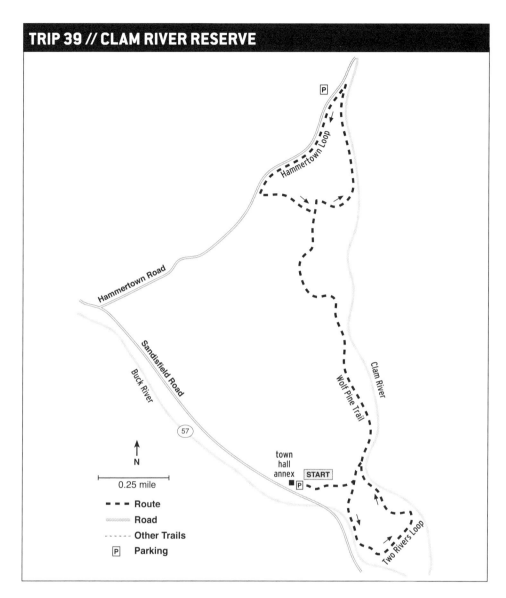

starflower and Canada mayflower, familiar flora of cool upland forests, bloom in spring. A large, spreading gray birch rises just off the trail on the right.

Although the land is densely wooded now, many signs of past use exist, including stone walls, former cart roads, old pine plantations and apple trees, and multitrunked trees (indicators of logging). Sheep farming was especially popular in the early to middle nineteenth century, before the wool market declined. Rocky soil (evidenced by scattered glacial boulders) and lack of a nearby railroad line made agriculture impractical here in the long term. Today nearly 90 percent of Sandisfield, the Berkshires' largest and least densely populated town, is forested.

Descend to a three-way junction at 0.2 mile, where the circuit portion of Two Rivers Loop begins. Turn right, following an old woods road through a mixed forest of hemlock, white pine, and hardwood. Clusters of winterberry add evergreen color to the forest floor. Continue past a side path on the right and through a seasonally wet area. Buck River, emanating from headwater near the Monterey town line, soon appears on the right, paralleling the highway. Sandisfield's post office is barely visible through the trees.

Bear left at the property boundary, remaining on Two Rivers Loop and heading away from Buck River, which merges with Clam River about a quarter-mile downstream. A few birches grow in the understory of an old pine plantation. Big-tooth aspen, named for its serrated, toothlike leaf edges, is adaptable to a variety of habitats, including stream edges and old fields. Continue along a stone wall to a sharp left turn onto the banks of the Clam River.

From headwater at the Otis town line, the Clam River flows southeast through Sandisfield to the confluence with the East Branch of the Farmington River in New Boston. The reserve protects 1.5 miles of frontage along this less known waterway. The name Clam River derives from the river's population of eastern pearl shell mussels ("clam" is a misnomer), which thrive in pristine coldwater streams favored by trout and salmon, their host fish. Larvae attach themselves to fish gills in late summer and grow in the oxygen-rich environment until the following May or June, when they drop off. Distinguished by their rough black or dark brown shells, eastern pearl shells can live more than 100 years but are vulnerable to habitat disturbance and climate change. The upper Farmington River watershed hosts one of southern New England's largest mussel populations, along with several other snail and crayfish species. The state of Massachusetts annually stocks the Clam and Buck rivers with trout.

Cross another knoll, pass a stone wall, and skirt a swampy area on the right. Shady hemlocks and pines offer welcome relief from summer heat, but be prepared for blackflies, mosquitoes, and other biting insects. Continue along the riverbank upstream to a posted map at the intersection with Wolf Pine Trail.

Turn right to continue north on Wolf Pine Trail toward Hammertown Road (a left turn leads to the trailhead for an easy 1.5-mile round trip). The trail initially follows a mostly level woods road, ideal for cross-country skiing, along the river's west banks. Look for tracks and droppings of white-tailed deer, which often use hemlock and pine groves as wintering areas. Moose also benefit from these extensive unbroken woodlands. Reach a large, old white pine with a broad base and multiple shooting trunks. Such specimens—known as "cabbage pines," "pasture pines," or "wolf trees"—colonized abandoned agricultural fields and then were likely infested by white pine weevils, causing the multiple trunks.

Bear left at an arrow marker, following the obvious path past a wet area where a hidden brook gurgles beneath mossy boulders. The well-drained soil sustains wildflowers including red trilliums, violets, and foamflowers. Some American Indian tribes used foamflowers, named for their foamy-looking white flower clusters, for pain relief and other medicinal purposes. After another brook crossing, the trail—clearly delineated with blazes and directional markers—briefly rejoins the woods road, passes a viewpoint above the river, and winds past another stone wall. Listen for the long, warbling song of diminutive winter wrens, especially around stream ravines.

As you progress north, the terrain becomes more rugged, though none of the sections are especially steep. Turn left at another marker to stay on Wolf Pine Trail and ascend the moderately steep valley slope for about 0.25 mile, heading away from the river. The path levels out in a wet area with a lush growth of violets. Veeries, small migratory thrushes that often nest along wooded riverbanks, have a distinctive (haunting to some) song of descending flutelike notes. Cross another brook and then climb easily through a pine grove.

After 1.2 miles on Wolf Pine Trail (1.9 miles overall), reach a posted map at the junction with Hammertown Loop. Turn right to begin a 1.6-mile circuit on Hammertown Loop. Descend to the Clam River on a switchback route that mitigates the steep grade. Walk through a growth of hobblebush, a shrub often found along stream banks and in rich, moist woods. Bear left to begin what is arguably the hike's most scenic segment, a pleasant 0.5-mile stretch following gently rolling terrain along the hemlock-lined riverbank. Pass a rocky chasm and the stone remains of an old mill, another artifact of past land use. The Clam River and the other Farmington River watershed tributaries powered many mills and tanneries during the nineteenth century, which was a time of economic prosperity in the region. Several mossy brooks cascade down the slopes above the river. Painted trillium, another characteristic species of moist ravines, emerges in May.

Shortly after passing a stone foundation, the footpath ends at Hammertown Road, a few hundred feet downstream from a bridge over the Clam River. Turn sharply left to continue the loop, following Hammertown Road (occasional traffic, unmaintained in

A tributary of Farmington River, Clam River meanders through a wooded valley in the remote hills of Sandisfield.

winter) uphill past a pullout and trail map on the left, where parking is available seasonally. Along the way you'll pass several brooks you crossed on the lower portion of the loop. Jack-in-the-pulpit, distinguished by its curved, hoodlike flower (the "pulpit") and long leaves, blooms along the road edge in spring, as do yellow violets, red trilliums, and other wildflowers.

After 0.7 mile on Hammertown Road, turn left at a gate and kiosk with another posted map and follow a woods road east past a wet area and the large stone foundation of a former country home. Continue along a stone wall lined with old sugar maples to the end of the loop at the junction with Wolf Pine Trail at 3.5 miles overall. Turn right and retrace your steps south along Wolf Pine Trail. The mostly downhill segments make for a fairly quick return to the riverside. When you rejoin Two Rivers Loop, follow the right branch on a gentle climb through hemlock-hardwood forest for a few hundred feet to the intersection at the start of the circuit. Turn right to return to the town hall annex's parking area.

DID YOU KNOW?

Clam River Reserve encompasses land donated by the conservationist Bob Thieriot in the late 1990s and additional parcels acquired by Berkshire Natural Resources Council between 2000 and 2012. Berkshire Natural Resources Council, MassWildlife, and the U.S. Department of Agriculture Natural Resources Conservation Service coordinated a 25-acre timber harvest off Hammertown Road (not visible from the hiking trails) in 2013 and 2014. The project created diverse habitats for wildlife, including endangered New England cottontail rabbits. Some red oaks were left as seed trees.

MORE INFORMATION

Open year-round. Access is free. Skiing, mountain biking, leashed dogs, and hunting in season are allowed. No restrooms are available. The Hammertown Road trailhead (not maintained in winter) is 1.5 miles east of the road's intersection with MA 57.

NEARBY

Sandisfield State Forest protects 4,200 acres of northern hardwood forests and wetlands, including 35-acre York Lake. Created by the Civilian Conservation Corps in the 1930s, the lake offers paddling, fishing, and an easy 2.2-mile loop trail. The York Lake entrance is at the intersection of MA 183 and East Hill Road in New Marlborough (mass.gov/locations/sandisfield-state-forest-york-lake).

40 CAMPBELL FALLS

An excellent outing for families, this easy trek leads past a small meadow, woodlands, and the ravine of a cascading brook to Campbell Falls, one of the most picturesque waterfalls in the Berkshires.

FEATURES

Location New Marlborough, MA; Norfolk, CT; and North Canaan, CT
Rating Easy
Distance 1.3 miles round trip
Elevation Gain 175 feet
Estimated Time 1.25 hours
Maps USGS South Sandisfield; Connecticut State Parks and Forests map: portal.ct.gov/-/media/deep/stateparks/maps/campbellfallspdf.pdf
GPS Coordinates 42° 02.559′ N, 73° 13.588′ W
Contact Connecticut State Parks and Forests, 860-424-3200, portal.ct.gov/DEEP/State-Parks/Reserves/Campbell-Falls-State-Park-Reserve

DIRECTIONS
From the intersection of MA 57 and Marlborough-Sandisfield Road in New Marlborough center, follow Marlborough-Sandisfield Road south for 1.3 miles. Turn left onto Norfolk Road and proceed 4.4 miles to the intersection with Campbell Falls Road, 100 hundred feet north of the Connecticut state line. Continue straight on Norfolk Road, which becomes CT 272 at the state line, for 0.1 mile. Turn right and follow Old Spaulding Road (also known as Spaulding Road or Tobey Hill Road) for 0.1 mile to the Connecticut park entrance on the right.

TRAIL DESCRIPTION
Scenic Campbell Falls lies within a secluded ravine in the Whiting River valley at the Massachusetts–Connecticut state line. Campbell Falls State Park Reserve, jointly owned by the states of Connecticut and Massachusetts, protects the falls and surrounding forests and wetlands. This hike, which starts at a parking area on Old Spaulding Road in Connecticut, follows an easy out-and-back trail along a brook ravine to the Massachusetts entrance on Campbell Falls Road, where a short path leads down to the falls. (To go directly to the falls, begin at the Massachusetts entrance.)

From a grassy field and picnic area at the Connecticut entrance, start the hike at a trail sign near the edge of the parking lot. Stroll through a small meadow where dense growths

TRIP 40 // CAMPBELL FALLS

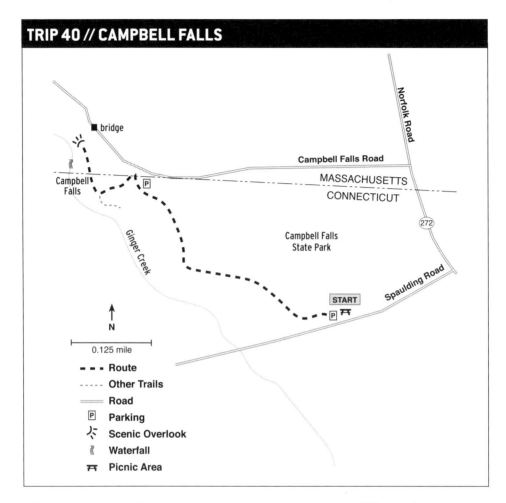

of goldenrod, spotted joe-pye weed, jewelweed, and other wildflowers bloom during summer. Though modest in size, the meadow serves as an important oasis for bees, butterflies, and pollinating insects amid the surrounding densely wooded hills of the southern Berkshires and northwestern Connecticut. Familiar butterflies include tiger swallowtails, which are active from May through early September, and monarchs, which feed on flowers during late summer and early autumn migrations. Watch for flocks of cedar waxwings, which favor old fields and shrubby thickets near rivers and streams.

Bear right at a trail marker and enter the woods on an unnamed but obvious path, heading generally northwest along the north side of Ginger Creek, a tributary of Whiting River. Calls and songs of eastern wood peewees and other migratory songbirds are most evident from late April to early July. Cross a wooden footbridge over the first of several seasonal brooks along the route. A few tall white pines rise amid predominantly hardwood forests. In late summer, look for white wood asters along the trail and forest edges. Unlike most woodland wildflowers that bloom in spring before deciduous trees leaf out, white wood aster, well adapted to shade, emerges late in the growing season. It serves as a host plant for checkerspots and other butterflies.

Descend wooden steps into a grove of eastern hemlock, a fire-intolerant species that thrives along streams and in moist ravines. Its shady evergreen foliage blocks light from reaching the forest floor, thus limiting growth of wildflowers and shrubs. Traverse another short footbridge at a mostly dry brook channel. An unmarked side path on the left leads roughly 300 feet past a stone wall to the banks of Ginger Creek, which makes a horseshoe-shaped bend as it winds along valley hills upstream from Whiting River. (Another short, unmarked path branches left here and leads farther upstream.) Ferns cap mossy boulders along the brook edge.

Return to the main trail and cross a boardwalk bridge over a rocky seasonal brook, where high flows after heavy rains have eroded a prominent channel on the steep slope. Just before the Massachusetts park entrance at the state line, another unmarked path on the left offers a short detour past a large, multitrunked white pine to an elevated perspective of Ginger Creek, looking upstream toward a small cascade.

At 0.4 mile, reach the Massachusetts entrance on Campbell Falls Road, where parking is available at pull-offs. A granite marker post, dated 1906, delineates the Massachusetts–Connecticut boundary. From a brown sign and arrow markers, make a quick 0.14-mile descent of Campbell Falls' steep ravine on an obvious wide trail built by Civilian Conservation Corps workers during the 1930s. After about 400 feet, the needle-covered route bends sharply right (another unmarked side path branches left along the slope above Ginger Creek). Pass another granite marker at the three-town boundary

In a remote valley near the Connecticut state line, the Whiting River drops 50 feet through a high gorge at Campbell Falls.

of Marlborough, Massachusetts; Norfolk, Connecticut; and North Canaan, Connecticut; continue down to the base of the ravine.

Enjoy a fine straight-on perspective of Campbell Falls, where Whiting River plunges 50 feet through a tall, narrow granite gorge in two drops, changing direction at the bottom of the larger, crescent-shaped upper cascade. The river's moderate size provides a healthy flow year-round; during spring high water, mist often drifts over the pool and rocks at the base of the falls. Ripples in the bedrock indicate erosion of soft minerals by the turbulent water over thousands of years. Look for red columbine wildflowers, which thrive in rocky habitats, blooming around the gorge in late spring. To the left, Ginger Creek merges with Whiting River downstream from the falls.

From the base of Campbell Falls, Whiting River meanders west and south through a deep valley along the state line to its confluence with the Blackberry River in North Canaan, Connecticut. All these waterways lie within the Housatonic River watershed.

Backtrack up the ravine to the Massachusetts trailhead; the moderately steep ascent gains about 100 feet in elevation. A quick 0.1-mile detour to the left on Campbell Falls Road leads past an unmarked path and fence to a stone road bridge at the crest of Campbell Falls. The steep slope visible across the valley to the southwest indicates the region's rugged topography. Cardinal flower, which thrives along river and stream banks and in other moist environments, blooms around the top of the falls in late summer. From the Massachusetts entrance, complete the hike by retracing your steps to the Connecticut trailhead.

DID YOU KNOW?

White Memorial Foundation of Litchfield, Connecticut, founded in 1913 by the conservationists Alain and May White, donated Campbell Falls Reserve to the states of Connecticut and Massachusetts in 1923.

MORE INFORMATION

Open 8 A.M. to sunset year-round; access is free. Leashed dogs are allowed. See portal.ct.gov/deep/state-parks/reserves/campbell-falls-state-park-reserve for an informative description of the geology of Campbell Falls State Park.

NEARBY

The Southfield Store, at 163 Norfolk Road in Southfield (a village of New Marlborough), offers breakfast and lunch. It's open 7 A.M. to 4 P.M. Monday through Saturday and 8 A.M. to 4 P.M. on Sundays. See thesouthfieldstore.com or call 413-229-5050 for more information.

41 EAST MOUNTAIN AND ICE GULCH

This out-and-back hike on the Appalachian Trail combines splendid views of the Housatonic Valley and Taconic Range with the cooling breezes emanating from the rocky cleft known as Ice Gulch. The return offers a second opportunity to take in the stunning vistas.

FEATURES

Location Sheffield and Great Barrington, MA
Rating Moderate to Strenuous
Distance 7.2 miles round trip
Elevation Gain 680 feet
Estimated Time 4 to 4.5 hours
Maps USGS Great Barrington; Appalachian Trail Conservancy online map: appalachiantrail.org/explore/hike-the-a-t/interactive-map
GPS Coordinates 42° 09.286' N, 73° 20.469' W
Contact AMC Western Massachusetts Chapter Massachusetts AT Committee, amc-wma.org/appalachian-trail-management-committee
Appalachian Trail Conservancy (New England Regional Office), 802-281-5894, appalachiantrail.org/explore/explore-by-state/massachusetts

DIRECTIONS

From the intersection of US 7 and Castle Street at the traffic signal in downtown Great Barrington, follow US 7 south for 1.25 miles. Turn left onto Brookside Road (which becomes Brush Hill Road and then Homes Road—labeled Home Road on some maps—in Sheffield) and proceed 2.0 miles to the Appalachian Trail crossing. Roadside parking is available on the left.

TRAIL DESCRIPTION

Follow the white-blazed Appalachian Trail (AT) northbound on a gentle ascent into woods of sugar maples, hickories, black birches, and massive white pines. Canada mayflower (wild lily of the valley) graces the forest floor. Old pine trees matured in what was once an open field. A residence is visible to the right, but the trail soon veers left, away from it (please stay on the footpath). Chunks of quartzite dot the ground; witch hazel and striped maple compose the understory. The AT meanders through this woodland but soon begins climbing more steeply.

TRIP 41 // EAST MOUNTAIN AND ICE GULCH

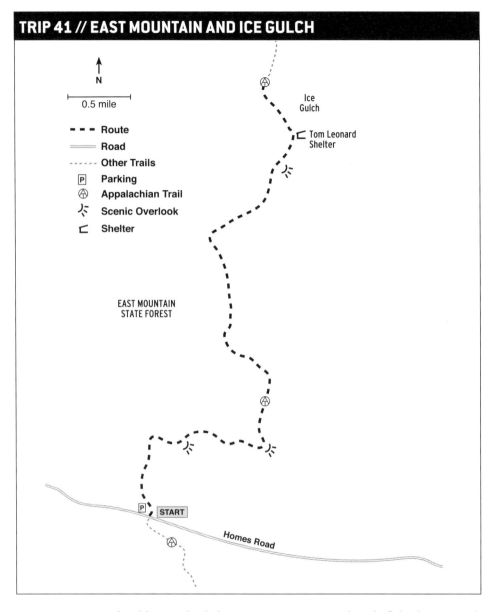

Arrive at gneiss boulders and a ledge outcropping covered with flaky brown rock tripes (lichens). The route leads up a stone staircase, the first of several. Here, vegetation such as chestnut oak, root sprouts of American chestnut, and lowbush blueberry indicates drier, more acidic soils that characterize oak-pine woods. A log across the trail ahead indicates a sharp turn to the right (watch for the white blazes). Climb along a ledge outcropping and turn right to amble over it. Listen for the *drink-your-tea* song of the eastern towhee.

At 0.6 mile, stride up a steep, sloping gneiss outcropping (use caution when wet) and glance back for screened views of the Taconics and Mount Everett. But better scenery

Cool air and a peaceful atmosphere emanate from the boulder-filled ravine known as Ice Gulch.

awaits. Huckleberry shrubs border the rock and soon become ubiquitous. Distinguish this blueberry relative by its resinous, sticky leaves and pinkish, rather than white, flowers. In late May or early June, you'll detect the sweet smell of mountain azaleas and their pink blossoms. Another pink flower to watch for this time of year is lady's slipper, an orchid.

The trail undulates under oaks and reaches a split boulder. Cross a short wooden span over the spring-fed stream flowing through the gap. Leathery bracken ferns now line the path. This forest has shorter-stature oak and red maple, but you'll soon pass taller trees in woodland with witch hazel in the understory. Winterberry, a native ground cover with shiny leaves and bright red fruits, is loaded with fragrant oil of wintergreen. Listen for the slow *beer-beer-bee* refrain of breeding black-throated blue warblers in late spring and early summer. They're partial to mountain laurel for nest sites.

Chestnut oaks dominate again atop the rocky spine of East Mountain. As the trail levels out, look for a low gneiss ledge on your right and admire the fabulous views from atop it (but be mindful of the sharp dropoff). The expansive scene across the Housatonic Valley to Mount Everett is exhilarating. Continue to follow the undulating AT north, past another split boulder; descend into a gully watered by a spring at 1.3 miles, and climb out. Arrive at another open vista atop an exposed ledge shared by two pitch pines. On a clear day, the views southwest to New York's Catskills are striking.

Pass another exposed boulder-top viewpoint at 1,790 feet (not as stunning as the previous two), briefly scramble over another outcropping, and reach a narrow woods road. Walk right 40 feet and then bear left to continue on the white-blazed AT. Wild sarsaparilla blooms here in late spring. Cross a moss-lined flow under an oak canopy and traverse undulating terrain. White oaks briefly mix with other oaks. Stride around a big, slanting boulder to screened views of the Taconics and listen for the ethereal, flutelike song of the hermit thrush. Drop into a damp spot where the rich, black soil beneath oaks nourishes wild geranium and interrupted fern. Soon, the closed canopy includes yellow birch, a northern hardwood. Oaks still dominate, and some, among a jumble of big boulders, are an impressive size. After a short climb, enter an area where mountain laurel and huckleberry proliferate. The first hemlocks make an appearance in a shallow cleft, while a bit farther, cinnamon fern fills a swale on the left. Negotiate more rocks, stride along a jutting ledge, and then walk through a seepage area. At 3.5 miles, a short, blue-blazed side path leads down to the Tom Leonard Shelter. Enjoy a pleasant vista just beyond the shelter on the left.

Follow the AT left for another 0.1 mile, across a brook, up and through a tight squeeze in the ledge, and along a sheer cliff face. The trail bears right for an evocative view of Ice Gulch, a boulder-filled ravine shaded by hemlocks. (*Caution*: Be careful around dropoffs; climbing into the gulch is unsafe and not recommended.) This is the turnaround point for the hike, so you may want to linger a bit to enjoy the cool air and peaceful atmosphere. When you're ready to start back, retrace your steps along the well-blazed AT to the trailhead, 3.6 miles distant.

DID YOU KNOW?

Tom Leonard was an AT Ridgerunner (a steward who patrols the trail, assists and educates hikers, and performs light trail maintenance) who passed away suddenly in 1985 at a young age. The lean-to shelter bearing his name was built in 1988 by volunteers of the Appalachian Trail Committee of AMC's Berkshire Chapter (now Western Massachusetts Chapter) with materials flown to the site via helicopter by the Air National Guard.

MORE INFORMATION

Open year-round; access is free. Mountain biking is not allowed. Skiing is permitted. The Appalachian National Scenic Trail is managed by the National Park Service and maintained by volunteers of the Appalachian Mountain Club's Western Massachusetts Chapter.

NEARBY

For a picnic meal after your hike, give The Bistro Box, on 937 South Main Street (US 7) in Great Barrington, a try. This little roadside stand offers tasty treats, including fresh milkshakes made with local ice cream. The stand is open seasonally, 11 A.M. to 4 P.M. Thursday through Tuesday (413-717-5958, thebistrobox.rocks).

42 JUG END STATE RESERVATION AND WILDLIFE MANAGEMENT AREA

Bucolic meadows with a stunning backdrop of ridges clothed in mixed woodlands beckon hikers to enjoy a landscape that evokes a time before commercial development. This is a great hike to take with young children and is a fine place to bird-watch or cross-country ski.

FEATURES

Location Egremont, MA

Rating Easy

Distance 2.9-mile loop

Elevation Gain 365 feet

Estimated Time 1.5 hours

Maps AMC Massachusetts Trail Map 2; USGS Egremont; Massachusetts Department of Conservation and Recreation map: mass.gov/doc/mt-washington-state-forest-trail-map/download

GPS Coordinates 42° 08.904′ N, 73° 26.995′ W

Contact Massachusetts Department of Conservation and Recreation, 413-528-0330, mass.gov/locations/jug-end-state-reservation-wildlife-management-area

DIRECTIONS

From the intersection of US 7 and MA 23/MA 41 in Great Barrington, turn onto MA 23/MA 41 and drive south for 4.0 miles. Turn left onto MA 41 South (at Mill Pond) and in 0.1 mile turn right onto Mount Washington Road. Follow it for 1.7 miles to Jug End Road on the left. Stay on Jug End Road for 0.5 mile and turn right into the large gravel parking area.

TRAIL DESCRIPTION

Blue-blazed Jug End Loop Trail begins at the far (south) end of the parking area near the concrete footing and ruins of a former massive cattle barn and silo. (In 1935, the barn was turned into a hotel that served a popular ski and winter sports resort called Jug End.) A brief climb leads to an old woods road; turn right, following blue blazes. Sugar maple, white ash, and black cherry form a canopy. Signs of former habitation include daffodil and yew plantings and lengths of rusty barbed wire. A substantial stone wall dissects the meadow below to your right. An old apple orchard is up the slope to your left.

TRIP 42 // JUG END STATE RESERVATION AND WILDLIFE MANAGEMENT AREA

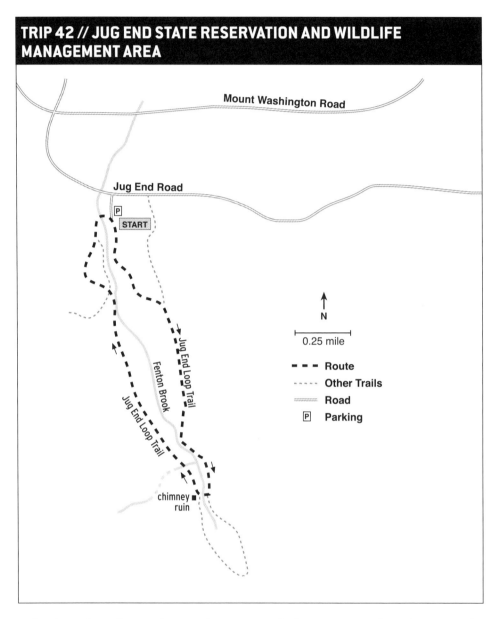

On the right, columnar big-tooth aspens rise before an easy, rolling descent, and a sizable sugar maple stands on the same side. Reach a field on the left bordered by apple trees. Walk easily along its right perimeter; in early May, the trees are heavy with pinkish-white blossoms. The flowering apples attract buzzing pollinators and birds that feed on insects.

Reenter deciduous woods of maple, cherry, ash, and birch that shade tall witch hazel shrubs. Traverse two small streams and soon arrive at a dark wall of planted Norway spruces. The path skirts the spruce plantation. No plant life exists in the total shade of the spruces, in contrast to the shrubs thriving in the forest opening. On your left is a brushy tangle of raspberry canes, cherry tree saplings, Japanese barberry shrubs, and multiflora roses. Chestnut-sided warblers prefer early successional habitats like this. Listen for their *pleased, pleased, pleased to meetcha* refrain in late spring and early summer. Native grapevines and the vines of round-leafed bittersweet, an invasive exotic, crowd the trail. Round-leafed bittersweet invades fields, edges, and woodlands, often forming dense growths that can smother native trees and shrubs. The grapevines cause no harm to the supporting trees.

You are soon surrounded by deciduous woodland of aspens, maples, ashes, and a few white pines. At a more open mowed field, the path hugs the woodland edge, where oaks, maples, and white birches—the latter in a row—flourish. As you pass through a bowl bordered by ridges, the fine view from your right (west) to left includes Mount Whitbeck, Mount Sterling, and, beyond the radio towers, Mount Darby. A number of ski runs once cut the slopes of Mount Sterling (elevation 1,980 feet). Following Jug End Loop Trail, bear left, reenter broadleaf woodland with some pine, and bear right onto an old woods road. More old barbed wire remains here.

Back in the forest, notice the copious sugar maple seedlings along a road—sometimes wet—cut deeply into the earth from years of use. Reach a mowed meadow on a hillside. (Some New England farmers joke that their cows have longer legs on one side of their bodies to graze on these hillsides.) Shad trees (juneberry) show white-petaled blossoms before they produce leaves in late April along the field margins. Pass a marble boulder near a big, spreading sugar maple and stroll past the end of a line of trees

Jug End Loop Trail skirts a large, sloping meadow, beyond which rises a ridgeline clothed in mixed hardwoods.

separating this meadow from another beyond it. The path continues to follow the upper field edge, and the sound of water flowing in the valley soon fills the air.

Head back into the forest and over a series of bog bridges across soggy ground. Here, you may find American woodcocks, which are chunky "shorebirds" with long bills perfectly suited to extract earthworms from moist soil. Below to the right is a shaded hemlock gorge from which the sound of flowing water is now unmistakable. As you walk among the hemlocks in summer, the cooler microclimate results from their deep shade. Gray schist litters the road. Red trillium blooms in spring around an old cellar hole on the right just before Fenton Brook becomes visible.

At the fork in the road, marked with a sign for the lower loop, bear right and follow blue blazes and stones to cross Fenton Brook at 1.5 miles. When the trail turns right, the ruins of a stone fireplace and chimney, seemingly out of place in the midst of a hemlock forest, mark the former location of a cabin, another artifact of the lost resort. Follow the old roadway under hemlock, ash, black birch, yellow birch, red maple, and oak to where mountain laurel appears. (If you have time for a longer hike, the upper loop offers an optional 1.2-mile extension.)

Descend easily on the old road to cross a rocky feeder stream on stones. One chunk of milky white marble has been elegantly polished by the flow. During the gradual downhill ramble, cross a handful of minor feeder streams. This open forest of maturing hemlocks—some tall and straight—is evocative, but soon sugar maple and white ash once again dominate. Violets—yellow, white, and purple—adorn the woods, and jack-in-the-pulpit holds forth under its canopy of maroon and green. Likewise, non-flowering plants, such as Christmas, sensitive, and lacy maidenhair ferns, grace the forest floor.

A rock wall on the left once kept in sheep. Approach Fenton Brook and bear left, then right, at another old roadway. Reach a brushy field, and at a Y intersection, turn right to continue on Jug End Loop Trail. A view of the ridge again appears as the path follows the brook downstream. Cross a short wooden span over a tiny flow to arrive at a T intersection. Diminutive yellow warblers and Baltimore orioles pour out their songs from perches in late spring and early summer.

Turn left at the junction, temporarily leaving Jug End Loop Trail, and walk along the field edge, bearing right to reach an obvious grass path. In addition to offering fine views, the meadows and other open areas provide habitat diversity for a variety of wildlife along the interface between field and forest. Bear right at the grass path, reach another Y intersection, and turn right again. Rejoin blue-blazed Jug End Loop Trail and follow it left, downstream, along Fenton Brook, past ancient Norway spruces as well as other ornamentals—forsythia, arbor vitae, and rhododendron. Turn right to cross the sturdy wooden bridge and return to the parking area.

DID YOU KNOW?

The name Jug End derives from the German word *Jugend*, meaning "youth." For 40 years, beginning in the 1930s, the property was a booming year-round resort and ski area known as Jug End, which no doubt appealed to young people in the vicinity.

MORE INFORMATION

Open sunrise to sunset year-round. Access is free. Skiing, leashed dogs, and hunting in season are allowed. Parking is permitted for day use only. Carry in, carry out rules apply.

NEARBY

Mill Pond, at the intersection of MA 23 and Mount Washington Road, is a favorite spot of local bird-watchers because it attracts an interesting variety of waterfowl and other birds that prefer wet habitats. Common gallinule (related to the American coot), a rare breeder in Massachusetts, has nested in the area. Pull off the pavement onto the wide gravel shoulder; no formal parking area exists. Viewing is best done with binoculars from your vehicle.

43 BASH BISH FALLS

A tale of two trails: The first segment combines an easy stroll to Massachusetts's most spectacular waterfall with a short, steep climb for a fine view of Bash Bish Gorge, New York's Harlem Valley, and the distant Catskill Mountains. The second is an out-and-back ascent to another overlook on South Taconic Trail. Both pay ample dividends.

FEATURES

Location Mount Washington, MA; Copake Falls, NY

Rating Easy to Moderate (falls and gorge only) or Moderate (with South Taconic Trail)

Distance 2 or 3.8 miles round trip

Elevation Gain 470 or 900 feet

Estimated Time 1.5 or 2.5 hours

Maps AMC Massachusetts Trail Map 2: C1; USGS Copake (NY), USGS Bash Bish Falls; Massachusetts Department of Conservation and Recreation map: mass.gov/doc/mt-washington-state-forest-trail-map/download; Taconic State Park map: parks.ny.gov/documents/parks/TaconicCopakeFallsAreaTrailMapNorth.pdf

GPS Coordinates 42° 07.020′ N, 73° 30.460′ W

Contact Taconic State Park, 518-329-3993, parks.ny.gov/parks/taconiccopake/details.aspx
Bash Bish Falls State Park, 413-528-0330, mass.gov/locations/bash-bish-falls-state-park

DIRECTIONS

From the junction of US 7, MA 23, and MA 41 in Great Barrington, proceed west on combined MA 23/MA 41 for 3.9 miles to Egremont, where MA 41 splits off to the left (MA 23 continues straight). Go left and follow MA 41 along the shore of Mill Pond, and then bear right onto Mount Washington Road (called East Street in Mount Washington). Drive for an additional 7.6 miles, following signs for Bash Bish Falls, to the signed intersection with Cross Road and turn right (Church of Christ chapel is on the opposite corner). Cross Road intersects West Street. Bear right onto West Street, which becomes fairly steep and winding. At the bottom of the hill, bear left to cross Wright Brook and turn left immediately onto Bash Bish Falls Road. Follow it for 2.4 miles into New York (passing the Bash Bish Falls State Park parking area in Massachusetts along

TRIP 43 // BASH BISH FALLS

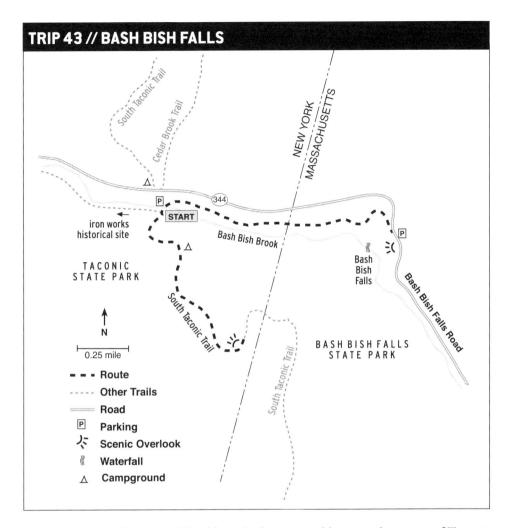

the way), where it becomes NY 344, to the large, paved lower parking area of Taconic State Park on the left.

TRAIL DESCRIPTION

At the parking area, two kiosks feature a detailed map and information about the locale's fascinating tourism and iron industry history. Walk down the gravel road bordered by hemlocks and sugar maples. Tall, autumn-blooming witch hazel shrubs line both sides of the path as it closely parallels Bash Bish Brook upstream. The frothy green water flows with a thunderous roar after rains or snowmelt. Shiny, platy schist protrudes from the gravel roadway and lines the stream; the route leads gently down to brook level, so you can take a closer look. Large red oaks, black oaks, and white ashes dot the hillside on your left, while the north-facing slope is shaded by hemlocks.

Just after a bench, a jutting schist boulder on the left offers eastern phoebes small, shelflike platforms upon which to build their moss-covered nests. But the brook's roar makes it almost impossible to hear birdsong. As the trail climbs gently to a second bench,

An overlook provides an elevated perspective of Bash Bish Falls's impressive 60-foot drop into a clear pool.

hardwoods intermix with hemlocks. The precipitous slope of Bash Bish Mountain, loden-green in hemlock attire, flanks the far side of the gorge. The path becomes a little rougher as it leads high above the surging stream. Note some large red oaks on the left. In winter, black-capped chickadees and tiny golden-crowned kinglets, hanging from the hemlock boughs in search of insects, may be among the few birds you'll find. After about 15 minutes, enter Bash Bish Falls State Park at the Massachusetts border.

Continue a gentle ascent on the obvious gravel road, skirting denser hemlock growth. Pass an intersection with a short gravel service road that leads left, up to a metal gate and the highway. Stay straight, guided by the roar of the falls, and arrive at a viewing area bordered by metal railings at 0.7 mile. The lookout provides a fine elevated perspective of 60-foot Bash Bish Falls, one of Massachusetts's best-known natural features. A granite outcropping splits the flow into twin cascades above an emerald pool. Angular slabs of schist surround the pool. In wet seasons, a feeder brook slants down the high-gradient slope from the left, adding its flow. Water tumbling over the falls originates from springs 1,300 feet up, in Mount Washington State Forest. (In winter, wind-blown mist artistically coats tree branches with ice.) If the path to the base of the falls is open, you can walk down stone steps for a closer look at the spectacle. Be extremely careful when conditions are icy or wet! (*Note*: The Massachusetts Department of Conservation and Recreation has seasonally closed access to the falls below the viewing area since 2020 due to overcrowding and littering.)

To continue to the overlook at the Bash Bish Falls State Park entrance in Massachusetts, from the viewing area follow a blue-blazed 0.3-mile path up the ravine's steep slope. (This trail path is the shortest route to the falls, but there is a 300-foot elevation gain.) Walk up wooden steps, then rock steps, and turn right onto a former woods road.

Cross a couple of seasonal flowages under impressive hemlocks, sugar maples, and ashes. Ascend fairly steeply toward the head of the ravine past schist boulders—some blazed with blue paint—to a twin-log bridge across the upper reaches of the feeder brook. The route continues to ascend under towering hemlocks that impart a primeval forest feel. Some are nearly 3 feet in diameter. Cross an intermittent drainage on rocks and walk a short distance on railroad-tie steps through a small stand of white birch to a kiosk and the paved upper parking lot, reached at approximately 1 mile. The kiosk informs visitors about the presence of the endangered eastern timber rattlesnake.

Head right, along the edge of the parking lot, and turn right at metal fencing to semi-scramble along the fence and up schist bedrock to a viewpoint above the gorge. Atop the crag are white pines, shrub-sized oaks, and a lone pitch pine. Common polypody ferns fill the crevices of the upturned schist, which contains milky quartz veins. From the vantage points along the metal railing (use caution), enjoy splendid vistas west down the gorge to the Harlem Valley and the distant Catskill Mountains. The falls are audible but not visible from here; the green mound of Bash Bish Mountain (1,890 feet) looms to the left, and oak-clothed Cedar Mountain (1,883 feet) forms the opposite wall of the gorge. (*Note*: Access to the upper gorge is prohibited; a former trail to the gorge and Bash Bish Mountain has been permanently closed.)

Retrace your steps about 1 mile past the falls to the lower parking area. When you return to the trailhead, several options are available for exploring this unusual area.

Described here is an out-and-back climb to a scenic lookout on a segment of long-distance South Taconic Trail, which passes through Taconic State Park and adjacent Mount Washington State Forest in Massachusetts. Iron Works Trail, leading to the Copake Iron Works historical site, is a worthwhile diversion (see final paragraph).

On the west side of the parking area, pick up white-blazed South Taconic Trail on the campground access road. Turn left, heading southbound, away from NY 344. (Blue-blazed Cedar Brook Trail, leading 1.0 mile to a waterfall on Cedar Brook, begins on the north side of the highway.) Cross a bridge over hemlock-shaded Bash Bish Brook at the junction with Iron Works Trail on the right. Continue past the overflow parking area to the campground entrance.

Turn right at a brown shower building and follow South Taconic Trail uphill along a cascading tributary stream. After a few hundred feet, bear left, away from the stream, and continue ascending the valley slope, passing a twin-trunked tulip tree. The deciduous trees here are significantly taller than those growing along the ridgetop, where the soil is much thinner and less hospitable. The trail levels out in a hemlock-shaded, bowl-like depression carpeted in spots by the long vines of the three-leafed hog peanut, a member of the bean family.

Pass the Taconic State Park boundary and bear left, making a steep ascent over rocks to a Y intersection at 0.9 mile, just west of the Massachusetts state line. Note an outcropping on the right covered with rock tripes—lichens that green up after absorbing moisture—and polypody fern. Blueberry and wintergreen border the path.

At the junction, turn left down a rocky blue-blazed side path leading about 200 feet to a partially open outcropping. Enjoy splendid long-distance views north and west to the alternating farm fields and forested ridges of the Harlem Valley, the village of Copake Falls, and the distant Catskill Mountains. Look for turkey vultures and ravens soaring past.

The ridgetop's upland forest communities include groves of oak-dominated hardwoods interspersed with hemlocks and white pines. Thin soil on the rocky slopes doesn't allow trees to grow very tall. Identify chestnut oak by its blocky bark and wavy-edged leaves. In fall, pines shed a third of their needles.

Return to the Y junction and resume walking on South Taconic Trail, which continues south along the ridge to Bash Bish Mountain's 1,890-foot wooded summit and Alander Mountain, about 3 miles from the trailhead (an option for a longer day hike). To complete this outing, retrace your steps down to the campground road. Watch your footing on the upper portion of the trail as you maneuver over rocks that may be slippery when wet.

When you return to the signed junction with Iron Works Trail at the bridge over Bash Bish Brook, consider taking a short detour on Iron Works Trail to the nearby Copake Iron Works Historic District, a designated National Heritage Area. The easy, obvious path parallels the brook downstream, passing interpretive stations at a charcoal exhibit and mill pond before reaching the iron works site in 0.3 mile.

DID YOU KNOW?
Bash Bish Falls became a popular tourist attraction in the nineteenth century. Jean Roemer, a college professor, built a large Swiss chalet–style mansion near the falls around 1860. The state of Massachusetts acquired the property in 1924 and established Mount Washington State Forest during the 1960s.

MORE INFORMATION
Both state parks are open sunrise to sunset year-round. Access is free. Leashed dogs are allowed. Swimming, diving, rock climbing, motorized or wheeled vehicles, and alcoholic beverages are prohibited. Portable restrooms available seasonally. The Taconic State Park campground is open from mid-May through mid-November as of 2024.

NEARBY
The Copake Iron Works Historic Site and Visitor Center are open year-round during daylight hours. A museum in the former engine house preserves an extensive collection of artifacts. The self-guided Iron Works Heritage Trail links many historical sites and other trails. A restored narrow-gauge railroad, which opened in 2023, offers free train rides from 2 to 4 p.m. on weekends from Memorial Day weekend to mid-October. See the Friends of Taconic State Park website (friendsoftsp.org/the-copake-iron-works-historic-district-2) for more information.

44 RACE BROOK FALLS AND MOUNT RACE

A hike of superlatives: a spectacular series of waterfalls, a stupendous laurel bloom mid-June to early July, and superb scenery from the southern Taconic ridgeline on Mount Race make this one of the most picturesque outings in the Berkshires.

FEATURES

Location Sheffield and Mount Washington, MA
Rating Strenuous
Distance 6.2 miles round trip (7.2 miles including out-and-back spur to Lower Race Brook Falls)
Elevation Gain 1,625 feet
Estimated Time 4 hours
Maps AMC Massachusetts Trail Map 2; USGS Bash Bish Falls; Massachusetts Department of Conservation and Recreation map: mass.gov/doc/mt-washington-state-forest-trail-map/download
GPS Coordinates 42° 05.368′ N, 73°24.667′ W
Contact Mount Washington State Forest, 413-528-0330, mass.gov/locations/mount-washington-state-forest

DIRECTIONS
From the junction of US 7, MA 23, and MA 41 in Great Barrington, proceed southwest on combined MA 23/MA 41 for 4.1 miles to where MA 41 splits off from MA 23 in Egremont. Turn left and follow MA 41 along the Mill Pond shore for 0.1 mile and then bear left to stay on MA 41 (Mount Washington Road bears right). Drive for 4.9 more miles (passing Berkshire School on the right at 3.1 miles) and park in a paved pull-off area on the right (west) side of the road.

TRAIL DESCRIPTION
Sign in at the kiosk trail register. A topographic map of the route and other information is posted here. Paper trail maps may also be available. (*Note*: You may encounter black bears and, occasionally, endangered timber rattlesnakes along this route, so be watchful.) A non-native mulberry tree near the kiosk produces sweet fruit relished by birds and mammals. Turn left and follow blue-blazed Race Brook Falls Trail down an initially eroded path and cross a shallow brook on stepping-stones (wading may be

TRIP 44 // RACE BROOK FALLS AND MOUNT RACE

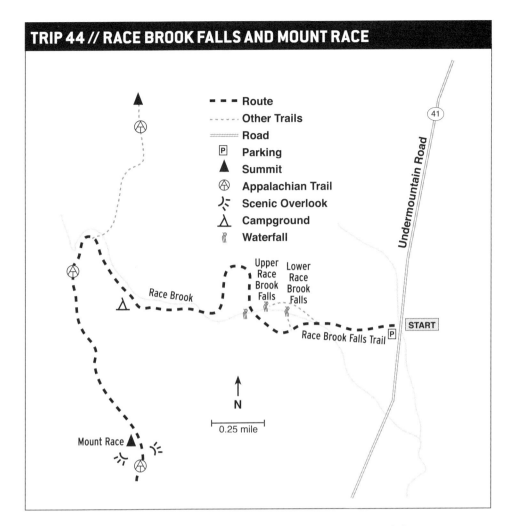

necessary after heavy rain or during spring runoff). The trail bears left past a wet area below white ashes and sugar maples. Traverse a rill and skirt the edge of a field on a narrow path through grasses, bedstraws, red clovers, and daisies in summer. A few red cedars are scattered about.

Enter a shady hemlock forest. As the path widens, note the presence of white pines, maples, and oaks—red, white, and chestnut. Chestnut oak sports wavy-edged leaves. The trail climbs gradually and then levels out. At 0.3 mile, reach a signed intersection with a side path to Lower Race Brook Falls, where you have the option now (which saves elevation gain at the end of the hike) or on the return of adding a mile to the route by bearing right on the 0.5-mile out-and-back spur to Lower Race Brook Falls. The detour is worth the effort. The spur path leads gradually uphill through mixed woods to giant boulders at the base of the lower falls, where Race Brook plunges over ledges. Retrace your steps to Race Brook Falls Trail after enjoying the charming cascade.

From the intersection, Race Brook Falls Trail continues left and uphill through hardwood-hemlock woods and mountain laurel shrubs toward the Appalachian Trail (AT),

2.0 miles away. Reach a moss-coated gneiss boulder along cascading Race Brook, guarded by sizable hemlocks. Bear right along the water for a short distance and then descend to the brook, crossing it on stones. On the opposite bank, turn left, then right, to begin the ascent. Hemlock roots crisscross the wide, well-blazed trail as it climbs higher and more steeply above the brook, which rushes along perhaps 60 feet below. American chestnut continues to root-sprout decades after blight effectively removed this magnificent species from southern New England's woodlands. As you move farther from the stream, a leafy forest of red maple, black birch, and oak forms a canopy over laurel thickets.

Reach a signed intersection for Lower Falls Loop Trail on the right, but stay straight on Race Brook Falls Trail up toward the falls campsite. The grade increases again, highlighted by ledge outcroppings. The route follows the steep hillside contour, but logs and rockwork ensure the treadway's integrity. In this mixed deciduous-evergreen forest, the songs of scarlet tanager and hermit thrush intermingle. Dead or significantly defoliated hemlock trees likely indicate effects of woolly adelgid infestation. These minute insects, aphids, have already killed many hemlocks in southern New England and the eastern United States, and they continue to spread north.

Pass a stream at the base of upper Race Brook Falls. Use caution around wet areas, as rocks are often slippery. The falls cascade down layered gneiss bedrock into a clear, green pool. Back on Race Brook Falls Trail, walk below a massive hemlock on the left and cross Race Brook—shallow here—on stones. Partway across, pause on a large, flat rock to take in the view of the high falls. This is one of the most impressive falls in the Berkshires, especially when the flow is high during early spring or after heavy rain.

Stride through a narrow gap between gneiss boulders and continue moderately upward under a leafy canopy. Listen for the loud, effervescent refrain of the tiny winter wren, a familiar species of wooded ravines. Turn left and ascend rock steps past a 25-foot-high ledge bedecked with leafy rock tripes, lichens that turn green when wet. After another steep section, stroll through an area that is very pretty in June with abundant mountain laurel.

The route levels out and turns left through more laurel. Enjoy peekaboo views of the Housatonic Valley through the trees. The sound of fast-moving water presages your return to Race Brook, where cooling breezes prevail in summer. Turn right to closely follow the crystal-clear mountain brook upstream and then turn left to cross a log bridge over the brook. Water striders skate across the glassy surface of pools. Emerald-green mosses coat the damp stones. Walk along the opposite bank, where you may see windblown trees that fell when their shallow roots separated from the tilted bedrock upon which they grew.

At a sign for Race Brook Falls Campsite, bear left and climb toward a long, low, wall-like outcropping, turning right before reaching it. Bear left and then right past wooden tent platforms to a posted map and campsite register. A privy stands nearby. You have covered 1.8 miles (or 2.8 miles with the side trip to Lower Race Brook Falls), and the AT is but 0.2 mile farther. Walk up under maple, beech, oak, and hemlock and then bear left and ascend schist stone steps. As Race Brook Falls Trail levels out and reaches a junction with the AT, enjoy even more amazing laurel in mid-June to early July. At the

Lower Race Brook Falls lies near the base of a long chain of waterfalls and cascades on the slopes of Mount Race.

junction, turn left (south) onto the white-blazed AT to head toward Mount Race, 1.1 miles distant on a sometimes-steep route. (Mount Everett's summit is 0.8 mile north via a steep ascent on the AT.) Carefully cross a wet spot on stones, cushioned by a bit of highly absorbent sphagnum moss, and climb again. A bit of scrambling is required but nothing major. The wheezy *drink-your-tea* refrain of the robin-sized black, white, and rust-colored eastern towhee indicates you've entered a shrubbier habitat.

The path follows bedrock outcroppings—some showing the polished gouges formed by the abrasive force of thick glacial ice. The white flowers of tiny three-toothed cinquefoil bloom in early summer in sunlit spots. The trees of this ridgetop woodland are short, owing to the thin soil and a brief growing season. Soon the first pitch pines appear and then patches of huckleberry. The pines take on a bonsai appearance. With the luxuriant laurel, lowbush blueberry, and shrubby bear oak, the scene is somewhat reminiscent of a Japanese garden. The trail remains fairly level amid more laurel (the state flower of nearby Connecticut).

Reach an outcropping some 20 feet high and climb it via natural rock steps. The gneiss melted and recrystallized under tremendous heat and pressure. These rock layers now stand on end. (The Taconics, among the oldest mountains in North America, formed from the collision of tectonic plates hundreds of millions of years ago.) Enjoy panoramic vistas from atop the rounded rock promontory of Mount Race at 2,365 feet. Looking back in the direction you came, you'll see the rounded form of Mount Everett about 2 miles north along the AT corridor. To the right is the saddleback profile of Mount Greylock, and New York's 4,000-foot-high Catskills form a blue ridgeline far to the west. Face south and look left to view the Twin Lakes lying across the state line in Salisbury, Connecticut. An uncommon forest of short-needled dwarf pitch pines, none more than 6 feet tall, grows on this rocky spine laced with white quartz swirls. For a more expansive scene, continue south and down along the AT, approximately 250 feet past a large rock cairn. From there the sights are truly inspiring.

When you're ready to descend, retrace your steps to Race Brook Falls Trail on the right. Watch carefully for the blue blazes, as some turns can be missed, especially at the last major brook crossing. Backtrack downhill to the junction with the side path to Lower Race Brook Falls and arrive at the trailhead.

DID YOU KNOW?

Some of the dwarf pitch pines along the bony Taconic ridgeline are more than 100 years old. Scant soil and harsh weather conditions severely limit their growth rate. Similar pitch pines on nearby Mount Everett have been dated at nearly 200 years of age!

MORE INFORMATION

Open year-round. Access is free. Pets must be leashed. Motorized vehicles, mountain bikes, horses, and alcoholic beverages are prohibited. Hunting is allowed in season, except along the AT corridor and near campsites. Camping and fires are allowed only at the Race Brook Campsite.

The AMC Western Massachusetts Chapter's Appalachian Trail Management Committee is responsible for maintenance, management, and protection of the nearly 90 miles of the AT in Massachusetts; volunteers do this work, with assistance from the Massachusetts Department of Conservation and Recreation.

NEARBY

The Shays' Rebellion monument in Sheffield, situated along the Appalachian Trail at the intersection of Egremont and Rebellion roads, commemorates an armed revolt by indebted farmers against the state and its wealthy merchants after the American Revolution. Captain Daniel Shays, a veteran of the Revolution and a farmer from Pelham, Massachusetts, was one of the rebellion's leaders. After rebels from Berkshire County and New York State marched on the nearby town of Stockbridge, a final battle with government militia—the bloodiest of the rebellion—was fought here in February 1787.

45 GUILDER POND AND MOUNT EVERETT

Scenic Guilder Pond is renowned for its profuse mountain laurel bloom, while ancient, pitch-pine-topped Mount Everett, the highest point in southern Berkshire County, offers sublime vistas.

FEATURES

Location Mount Washington, MA
Rating Moderate
Distance 4 miles round trip
Elevation Gain 825 feet
Estimated Time 2.5 to 3 hours
Maps AMC Massachusetts Trail Map 2; USGS Bash Bish Falls; Massachusetts Department of Conservation and Recreation map: mass.gov/doc/mt-washington-state-forest-trail-map/download
GPS Coordinates 42° 6.220' N, 73° 27.091' W
Contact Mount Everett State Reservation, 413-528-0330, mass.gov/locations/mount-everett-state-reservation

DIRECTIONS
From the intersection of US 7, MA 23, and MA 41 in Great Barrington, proceed west on combined MA 23/MA 41 for 4.1 miles and turn left at Mill Pond in Egremont to follow MA 41 for 0.1 mile to Mount Washington Road on the right (becomes East Street in Mount Washington). Drive for 7.5 miles and turn left at the sign for Mount Everett State Reservation. Follow the gravel entrance road for 0.1 mile to an iron gate. Park along the right side of the gravel turnout. It is possible to drive all the way to Guilder Pond Picnic Area below Mount Everett's summit when the road is open seasonally and start the hike from there, but this trip begins at the lower entrance road gate.

TRAIL DESCRIPTION
From the iron gate at the western end of the gravel entrance road, stroll steadily uphill on the gravel road through a mixed forest of oak, maple, birch, beech, white pine, and hemlock. Mountain laurel is in evidence almost immediately, especially from late June to early July when it blooms. Some bushes are more than 12 feet tall. The road winds under a shady canopy of eastern hemlocks, as does Guilder Brook a bit farther on the left.

TRIP 45 // GUILDER POND AND MOUNT EVERETT

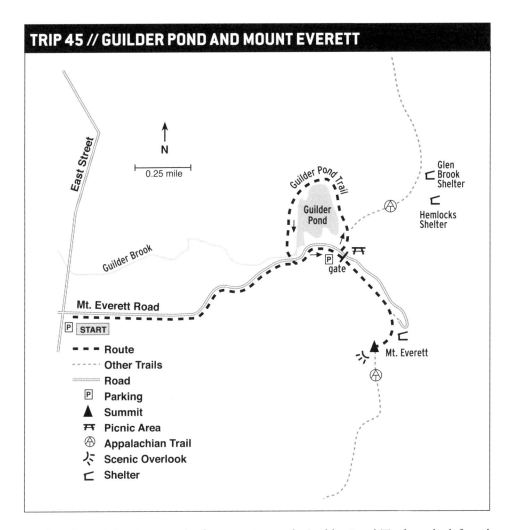

After about 0.8 mile, pass the first junction with Guilder Pond Trail on the left and arrive at its namesake waters. At 2,042 feet above sea level, Guilder Pond is one of the highest natural water bodies in the commonwealth. Many sources place it second, but Tilden Swamp in Pittsfield State Forest, flooded by beavers in the mid-1990s, may be a few feet higher (2,150-foot Berry Pond, also in Pittsfield State Forest, is the highest). Patches of sweetgale, leatherleaf, and sphagnum moss have colonized the shore. Black whirligig beetles gyrate on the water's surface in summer. Regardless of elevation, the pond is a beautiful sight, especially when fringed with white and pink blossoms of mountain laurels in early summer. Later you'll walk completely around it. For now, continue on the gravel road another 0.2 mile to Guilder Pond Picnic Area.

At the far left end of the picnic area is the second (eastern) junction with Guilder Pond Trail, which you'll use upon your return. To continue to Mount Everett, follow the white-blazed Appalachian Trail (AT) at a large sign (maps may be available at the kiosk on the right) up into beech, maple, yellow birch, and oak woodland on a steady incline. After just 0.1 mile, reach the gravel summit road and turn left. Walk 100 feet and turn right to continue on the AT, which ascends on a rocky path. Striped maple (moosewood) is an abundant small tree here. Wood sorrel (with cloverlike leaves and white, pink-veined summer blossoms), *Clintonia* (blue-bead lily), and Canada mayflower also grow in the rich soil.

The summit road parallels a footpath on the left. The AT bears right, climbs a short distance, turns left, and ascends a stone "stairway" adjacent to rocky outcroppings. Blue-green spinulose wood ferns soften the sharp angles below yellow birch and mountain ash.

At a short, rocky side path, bear left to a bench and shelter in a grassy clearing that offers an expansive vista all the way to Mount Greylock, 37 miles north. When you look at this peak from a distance, it's easy to imagine how its other name—Saddleback Mountain—came to be.

Return to the AT, which resumes its uphill climb before leveling out briefly. Mountain azaleas put on quite a show in May. In late June and early July, mountain laurel (Connecticut's state flower), festooned with clusters of white-and-pink blossoms, crowds the path. The modest leaves of trailing arbutus (Massachusetts's state flower) beneath the laurel are easy to overlook. The hike is so close to the Connecticut border here, it's fitting that the two state flowers are in such close proximity as well. Adding much to the overall ambiance are shrubby red maple, mountain ash, wild raisin, huckleberry, and lowbush blueberry. The latter two also offer tasty treats.

After a wooden sign indicating 0.1 mile to the summit, tread over schist bedrock that stands on end due to the collision of continental plates hundreds of millions of years ago when these mountains formed. The thin soil atop the bedrock provides nourishment for bear oak (or scrub oak), also found on Cape Cod. Its tough, leathery leaves and tiny acorns limit water loss in this harsh environment. At a blue blaze on the right, step up onto a ledge outcropping and viewpoint to gaze eastward over the Housatonic Valley, the Berkshire Plateau beyond, and the Twin Lakes just over the Connecticut–Massachusetts border. You might even be able to identify the sloping meadow atop Hurlburt's Hill at Bartholomew's Cobble in Sheffield (Trip 48).

Continue on the AT to Mount Everett's summit, approximately 1.7 miles from the trailhead. Short, stiff-needled pitch pines surround concrete footings at the site of the former summit fire tower at approximately 2,610 feet. The tower, erected in 1915, fell into disrepair and was removed by helicopter in 2003. The summit is an unusual and fragile environment; please remain on the trail and bedrock to avoid trampling the vegetation. Studies of the forest have revealed that some of the gnarled dwarf pitch pines are between 100 and 200 years old—an old-growth forest in miniature! Though vegetation limits views from the summit, look to the west and southwest for the ridgeline of New York's Catskill Mountains, roughly 50 miles away.

From the summit, retrace your steps north on the AT to Guilder Pond Picnic Area and turn right at 2.3 miles to follow the joint AT/Guilder Pond Trail, marked with both white and blue blazes. Ignore the almost-immediate unmarked side path on the left and continue straight through northern hardwoods blended with hemlocks, oaks, and laurels. At a three-way intersection, where bog bridges lead through a seasonally damp area, turn left to follow blue-blazed Guilder Pond Trail (the AT branches right to the

A loop trail leads to several perspectives of Guilder Pond, one of the highest water bodies in Massachusetts.

Hemlocks and Glen Brook shelters and Mount Bushnell). Based on their girth, some hemlocks appear to have attained an advanced age. The needle-cushioned path undulates through and around old mountain laurels that tower over your head. The woodland is filled with the songs of vireos, warblers, and thrushes in summer.

After passing through a fern glade dominated by New York fern (the fronds taper to a point at the bottom as well as the top), ascend a rocky ledge on stone steps that bring you to a viewpoint that looks out across the pond to the rounded "Dome of the Taconics," as Mount Everett is known. A beaver lodge is visible on an island in the pond; you may be surprised to see that industrious beavers have cut stumps quite high up the slope. However, hemlocks and oaks are not among their preferred foods. Continue past a ledge that runs parallel to the trail. The schist of the bedrock along the shore is laced with the white veins of milky quartz.

To your left are a concrete water control structure, wooden decking, and a culvert that transports water under an old beaver dam to the pond's outlet stream—Guilder Brook. Water from this side of the mountain eventually finds its way into the Hudson River. Cross a single-log span over Guilder Brook and rejoin the gravel entrance road at Guilder Pond Trail's western end at approximately 3.2 miles. Turn right and walk about 0.8 mile back to the iron gate near the western end of the entrance road.

DID YOU KNOW?
Mount Everett is named for Edward Everett, the fifteenth governor of Massachusetts, who served from 1825 to 1835. The geologist Edward Hitchcock suggested the name in 1841. Up until that time, the mountain was known as "Bald Mountain" or "the Dome."

MORE INFORMATION
Open sunrise to sunset, year-round. Access is free. Skiing and leashed dogs are allowed. Hunting, overnight parking, motorized off-road vehicles, and alcoholic beverages are prohibited. A boat launch for canoes and kayaks is available at Guilder Pond.

The AMC Western Massachusetts Chapter's Appalachian Trail Management Committee is responsible for maintenance, management, and protection of the nearly 90 miles of the AT in Massachusetts; volunteers do this work, with assistance from the Massachusetts Department of Conservation and Recreation.

NEARBY
Pick organically grown blueberries, in season, at Blueberry Hill Farm, 100 East Street, in Mount Washington. The farm's 10 acres contain several types of highbush blueberries, including heirloom varieties developed in the 1930s. Visit the farm's website or Facebook page for dates, hours, and other information (413-528-1479; austinfarm.com).

46 ALANDER MOUNTAIN TRAIL

Alander Mountain is one of the most scenic summits in the Berkshires. Throw in a roaring mountain brook and attractive mixed woodland alive with birds, and this hike is a real winner.

FEATURES

Location Mount Washington, MA

Rating Moderate

Distance 5.8 miles round trip

Elevation Gain 790 feet

Estimated Time 3 to 4 hours

Maps AMC Massachusetts Trail Map 2; USGS Bash Bish Falls, USGS Copake (NY); Massachusetts Department of Conservation and Recreation map: mass.gov/doc/mt-washington-state-forest-trail-map/download

GPS Coordinates 42° 5.185′ N, 73° 27.725′ W

Contact Mount Washington State Forest, 413-528-0330, mass.gov/locations/mount-washington-state-forest

DIRECTIONS

From the intersection of US 7, MA 23, and MA 41 in Great Barrington, proceed southwest on combined MA 23/MA 41 for 4.1 miles. Turn left onto MA 41 South at Mill Pond, and in 0.1 mile, turn right onto Mount Washington Road (becomes East Street in Mount Washington). Follow it for 9.1 miles (past the entrance to Mount Everett State Reservation) until you come to the Mount Washington State Forest headquarters on the right. Follow the driveway around to the right and the large gravel parking area.

TRAIL DESCRIPTION

This out-and-back trek follows blue-blazed Alander Mountain Trail on a relatively gentle ascent of Alander Mountain (the route briefly coincides with long-distance South Taconic Trail at the summit). From the trailhead and kiosk, walk across the mowed field, where lowbush blueberries and tiny, four-petaled bluets attract pollinators in spring. Hunts Pond, with its resident Canada geese, lies serenely in a bowl to the left. Enter woods of eastern hemlock, where Canada lilies bloom in May. Listen for the *weeta-weeta-weeteo* song of the black, yellow, and white magnolia warbler and for the buzzy notes of the black-throated green warbler in spring and early summer. After strolling through mixed woods, amble down through a second field, where fiery wood

TRIP 46 // ALANDER MOUNTAIN TRAIL

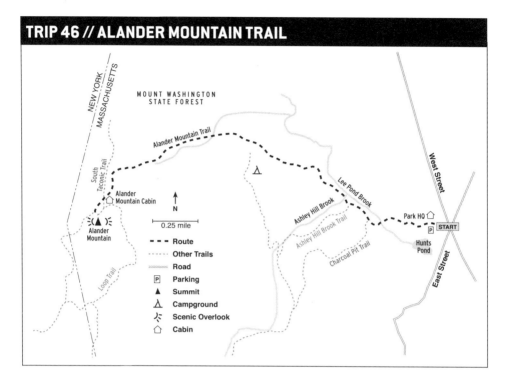

lilies brighten the brushy meadow in July. Alander Mountain, your destination, is visible roughly 2 miles to the west.

At the far end of the meadow, cross a wooden bridge over Lee Pond Brook and turn right onto an old roadway. A stone foundation lies adjacent to the brook. At 0.6 mile, stay straight at the intersection with Charcoal Pit Trail on the left. This forest was clear-cut between the late 1700s and mid-1800s to make charcoal—fuel for the many iron furnaces in the area. Note the significant yellow birch on the left, perhaps one of the first to grow back after the last clear-cut. The bark of young trees is much brassier. Reach the signed junction with Ashley Hill Brook Trail on the left; that trail leads south to Connecticut, but you will remain on blue-blazed Alander Mountain Trail.

A short descent through hemlocks brings you to cascading Ashley Hill Brook (first audible from some distance away), just above its confluence with another high-gradient stream. Cross a well-built wooden bridge over the roaring flow. The water has polished the schist bedrock to a silvery patina.

Arrive at the stone remnants of a millrace, which once conveyed water to a mill's waterwheel. Across the stream, water cascades down small falls to join the main flow. Alander Mountain Trail now ascends along an old woods road under the dense shade of deep green hemlocks as the slope drops off sharply to the right. Shade-tolerant American beech, recognizable by its smooth gray bark, joins the conifers, along with yellow birch and red oak. Striped maple, black birch, and black cherry also grow here. Striped maple has green bark; black cherry has scaly bark; young black birch has dark, shiny bark.

A sign on the right indicates that the primitive campground is 0.5 mile away. Alander Mountain Trail continues on level ground through mixed woodland (spring beauty

A group of hikers enjoy a snack and expansive three-state views from Alander's open summit.

blooms here in early May with five delicate white petals veined with pink) but then steepens as you bear left. Former heavy use and flowing water have eroded the rocky road. The rocks are schist, the tough material that makes up the Taconic Mountains. At 1.6 miles, a side path leaves to the left, uphill toward the primitive campground. Continue straight on Alander Mountain Trail and soon find yourself among mountain laurel shrubs. Laurel boughs support the nests of black-throated blue warblers in spring and summer. Listen for the warblers' *beer-beer-bee* songs during the breeding season. After crossing a generally dry, stony streambed, the trail briefly parallels a brook through a shallow hemlock gorge.

Cross a small stream on rocks. Pass more laurel and enter a maple and oak forest. The small stream is now on your left. Reach a landing that may be a former charcoal-making site. One clue is that the earth is black from years of use. This is a suitable spot to pause for a moment; the trail turns right and climbs sharply from here. Head uphill and bear left under hemlocks in an especially attractive woodland. A small metal sign affixed to a hemlock warns that the stream is the last source of water during the dry season. (Should you use it, be sure to purify it first!)

Walk up through lush laurel and along a ledge outcropping that parallels the trail on the right. Ahead sits a cabin where hikers may spend the night. Wood smoke aroma permeates the structure, and a rock tied to a rope serves as a clever counterweight that closes the door behind you. The cabin was originally built in the early 1920s for observers at the fire tower that stood on Alander's summit from around 1928 to 1930. (The tower was dismantled and moved to New York, where it stood on Washburn Mountain in Copake Falls before being relocated again to Beebe Hill.) From the cabin and a sign for Alander Mountain Trail, Alander Mountain Summit, and South Taconic Trail, ascend shist outcroppings to an intersection with a small rock cairn and sign at 2.8 miles. Turn left and follow combined Alander Mountain Trail and South Taconic Trail through brushy scrub oak (bear oak) toward the splendid open rock summit of 2,239-foot Alander Mountain. The footings of the former fire tower are still obvious on the banded schist.

Lowbush blueberry and glossy-leafed bearberry both produce delicate, bell-like, whitish blossoms in May. Listen for the hoarse *chewink* call and the sweet whistled *drink-your-tea* song of the eastern towhee, a large black, white, and rust-colored member of the sparrow family. Gaze skyward for migrant hawks in spring and fall, and watch for turkey vultures in every season except winter.

This summit is the most open and, arguably, the most spectacular in the region, and it offers wonderful views of the Catskill Mountains, some 45 miles to the west (right). Nearby, behind you, is the rounded form of Mount Everett (Trip 45). To your left is an undulating wooded ridge with three bumps: Mount Ashley is on the left, Mount Frissell is in the middle, and Mount Brace (at the New York–Connecticut state line) is on the right (see Trip 50). Note the rock cairn on Mount Brace's open summit. Ahead, below you, lies the Hudson River valley. New York's Route 22 is the ribbon of blacktop that runs south and north along the western side of the Taconics, one of this country's oldest mountain ranges, at approximately 400 million years.

When you're ready to descend, retrace your steps on combined Alander Mountain Trail and South Taconic Trail to the intersection near the cabin; then turn right to follow blue-blazed Alander Mountain Trail back to the trailhead. (South Taconic Trail continues north along the ridge past more scenic vistas to Bash Bish Falls State Park's New York entrance (Trip 43).

DID YOU KNOW?

This area of the southern Taconics was disputed by early Dutch and English colonists. Violence ensued following the murder of an English settler over a land claim in 1755. Forty proprietors subsequently established a plantation on the range in an attempt to legally control the land. The town of Mount Washington was established in 1779.

MORE INFORMATION

Open sunrise to sunset, year-round. Access is free. Leashed dogs are allowed. Motorized vehicles and alcoholic beverages are prohibited. A portable toilet is available at the parking lot.

NEARBY

Mount Washington's diminutive town center, at the intersection of East Street and Cross Road, includes the historical First Church of Christ (116 East Street) and the town hall/library (118 East Street). The church hosts a popular annual fair on the first Saturday in August.

FEEDING THE FIRES OF INDUSTRY

In the mid-nineteenth century, Massachusetts was only 25 percent shaded by a forest canopy. Fully 75 percent of the state was devoid of tree cover. The process had begun in earnest during the previous century, when the ancient forests that had greeted the first European settlers were systematically cut. Of course, early colonists used timber for house construction and firewood, and they cleared the land for agricultural use, but not until the Industrial Revolution did the wholesale clear-cutting of Massachusetts woodlands move into high gear.

Early in the life of the young nation, the Berkshires were the center of a booming iron industry. In his book *Exploring the Berkshire Hills: A Guide to Geology and Early Industry in the Upper Housatonic Watershed* (Valley Geology Publishing, 1995), the historian and geologist Ed Kirby chronicles this little-known period when America's industrial epicenter was right in Massachusetts. Iron was discovered in 1731, and eventually there would be 43 blast furnaces processing locally mined ore. Ironworkers manufactured cannons and cannon balls for the American Revolution and, later on, wheels for railroad trains. Not until large quantities of a higher-quality grade ore were discovered in the upper Midwest did the prominence of the Berkshires industry diminish.

The fires of the mammoth Richmond Furnace, which had once operated 24 hours a day, went out for good in 1923. The fuel that fired the blast furnaces was not coal but locally produced charcoal (made from wood), which was more abundant and therefore cheaper. Thousands upon thousands of forested acres were cleared to make charcoal to feed the insatiable furnaces.

Charcoal making was a laborious proposition. Workers called colliers cut up to 30 cords of wood that required seasoning for a year to dry it. Later, the colliers constructed a mound from the cords of wood in the shape of a wigwam, which was covered with ferns and sod to slow the combustion process, while vents at the base of the mound controlled airflow. The smoldering mound was tended for four weeks as the wood slowly transformed into charcoal.

Of course, at first, the furnaces burned charcoal from the abundant woodlands close at hand, but as those supplies were exhausted, sources farther away from the furnaces were required. Eventually, with local forests decimated, people had to import charcoal from elsewhere, making it more expensive than coal. But by then the landscape had virtually been laid bare. Today's woodlands are only now recovering from the far-reaching effects of the iron industry.

47 LIME KILN FARM WILDLIFE SANCTUARY

This biologically diverse property in the Housatonic Valley, almost in the shadow of Mount Everett and the Taconic Range, boasts rolling hayfields with magnificent vistas and hardwood forest alive with songbirds. This is a fine walk for families with small children.

FEATURES

Location Sheffield, MA

Rating Easy

Distance 1.8 miles round trip

Elevation Gain 135 feet

Estimated Time 1.5 hours

Maps USGS Ashley Falls; Mass Audubon map: massaudubon.org/places-to-explore/wildlife-sanctuaries/lime-kiln-farm/trails

GPS Coordinates 42° 04.963′ N, 73° 21.766′ W

Contact Mass Audubon, 413-637-0320, massaudubon.org/places-to-explore/wildlife-sanctuaries/lime-kiln-farm

DIRECTIONS

From the north: From the center of Sheffield, at the U.S. Post Office, travel south on US 7 for 1.1 miles. Turn right onto Silver Street (blue-and-white sanctuary sign) and follow it for 1.1 miles to the sanctuary entrance and crushed-stone parking lot (room for twelve vehicles) on the right.

From the south: From US 7 at the Connecticut border, drive north on US 7 for 3.6 miles to Silver Street on the left (blue-and-white sanctuary sign) and follow the directions above.

TRAIL DESCRIPTION

From the parking lot, enjoy a wonderful view of Mount Everett (elevation 2,624 feet), 3 miles away. An information sign includes a map with trail details (paper copies are available as well) and a donation box. Blue blazes indicate the outbound travel route, and yellow ones indicate the return route. Portions of the trail near the entrance may be seasonally wet due to increased beaver activity and spring flooding; the sanctuary is working on a solution as of 2024.

TRIP 47 // LIME KILN FARM WILDLIFE SANCTUARY

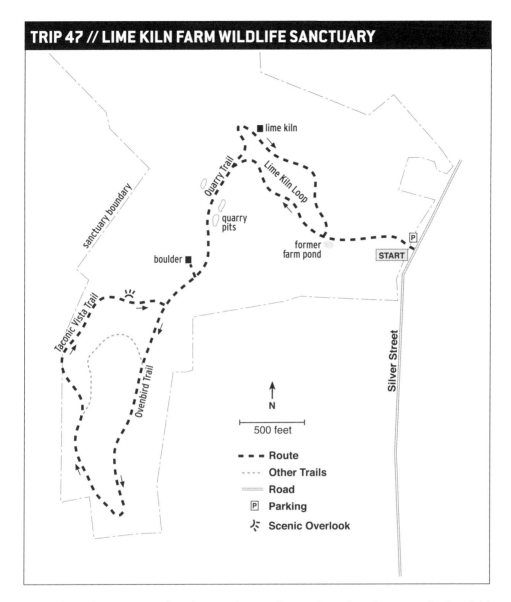

Amble under a canopy of apple trees down a former dairy farm lane—with a hayfield to the right and marsh to the left—where sweet flag thrives. This relative of jack-in-the-pulpit has cattail-like leaves and greenish-yellow flower spikes the size and shape of your pinkie. Pink-flowering hairy willow herb fills the wetlands in summer. Arrive at a former farm pond on the left, just before a trail junction.

Here, the circuit portion of Lime Kiln Loop begins. Continue straight up on the path into another hayfield, following blue blazes and passing weathering marble outcroppings on the right. Marked by a signpost, the path soon bears right and briefly enters regenerating woody vegetation that includes columnar eastern red cedars (junipers) and invasive exotic autumn olive trees that sport silvery-red fruits. Emerge into the field again, turn right, and then bear left at another signpost. Follow the broad path over soggy ground and pass a small quarry area on the left, largely hidden by woody growth.

The trail leads gently uphill and passes several corky-barked hackberry trees, unusual in these parts. Two species of butterfly caterpillar—hackberry emperor and tawny emperor—feed exclusively on hackberry leaves. Bear left and look for the concrete footings of a former trestle on the right, over which marble rock was conveyed to the top of the lime kiln (not visible from here). A few feet farther, a wooden bench provides a fine spot for a snack as you survey a large, sloping hayfield and its Taconic Mountains backdrop. Sanctuary hayfields are cut annually by a neighboring dairy farmer, but not until late summer, giving grassland-nesting birds time to breed.

At this point, Lime Kiln Loop turns right and follows the field edge down past the lime kiln and back to the parking lot; turn left instead to follow Quarry Trail, a wide former roadway. Pass a monument to the three women who formerly lived on the property and are responsible for its donation as conservation land in 1990. Reenter the woodland edge and soon bear left. Reach several former marble quarry pits. The largest is often filled with water and may serve as a vernal pool. Red-and-yellow blossoms of columbine grace the trail's borders in June.

Continue along the wide, grassy path, where round-leafed bittersweet vines drape the trees. This invasive exotic is a real curse as it strangles native trees and robs them of sunlight. In fall, the yellow fruit husks split open, revealing bright red-orange fruits that are consumed and spread by birds, such as cedar waxwings and robins. Before long, enter deciduous woodland and arrive at signed Boulder Spur on the right. Walk a short distance down this side path for a close look at an imposing angular glacial erratic. A bench faces the Taconics.

Back at Quarry Trail, turn right to continue. At 0.5 mile, reach a junction with Taconic Vista Trail on the right, where a 0.8-mile loop begins. Continue straight on Ovenbird Trail—an old farm road passing through mixed woodland that includes hemlock and white pine. Keep straight at an intersection where Ovenbird Trail splits to form a loop. Interestingly, yellow-rumped warblers nest among the pines on the left, although they are much more apt to choose high-elevation nest sites in the Berkshires.

Ovenbird Trail eventually turns right and makes its way along the property line. This path through woodland of oak, black birch, big-tooth aspen, hemlock, and witch hazel parallels a linear ledge outcropping rising on the right. At a signed junction, bear left on Taconic Vista Trail, leaving the Ovenbird Trail loop. Follow Taconic Vista Trail as it winds over and around the end of the ledge softened by moss. Even after heavy snowfall, the ground is relatively bare below the hemlocks because their dense foliage intercepts and holds much of the fluffy white stuff. These hemlocks are threatened by hemlock woolly adelgids, aphids that continue to gradually spread across the Berkshires, especially in years with mild winters.

After passing a large fallen hemlock trunk cut to make way for the trail, walk through a patch of Christmas fern before turning right to follow an old barbed wire fence line up into mixed woodland that includes yellow birch. At a signpost marked "Vista," turn left and walk a few feet to the upper edge of a hayfield that affords a stunning vista north and west of the Berkshire Hills and Taconic Mountains. This field is loaded with butterflies and dragonflies in summer.

Continue gently uphill on the main path. Taconic Vista Trail soon rejoins Quarry Trail. Turn left and follow the yellow blazes back to the monument to the property donors and the junction with Lime Kiln Loop on the right.

Instead of turning right to retrace your steps past the bench, however, stay straight and walk along the large field edge down to a signpost. After leaf fall, the 40-foot-high lime kiln, a concrete cylinder, is visible to your right. At the signpost, turn right and approach the former kiln. Built in 1909, this enterprise lasted only three years before it was abandoned. Marble rock was dumped in the top of the kiln and cooked at 1,400 degrees to drive out all the moisture. The rock was reduced to powdery lime, used in agriculture and many industrial applications. (Be sure to stay clear of the kiln and adjacent structures.)

Past the kiln on the left stand two enormous hemlocks that must be several hundred years old. Continue to follow Lime Kiln Loop along an old road lined by prickly ash shrubs. While the shrub is not an ash at all, the branches are certainly prickly—avoid contact with them. Walk along the left margin of another field and turn right where a couple of deciduous conifers—American larches (tamaracks)—stand. Their needle

The rounded mass of Mount Everett, the highest point in the southern Berkshires, presents a picturesque image from the sanctuary's parking lot.

tufts turn yellow in fall before dropping off. Pass shrubby wetlands on your left, where alder flycatchers nest in summer. Their breeding "song" is a rapid, hiccuping *fee-bee-o*.

In summer and fall, American woodcocks sometimes flush from beneath the brushy growth to the right of the path just before Lime Kiln Loop ends near the farm pond. When you complete the loop, turn left to stroll back to your vehicle.

DID YOU KNOW?

Lime Kiln Farm (248 acres) is part of the much larger 13,750-acre state-designated Schenob Brook Area of Critical Environmental Concern (ACEC), established in 1990. The Schenob Brook ACEC and its associated wetlands make up one of the most significant natural communities in Massachusetts, featuring the largest continuous calcareous seepage marsh (open, unforested wetlands with scattered shrubs), the finest examples of calcareous fens in southern New England, and more than 40 state-listed rare species.

MORE INFORMATION

Open dawn to dusk, year-round. Access is free, but donations are appreciated. The site has no restrooms or visitor facilities. Dogs, vehicles, mountain bikes, horses, hunting, fishing, trapping, and collecting are prohibited. The property is managed by Mass Audubon's Pleasant Valley Wildlife Sanctuary (see Trip 25) at 472 West Mountain Road in Lenox.

NEARBY

Sheffield Covered Bridge, destroyed by fire in 1994 and rebuilt in 1998, is a 93-foot-long lattice truss bridge across the Housatonic River. It's one of only seven historical covered bridges remaining in Massachusetts. The original, constructed in 1854, was the oldest covered bridge in the state until it burned. The bridge, open only to pedestrian traffic, is 0.8 mile north of the center of Sheffield, on the east side of US 7.

48 BARTHOLOMEW'S COBBLE RESERVATION

Long beloved by botanists and fern enthusiasts, Bartholomew's Cobble offers terrific bird-watching and wildflower-viewing opportunities, interesting geology, and fabulous panoramic vistas from the crest of Hurlburt's Hill.

FEATURES

Location Sheffield, MA

Rating Moderate

Distance 3.5 miles round trip

Elevation Gain 310 feet

Estimated Time 2 to 2.5 hours

Maps USGS Ashley Falls; The Trustees of Reservations map: thetrustees.org/wp-content/uploads/2023/09/bartholomews-cobble-trail-map.pdf

GPS Coordinates 42° 03.452′ N, 73° 21.042′ W

Contact Bartholomew's Cobble, 413-229-8600, thetrustees.org/place/bartholomews-cobble

DIRECTIONS

From the center of Sheffield (at the U.S. Post Office), proceed south on US 7 for 1.7 miles to the intersection with US 7A. Turn right onto US 7A and follow it for 0.4 mile. Turn right onto Rannapo Road, cross the railroad tracks, and drive 1.5 miles to Weatogue Road on the right. Turn right onto Weatogue Road and continue for 0.1 mile to the reservation's gravel parking area on the left.

TRAIL DESCRIPTION

Check in at the visitor center or, if the center is closed, examine the kiosk with map at the trailhead to the left. Trail intersections are signed. From the kiosk, walk left and follow Eaton Trail, a short path that leads up past junipers (eastern red cedars) to the smaller cobble. Cobbles are composed primarily of erosion-resistant quartzite rock and softer marble. The amalgamation of these two rock types and the soils they produce gives rise to great botanical biodiversity here. Note the large rock outcroppings, capped by polypody ferns, on both sides of the trail. Delicate maidenhair spleenwort, just one of 43 ferns and allied species to be found in this botanist's wonderland, thrives at the

TRIP 48 // BARTHOLOMEW'S COBBLE RESERVATION

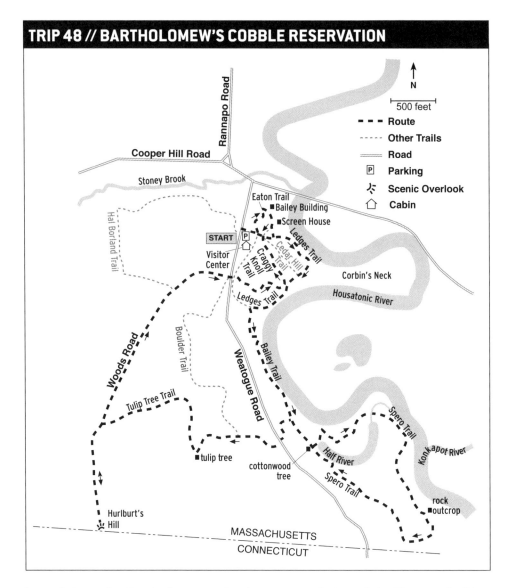

base of the rocks. Reach the top and enjoy a screened view of the Housatonic River valley from a well-placed wooden bench.

Bear left and proceed downhill, still under junipers, to the old Bailey Building, a former museum. Bear right under white pines on a wide path and soon arrive at an intersection where the trail splits. Follow either fork to the nearby intersection with red-blazed Ledges Trail, shaded by eastern hemlocks and white pines. Invasive garlic mustard is also prevalent, unfortunately. Turn left onto Ledges Trail and head toward the Housatonic River. The larger of two moss-and-fern-covered quartzite cobbles hems in the path on the right. Steps lead down to the edge of the floodplain, where spring's rising waters deposit silt. This flat pasture, nearly encircled by the river, is known as Corbin's Neck. One day it may be cut off by the flow and become an oxbow pond.

Watch for fish-hunting ospreys here during their spring and fall migrations; you can see bald eagles in winter.

In early spring, look for the pleated leaves of false hellebore rising from the silt, and find the dainty pantaloons of dutchman's breeches closer to the cliff face. The latter are ephemeral wildflowers that bloom in midspring, before unfurling tree leaves shade the ground. White ashes predominate, and maples are present, too. Bear right and climb to the Cedar Hill Trail intersection under large oaks; continue left on Ledges Trail, which skirts the larger cobble. After a few steps up, note the massive white ash, more than 3 feet in diameter, on the right. Past Corbin's Neck, follow Ledges Trail above and adjacent to the Housatonic and along a marble-and-quartzite cliff face topped by junipers. Sinewy ironwood, hop hornbeam (both have hard wood), and birch clothe the slope down to the water's edge.

At a small clearing at 0.3 mile, turn left onto blue-blazed Bailey Trail and cross a small brook. Skunk cabbage and red osier dogwood thrive in the moist soil. A "hairy" poison ivy vine snakes up a black cherry tree on the right. A bit farther, large wild grapevines hang from the trees. Follow the river downstream, traverse a few small feeder streams, and walk beneath some sizable white pines until you reach the Spero Trail/Tulip Tree Trail junction. Continue straight, following Spero Trail (also blue blazed) under more towering pines. Listen for the sweet trill of pine warblers during spring and early summer. Shallow pools dot the floodplain in spring.

At 0.7 mile, arrive at Half River, an oxbow pond that was once part of the river's main stem. Here, the Spero Trail loop begins. A cottonwood of truly monumental proportions dominates the intersection. This giant, hollow at its base, is more than 6 feet in diameter. Turn left and tread through a floodplain dominated by silver maples tolerant of periodic inundation and then walk along the edge of a wet meadow, the site of recent floodplain forest restoration work. Depending on how wet the meadow is, it may not always be passable. If the trail is flooded, backtrack to the giant cottonwood tree and turn left, then return along that stretch of Spero Trail.

Climb out of the floodplain and bear left at the signed fork to remain on Spero Trail. An angular schist outcropping juts from the oak woodland on the left. Schist is considerably harder than the eroded marble bedrock that underlies the river valley. Enjoy a wonderful view south into Connecticut upon reaching another meadow and then begin a gradual climb on Spero Trail into a forest of hemlock, pine, and black birch. The cooling effect of deep evergreen shade is readily apparent under hemlocks as you head back to Half River. Check the protruding logs for basking painted turtles.

After crossing a boardwalk spanning a trickle, find yourself once more among quartzite boulders. Striking emerald-green mosses pad the surface of one low, vertical rock face on the left. Maidenhair fern and round-lobed *Hepatica* do well in the nutrient-rich soil at the bottom of the slope a bit farther along. When you reach the giant cottonwood at the end of the loop, retrace your steps for a short distance to the intersection with Tulip Tree Trail.

Turn left onto Tulip Tree Trail and begin a 0.9-mile trek to Hurlburt's Hill, ascending moderately through pines and hemlocks to gravel Weatogue Road. Cross it and follow Tulip Tree Trail up into rocky, mixed woodland of oak, ash, hemlock, and pine.

Turn left at the intersection with Boulder Trail to remain on Tulip Tree Trail. After traversing a series of bog bridges, pause to marvel at a massive tulip tree more than 3 feet in diameter, with a spreading crown. This imposing species, near its northern range limits in the southern Berkshires, is the largest species of our eastern forests. The path may be a bit muddy here during wet weather. Bits of rusted barbed wire and a luxuriant growth of invasive Japanese barberry and multiflora rosebushes indicate former disturbance by humans and livestock.

As you enter a small field, be on the lookout for wild turkey and ruffed grouse, two game birds that thrive in a mosaic of habitats. Bear left and walk up to Tractor Path, an old farm road. Turn left to follow it steadily up an obvious mowed path toward the summit of Hurlburt's Hill. Bluebird nest boxes on wooden posts flank the trail. Splendid scenery unfolds as you ascend the hillside hayfield. Near the crest at 2.5 miles, two wooden benches facing north offer a magnificent 180-degree vista with unobstructed views of Mount Everett (Trip 45) and the southern Taconics to the northwest and East Mountain (Trip 41) to the northeast. This is also a fine site from which to spot southward-migrating hawks in fall. An interpretive panel identifies both distant landscape features and the hawks that one might see. A stone monument just to the right marks the state line.

The larger of two moss- and fern-capped quartzite cobbles is skirted by Ledges Trail.

Retrace your steps down the hill, past the intersection with Tulip Tree Trail, and enter pine, hickory, ash, and cherry woods with Japanese barberry and another invasive exotic: winged euonymus. Both escaped from cultivation long ago. A few old apple trees along the field edge produce fruit for deer and other wildlife. Continue steadily downslope and cross Weatogue Road at 3.2 miles. Pass the intersection with Ledges Trail and continue straight on Craggy Knoll Trail. Walk under junipers—some dead—up to the top of the larger cobble. Ledges heavily padded with mosses and ferns rise on the left. The rock has been intriguingly eroded over eons. In late spring, the delicate pink blossoms of herb-Robert are ubiquitous. Finally, descend rather steeply from the promontory around a quartzite boulder, reaching the intersection with Cedar Hill Trail and Ledges Trail. Turn left here to return to the visitor center.

DID YOU KNOW?
The reservation's twin cobbles originated some 500 million years ago. During those ancient times, layers of sediment pushed upward. (Quartzite is metamorphosed beach sand, and marble is metamorphosed limestone composed of the shells of sea creatures.) The property is named for George Bartholomew, a farmer who purchased the land in the late nineteenth century.

MORE INFORMATION
Trails are open sunrise to sunset, year-round. The museum and visitor center are open year-round; hours vary seasonally (call 413-298-8600, for details). Entrance fees for non-members of The Trustees of Reservations: adults, $5; children 6 to 12, $1. Access is free to Trustees members. Pets and mountain biking are not permitted. Public programs are presented on a regular basis. Limited seasonal bow hunting is allowed, with written permission as part of a deer management program administered by The Trustees.

NEARBY
Visit historic Ashley House on Cooper Hill Road adjacent to Bartholomew's Cobble. Also owned by The Trustees of Reservations, it is on the National Register of Historic Places. The home, built in 1735, was the residence of Colonel John Ashley, who amassed a 3,000-acre estate in the eighteenth century. It was also the residence of Mum Bett, an enslaved African American who sued Ashley for her freedom in 1781 and won, effectively ending slavery in Massachusetts. The grounds are open daily year-round. The house is open regularly for tours (preregistration required); see thetrustees.org/place/ashley-house or call 413-298-3239 for dates and other information.

49 SAGES RAVINE AND BEAR MOUNTAIN

A journey into a charming chasm—a veritable mile of delights—contrasts with a short but tough climb to Connecticut's loftiest perch, offering sublime views.

FEATURES

Location Mount Washington, MA; Salisbury, CT

Rating Strenuous

Distance 3.9 miles round trip

Elevation Gain 915 feet

Estimated Time 2.5 to 3 hours

Maps USGS Bash Bish Falls; AMC Massachusetts Trail Map 2; Massachusetts Department of Conservation and Recreation map: mass.gov/doc/mt-washington-state-forest-trail-map/download

GPS Coordinates 42° 02.959′ N, 73° 28.011′ W

Contact Appalachian Trail Conservancy (New England Regional Office), 802-281-5894, appalachiantrail.org/explore/explore-by-state/massachusettsMassachusetts
AMC Western Massachusetts Chapter Massachusetts AT Committee, amc-wma.org/appalachian-trail-management-committee
AMC Connecticut Chapter AT Committee, ct-amc.org/trails

DIRECTIONS

From the intersection of US 7, MA 23, and MA 41 in Great Barrington, proceed southwest on combined MA 23/MA 41 for 3.9 miles. Turn left onto MA 41 South (at Mill Pond) in Egremont. Follow MA 41 for 0.1 mile before bearing right onto Mount Washington Road. Follow Mount Washington Road (later becomes East Road) for 11.4 miles, past the entrances to Mount Everett State Reservation (7.3 miles) and Mount Washington State Forest (8.8 miles). The last 2.3 miles are on gravel. A small parking area, with space for about five vehicles, is on the left, approximately 100 feet beyond the 1906 granite marker signifying the Massachusetts–Connecticut border. Be sure not to block the metal gate. The road may be closed in winter. Additional parking is available 150 feet back the way you came.

TRIP 49 // SAGES RAVINE AND BEAR MOUNTAIN

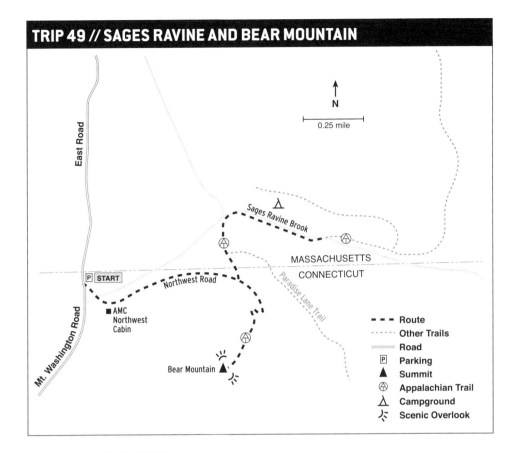

TRAIL DESCRIPTION

From the parking area, walk around the metal gate on wide, grassy Undermountain Trail (also known as Northwest Road), marked with blue blazes. Showy mountain laurel (the Connecticut state flower) is profligate to the right, while dense ferns—tall interrupted fern and shorter New York and hay-scented ferns—populate a glade on the left. At the trail fork, stay left to remain on Undermountain Trail and cross a feeder stream on stones. The right fork leads to AMC's Northwest Camp, wonderfully situated on a rise under hemlocks (please respect posted signs and do not visit the cabin without a reservation; see ct-amc.org/nwcamp for information). Sages Ravine Brook soon becomes visible to your left; the forest diversifies into mixed hemlock and beech woods and then virtually pure deciduous growth.

It doesn't take long to come upon the first cascade on the old, built-up roadway, but this is only a teaser. Cross a plank bridge over another feeder stream just before the narrowing path turns rocky and the grade increases through laurels. American beech sprouts, striped maples, and laurels fill the space between yellow and black birches, then maples, ashes, and oaks. Soon you're treading on level ground through open woodland along the base of Bear Mountain, which you'll climb later. Multitrunked oaks hint at past logging.

A sign on the left announces that you've entered the 500-foot-wide Appalachian Trail (AT) corridor, and within moments you reach the fabled footpath at 0.8 mile. Here, you have a choice: turn right to scale Bear Mountain first or turn left to visit Sages Ravine. For the latter, turn left and stride downhill under a mixed evergreen-deciduous canopy to arrive at a wooden sign that states, "You are entering a very fragile environment. Please camp at designated sites only. Help this area to recover from overuse and abuse. Thank you." Here, blue-blazed Paradise Trail diverges to the right; turn left to continue on the white-blazed AT as it proceeds moderately downhill through a thick stand of striped maple saplings and over stone steps toward Sages Ravine Brook.

The grade eases along the brook, where the path bears right and runs along steep ledge faces. The next mile or so is without doubt one of the loveliest stream strolls in the region. Spinulose wood fern blankets the lower reaches of the mountain as you arrive at large stepping-stones that lead across the stream to hemlock-shaded Sages Ravine Campsite. But instead of crossing the brook, continue straight ahead on the AT, now a rocky, narrow path along the water's edge. Pools that harbor native brook trout are interspersed with little cascades. Some "brookies" here attain all of 6 inches in length.

At one point, a large pool is hemmed in by sheer ledges. As you proceed downstream, the scene becomes progressively more enchanting, so take your time moving through the ravine. American yew caps boulders. Wood sorrel, with cloverlike leaves, thrives in patches on the forest floor under hemlocks. A high-gradient tributary empties into Sages Ravine Brook, and a laurel shrub marks the confluence. The AT climbs jauntily above the rock-lined chasm. From above, you can see that the water has scoured the sides of the vertical walls.

Cross a flow that bounces precipitously down the right slope from one rock ledge to the next in multiple cascades. It's only a sideshow to the main act but a delight nonetheless. These rocky tributaries cause the main stream to flow with even more gusto. Work your way down through angular schist boulders. The battlements of a formidable ledge rise above on the right slope. The path descends to the brook's bank again at a 3-foot-high falls, and the volume of water charging down the ravine is impressive. Continue to another plunge, where the brook makes a serpentine bend under hemlocks. This second cascade, which is actually split into two, is more than 12 feet high. Viewed upstream from an elevated location, the falls align themselves into a truly sublime scene. Note the trough to the right that the torrent has gouged into tilted bedrock during flood events.

After reaching a lofty height of about 45 feet above the churning flow, descend on expertly constructed stone steps to a cool microclimate. Here grows long beech fern, a small fern identified by its bottom two leaflets, which point downward. A sign affixed to a tree on the right welcomes hikers to Connecticut. (You are actually in Massachusetts here but only about 1,000 feet north of the state line.) The AT crosses the brook on large stones, but this is the turnaround point for this portion of the hike (approximately 1.5 miles from the trailhead). The good news is that you'll have a second opportunity to revel in the many delights of Sages Ravine. Retrace your steps to the signed intersection with Undermountain Trail, where you first began hiking on the AT, at 2.6 miles.

Gazing up Sages Ravine Brook from an elevated perch reveals a series of falls and cascades in a sublime setting.

Now it's time for a very different hiking experience. If your energy level is low by this point, put off the ascent of Bear Mountain's steep north face for another day, as it gains more than 500 vertical feet in 0.3 mile. Otherwise, forge on, following the white-blazed

TRIP 49 // **SAGES RAVINE AND BEAR MOUNTAIN**   267

AT along the slope contour under a deciduous forest canopy. Descend and then climb a series of stone staircases over slanting bedrock. The path zigzags up the steep gradient. Negotiate rock ledges that have some easy handholds to aid your progress. White blazes are few heading up, and the going can be tricky, so watch your footing; this hike is certainly not recommended during icy or wet conditions.

A few herbaceous dogwoods—bunchberries—have gained a foothold in the scant soil, while mountain azalea, common polypody fern (the little one clinging to rocks), and lowbush blueberry eke out a living in sun-dappled spots. The first pitch pines appear on the right, as does more laurel, loaded with blossoms in late June and early July. Ascend more bedrock, but not as steeply. Glaciers scoured this stone some 14,000 years ago. If you have a compass—and you should—note that the grooves line up north–south, the direction of the flow of the glacier's mile-thick ice sheets.

An evocative pine-resin aroma wafts in the air of sunny gaps as you near the summit. Blueberry and related huckleberry shrubs (note huckleberry's shiny resin dots on the undersides of its leaves) populate the area, as do gray birches, oaks, and cherry trees. A stone tower, appearing as a giant rock cairn, sits atop Bear Mountain, the highest summit (2,316 feet) entirely within Connecticut's boundaries. The tower has been rebuilt three times.

Climb the mound of schist flagstones from the back for superb views—some stones are loose, so tread carefully. To the near north are Mount Race (Trip 44) and Mount Everett (Trip 45) along the AT, while the Housatonic River valley and Twin Lakes in Connecticut lie seemingly at arm's length to the east. On a completely clear day, portions of five states—Massachusetts, Connecticut, New York, Vermont, and New Hampshire—may be visible. When you're ready to leave, retrace your steps (proceed carefully down the steep rocks) to Undermountain Trail on the left and follow it back to the parking area.

DID YOU KNOW?

A plaque placed on the summit tower in 1885 refers to Bear Mountain as being the highest point in Connecticut. It has since been discovered that the state's actual high point (highest elevation) is on the south slope of Mount Frissell at 2,380 feet. The summit of that peak is across the border in Massachusetts.

MORE INFORMATION

Open year-round. Access is free. Camping is permitted only in designated areas. Carry in, carry out rules apply. Motorized vehicles, horses, hunting, and fires are prohibited. The AMC Western Massachusetts Chapter's Appalachian Trail Management Committee is responsible for maintenance, management, and protection of the nearly 90 miles of the AT in Massachusetts; volunteers do this work, with assistance from the Massachusetts Department of Conservation and Recreation. The AT south of Sages Ravine is maintained and managed by the AMC Connecticut Chapter's AT Committee.

NEARBY

The site of the boyhood home of Black intellectual and civil rights leader W.E.B. Du Bois (1868–1963) is just south of the MA 71 intersection along MA 41/MA 23 in Great Barrington. Designated as a National Historic Site, the location contains foundation remnants of Du Bois's grandfather's home, where Du Bois spent his first five years; an informational kiosk and self-guided interpretive trail; and a commemorative boulder. The 5-acre property was donated to the state in 1987 and is administered by Housatonic Heritage and the University of Massachusetts Amherst (duboisnhs.org).

50 ROUND MOUNTAIN, MOUNT FRISSELL, AND BRACE MOUNTAIN

This rugged but fairly short out-and-back trek offers a special opportunity to traverse three distinctive summits in three states. Attractions include many scenic views, Connecticut's highest elevation, and a three-state historical boundary marker.

FEATURES

Location Mount Washington, MA; Salisbury, CT; Millertown, NY

Rating Moderate to Strenuous

Distance 4.4 miles round trip

Elevation Gain 1,425 feet

Estimated Time 3.5 hours

Maps AMC Massachusetts Trail Map 1; USGS Bash Bish Falls; Massachusetts Department of Conservation and Recreation map: mass.gov/doc/mt-washington-state-forest-trail-map/download

GPS Coordinates 42° 02.959′ N, 73° 28.011′ W

Contact Mount Washington State Forest, 413-528-0330, mass.gov/locations/mount-washington-state-forest
Taconic State Park, 518-329-3993, parks.ny.gov/parks/taconiccopake

DIRECTIONS

From the junction of US 7, MA 23, and MA 41 in Great Barrington, proceed west on combined MA 23/MA 41 for 3.9 miles to South Egremont. At Mill Pond, turn left and follow MA 41 for 0.1 mile; then turn right onto Mount Washington Road. Follow Mount Washington Road (becomes East Street in the town of Mount Washington) for 11.4 miles, passing the entrances to Mount Everett State Reservation on the left at 7.3 miles and Mount Washington State Forest on the right at 8.3 miles (stay straight at the Union Church). The last 2.3 miles are on gravel. Parking is available at the trailhead and a small lot on the left, about 100 feet beyond the Connecticut state line.

TRAIL DESCRIPTION

The southern Taconic Mountains' many natural treasures include Round Mountain, Mount Frissell, and Brace Mountain, a trio of rolling summits clustered along the three-state boundary of Massachusetts, Connecticut, and New York. Mount Frissell is well known for its unusual distinction of being Connecticut's highest elevation even though

TRIP 50 // ROUND MOUNTAIN, MOUNT FRISSELL, AND BRACE MOUNTAIN

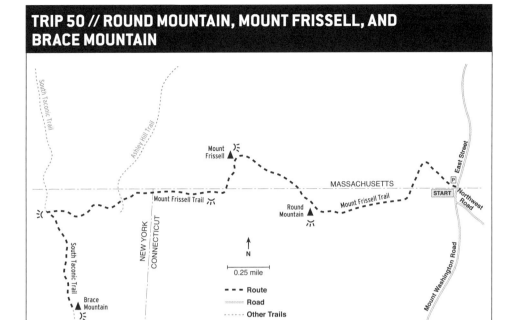

its summit is in Massachusetts. This hike combines Mount Frissell Trail, which traverses several steep and rocky slopes on Round Mountain and Mount Frissell, and a segment of South Taconic Trail leading to Brace Mountain. You can turn back at any point for a shorter outing (1.2 miles round trip for Round Mountain, 2.2 miles for the Connecticut high point and vista on Mount Frissell, and 2.8 miles for the three-state marker).

From the trailhead on the west side of East Street, follow red-blazed Mount Frissell Trail into the woods and along the south side of a swampy area, where yellow and chestnut-sided warblers breed in spring and summer. Evergreen eastern hemlocks and mountain laurels shade the rocky path before you enter hardwood forest dominated by red oak and chestnut oak, characteristic of the southern Taconic Mountains. Watch for black-throated blue warblers, with calls sounding like *sir-sir-sir-please*, in and around shrubby growths.

Bear left, entering Connecticut at the first of several state line crossings, and begin ascending at an initially gentle grade. Painted trilliums, named for their three-part white flowers with pink markings, bloom in May and then produce scarlet berries (mildly toxic to humans) in late summer and early autumn. After a 0.4-mile warm-up, the character of the hike changes rather abruptly as you begin a steep, rocky ascent of Round Mountain's eastern slope. Carefully work your way around and over several sections of exposed rock (free hands are helpful in places). Near the crest of the climb, gaze back for a fine view overlooking nearby Bear Mountain and the hills to the east.

Continue through stunted scrub oaks and birches and abundant blueberries, all well adapted to the ridgetop's thin soil, to the 2,289-foot summit at 0.6 mile. The blueberries display tiny, bell-shaped white flowers in spring before the tasty fruits ripen in summer. Several outlooks offer perspectives across the region, including nearby Mount Frissell and Brace Mountain, your next destinations, to the west-southwest. Other landmarks include Mount Everett and Mount Race to the north, Mount Greylock on the distant northern horizon, and Riga Lake and Mount Riga Forest Preserve to the south. The oak forests on the surrounding slopes show mostly russet hues when fall foliage peaks in mid to late October. Common yellowthroats, easily identified by their *witchity-witchity-witchity* song, frequent the shrubby vegetation during spring and summer.

Continue west on Mount Frissell Trail, descending to the narrow gap (less than 100 feet wide) between Round Mountain and Mount Frissell, through growths of paper birches and mountain laurels. Look for pink lady's slippers blooming along trail edges in late spring. These orchids are well adapted to a variety of habitats with acidic soils. Make a steep (but thankfully short) 0.1-mile ascent of Mount Frissell, crossing back into Massachusetts about halfway up the slope. When the grade levels, take a moment to catch your breath and enjoy an easterly view to Round Mountain and Bear Mountain. At the wooded 2,453-foot summit, a trail register in a metal box is just off the trail on the right. Tiger swallowtail butterflies frequent the hilltops and open woods of this area in spring and summer.

Follow Mount Frissell Trail as it curves left (south) down to an open ledge with splendid 180-degree southerly vistas of Riga Lake and the surrounding hills. At the state line, a United States Geological Survey (USGS) survey marker and another trail register denote Connecticut's highest elevation at 2,380 feet. Many "highpointers" (see "Did You Know?") hike the trail just to reach this spot. Bear Mountain, roughly 1.5 miles to the southeast, is Connecticut's highest summit at 2,316 feet.

Continue west along the Massachusetts–Connecticut state line through more shrubby ridgetop vegetation. Two openings along the path afford westerly views to New York and the distant Catskill Mountains. From the second lookout, carefully descend another section of exposed rock. The terrain is much gentler from this point to Brace Mountain. Pink-and-white blooms of mountain laurel, which thrive in dry, rocky, oak woods, peak in June here.

At 1.4 miles, reach a stone pillar at the boundary of Massachusetts, New York, and Connecticut, one of 65 places in the United States where three states meet. (Because of a long-standing historical dispute over the location of Connecticut's western border, only Massachusetts and New York are marked on the monument, which was erected in 1898.) Enter New York's Taconic State Park and pass the signed intersection with Ashley Hill Trail, which leads north into adjacent Mount Washington State Forest.

Bear right and follow Mount Frissell Trail past a discontinued trail and a boulder capped with lichens and Canada mayflowers. Ascend easily past blueberry shrubs and over exposed rock up to the Taconic ridge's western escarpment. The *drink-your-tea* call of eastern (or rufous-sided) towhees is a familiar sound in shrubby growths and thickets during spring and summer. In mountain settings, these birds are most common on mild south- and west-facing slopes. Mountain azaleas and pink lady's slippers add splashes of color to forest edges in late spring.

At 1.8 miles, reach Mount Frissell Trail's western terminus at the junction with long-distance South Taconic Trail. Straight ahead is a westerly view across farm fields in the Harlem Valley to the Catskills. Alander Mountain's summit is 3.7 miles north of the junction. Turn left and follow white-blazed South Taconic Trail along the ridge toward Brace Mountain, just 0.4 mile away on a well-maintained path. Pass the junction with an unmarked woods road, leading southeast approximately 1.5 miles to East Street, on the left. Nannyberry, a shrub in the viburnum family with tiny white flower clusters and blue-black berries, grows in rocky uplands and forest edges.

A gentle climb to Brace Mountain's grassy, open top completes your three-summit, three-state trifecta. The 2,311-foot peak, capped by a large rock cairn and wind sock, is the highest point of South Taconic Trail and New York's Dutchess County. Enjoy sweeping vistas in all directions, including the Catskills and Hudson River valley to the west, Bear Mountain on the east side of the range, Alander Mountain to the north, Mount Frissell and distant Mount Greylock northeast, and the southern end of the Taconic uplands to the south. Westerly breezes provide welcome relief on hot summer days. Brace Mountain is a popular destination for hang gliders and paragliders, thanks to the thermal currents along the ridge and its gradual topography.

The summit marks the end of this out-and-back hike (you can extend the trip by exploring South Taconic Trail, but be sure to save enough time and energy for the return).

A scenic section of South Taconic Trail links Brace Mountain and Mount Frissell Trail near the boundaries with New York and Connecticut.

Retrace your steps to Mount Frissell Trail and turn right to return to the trailhead, crossing back over Mount Frissell and Round Mountain. Use caution descending the steep sections. The return route entails roughly 475 feet of elevation gain, but the last 0.4-mile segment is easy after you descend Round Mountain.

DID YOU KNOW?

"Highpointing"—ascending to the highest natural elevations within geographic areas, such as states, countries, or continents—became popular in the late nineteenth century. Arthur Marshall was the first known person to reach the highest points of all 48 continental states. His quest began at Mount Rainier in Washington State in 1919 and ended at Hoosier Hill in Indiana in 1936.

MORE INFORMATION

Open sunrise to sunset, year-round. Access is free. No restrooms are available. Mountain biking, skiing, leashed dogs, and hunting in season are allowed.

NEARBY

Kenver, at 39 Main Street (MA 23) in South Egremont, is the Berkshires' largest winter sports store. See kenver.com or call 413-528-2330 for products, events, sales, hours, and other information.

APPENDIX: INFORMATION AND RESOURCES

CAMPING

From Mount Greylock's upper slopes to secluded backcountry sites in the southern Taconic Mountains, the Berkshires offer a variety of options for campers. Public campgrounds generally offer basic amenities, including restrooms, showers, swimming, beaches, boat launches, and picnic areas. In addition to the public sites listed here, many privately owned campgrounds offer extra features, such as playgrounds, family activities and events, and RV hookups.

The camping season generally runs from May to September or mid-October; specific dates vary by location. Reservations for Massachusetts state forest and state park campgrounds can be made anytime from six months to one day in advance through Reserve America (reserveamerica.com). For all campgrounds, public or private, be sure to contact the management ahead of time to confirm availability and amenities.

BEARTOWN STATE FOREST
69 Blue Hill Road
Monterey, MA 01245
413-528-0904; mass.gov/locations/beartown-state-forest
Twelve primitive sites at Benedict Pond (some universally accessible); no showers or flush toilets; available year-round; campground office open mid-May to mid-October.

CLARKSBURG STATE PARK
1199 Middle Road
Clarksburg, MA 01247
413-664-8345; mass.gov/locations/clarksburg-state-park
Forty-five sites at Mausert Pond.

MOHAWK TRAIL STATE FOREST
175 Mohawk Trail (MA 2)
Charlemont, MA 01339
413-339-5504; mass.gov/locations/mohawk-trail-state-forest
Forty-seven seasonal sites, six log cabins available year-round, near Cold River andthe Mohican–Mohawk Trail.

MONROE STATE FOREST
Tilda Hill Road
Monroe, MA 01247
Dunbar Brook Trailhead
River Road
Florida, MA 01247
413-339-5504 (Mohawk Trail State Forest); mass.gov/locations/monroe-state-forest
Three primitive shelters at Dunbar Brook, Ridge, and Smith Hollow; no facilities.

MOUNT GREYLOCK STATE RESERVATION
30 Rockwell Road
Lanesborough, MA 01237
413-499-4262; mass.gov/locations/mount-greylock-state-reservation; mass.gov/location-details/camping-at-mount-greylock
Eighteen sites (four-person limit) and nine group sites (twelve-person limit); reservations required Memorial Day weekend to Columbus Day/Indigenous Peoples' Day. Off-season camping available November to mid-May (first come, first served; no fee; registration recommended). Five primitive shelters at Deer Hill, Wilbur's Clearing, Bellows Pipe, Peck's Brook, and Mark Noepel (first come, first served; twelve-person limit; no fee; registration recommended). Bascom Lodge at the summit offers accommodations and meals for up to 34 people; open mid-May to late October.

MOUNT WASHINGTON STATE FOREST AND MOUNT EVERETT STATE RESERVATION
545 East Street
Mount Washington, MA 01258
413-528-0330; mass.gov/locations/mount-washington-state-forest
Wilderness camping allowed year-round at designated sites and lean-tos (see map at mass.gov/doc/mt-washington-state-forest-trail-map/download); first come, first served; no fee; five-person limit.

OCTOBER MOUNTAIN STATE FOREST
317 Woodland Road
Lee, MA 01238
413-243-1778; mass.gov/locations/october-mountain-state-forest
Forty-three sites, three yurts; open mid-May to mid-October.

PITTSFIELD STATE FOREST
1041 Cascade Street
Pittsfield, MA 01201
413-442-8992; mass.gov/locations/pittsfield-state-forest
Thirteen sites at Berry Pond at summit, nineteen sites at Parker Brook, six sites at Bishop Field. Group sites at Bishop Field (twenty-person limit) and Lulu Brook (50-person limit).

SAVOY MOUNTAIN STATE FOREST
260 Central Shaft Road
Florida, MA 01247
413-663-8469; mass.gov/locations/savoy-mountain-state-forest
Forty-five seasonal sites, four log cabins available year-round, at South Pond.

TACONIC STATE PARK COPAKE FALLS CAMPGROUND
253 NY Route 344
Copake Falls, NY 12517
518-329-3993; parks.ny.gov/parks/taconiccopake
One hundred and six sites, including 70 tentsites and 3 cabin areas, at state line near Bash Bish Falls, South Taconic Trail, and Copake Iron Works Museum.

TOLLAND STATE FOREST
410 Tolland Road
East Otis, MA 01029
413-269-6002; mass.gov/locations/tolland-state-forest
Ninety-three sites and RV facilities at scenic peninsula on Otis Reservoir, open mid-May to mid-October.

OTHER STATE PARKS

NATURAL BRIDGE STATE PARK
McAuley Road
North Adams, MA 01247
413-663-6392 (413-499-7003 off-season); mass.gov/locations/natural-bridge-state-park
Marble arch bridge on Hudson Brook; open weekends Memorial Day to Columbus/Indigenous Peoples' Day; parking fee.

WAHCONAH FALLS STATE PARK
68 Wahconah Falls Road
Dalton, MA 01226
413-442-8992; mass.gov/locations/wahconah-falls-state-park
Forty-eight-acre park at scenic Wahconah Falls; picnic area; open year-round; free.

OUTFITTERS

AMC WESTERN MASSACHUSETTS CHAPTER
amc-wma.org/paddling-committee.cgi
Whitewater and quietwater trips.

ARCADIAN SHOP
91 Pittsfield Road (US 7/20)
Lenox, MA 01240
413-637-3010; arcadian.com
Bike, cross-country ski, snowshoe rentals; outdoor clothing, accessories.

BARRINGTON OUTFITTERS
289 Main Street
Great Barrington, MA 01230
413-645-5248; barringtonoutfitters.net
Outdoor gear, shoes, clothing, furniture.

BERKSHIRE BIKE AND BOARD
29 State Road
Great Barrington, MA 01230
413-528-5555; berkshirebikeandboard.com

502C East Street
Pittsfield, MA 01201
413-445-8888; berkshirebikeandboard.com
Bike rentals and service.

BERKSHIRE OUTFITTERS
169 Grove Street
Adams, MA 01220
413-743-5900; berkshireoutfitters.com
Cross-country ski, bike, canoe, kayak rentals; outdoor gear and accessories.

BERKSHIRE U-DRIVE BOAT RENTALS
1651 North Street
Pittsfield, MA 01201
413-281-4196; berkshireudriveboatrentals.com
Canoe, kayak, and boat rentals. On Pontoosuc Lake.

CLARKE OUTDOORS
163 US Route 7
West Cornwall, CT 06796
860-672-6365; clarkeoutdoors.com
Canoe, kayak, and raft rentals; paddling gear. On Housatonic River.

CRAB APPLE WHITEWATER
2056 Mohawk Trail
Charlemont, MA 01339
800-553-7238; crabapplewhitewater.com
Rafting tours on Deerfield River.

DICK'S SPORTING GOODS
635 Merrill Road
Pittsfield, MA 01201
413-395-0870; dickssportinggoods.com
Wide selection of outdoor apparel, equipment, footwear.

THE GREAT OUTDOORS
78 Main Street
Charlemont, MA 01339
413-834-2213; greatoutdoorstubing.com
Outdoor and sporting goods and accessories, tube rentals, river shuttles, and parking. On Deerfield River.

KENVER
39 South Main Street (MA 23)
South Egremont, MA 01258
413-528-2330; kenver.com
Bike rentals, outdoor gear, and accessories.

NATURE'S CLOSET
61 Spring Street
Williamstown, MA 01267
413-458-7909; naturescloset.net
Outdoor apparel, accessories, and footwear.

ONOTA BOAT LIVERY
463 Pecks Road
Pittsfield, MA 01201
413-442-1724; onotaboat.com
Canoe, kayak, boat, and pontoon rentals. On Onota Lake.

SKI FANATICS
65D North Main Street
Lanesborough, MA 01237
413-443-3023; skifanatics.com
Ski and snowboard rentals.

ZOAR OUTDOOR
7 Main Street
Charlemont, MA 01339
413-339-4010; zoaroutdoor.com
Kayaking, rafting, rentals, tours, and instruction. On Deerfield River.

SKI AREAS

BERKSHIRE EAST MOUNTAIN RESORT
66 Thunder Mountain Road
Charlemont, MA 01339
413-339-6618; berkshireeast.com
Downhill skiing, whitewater rafting on Deerfield River, zip line tours, tree house trail and adventure park, mountain biking.

BOUSQUET MOUNTAIN
101 Dan Fox Drive
Pittsfield, MA 01201
413-442-8985; bousquetmountain.com
Downhill skiing, water slides, adventure park, disc golf; trailhead for Mahanna Cobble Trail and High Road.

CANTERBURY FARM
1986 Fred Snow Road
Becket, MA 01223
413-623-0100; canterbury-farms.com
Groomed ski and snowshoe trails, ice skating, equipment and kayak rentals, lessons; near October Mountain State Forest.

JIMINY PEAK MOUNTAIN RESORT
37 Corey Road
Hancock, MA 01237
413-738-5500; jiminypeak.com
Downhill skiing, aerial adventure park, mountain biking.

MAPLE CORNER FARM
794 Beech Hill Road
Granville, MA 01034
413-357-8829; maplecornerfarm.com
Groomed cross-country ski and snowshoe trails, rentals, lessons; blueberry picking in summer.

NOTCHVIEW (THE TRUSTEES OF RESERVATIONS)
83 Old Route 9
Windsor, MA 01270
413-684-0148; thetrustees.org/place/notchview
Twenty-five miles of groomed and ungroomed ski trails; snowshoeing; rentals and food at Budd Visitor Center. Open year-round; skiing and snowshoeing daily 8 A.M. to 4:30 P.M. December to April.

OTIS RIDGE
159 Monterey Road
Otis, MA 01253
413-269-4444; otisridge.com
Downhill skiing and lessons.

SKI BUTTERNUT
380 State Road
Great Barrington, MA 01230
413-528-2000; skibutternut.com
Downhill skiing, rentals, lessons.

INDEX

A

Adams, MA, hikes near, viii–ix, 24–29, 32–37, 43–47, 78–83, 84–89
Alander Mountain Trail, xii–xiii, 249–252
Alford, MA, hikes near, xii–xiii, 188–193
Alford Springs, xii–xiii, 188–193
AMC Noble View Outdoor Center, 203
Ames, Tad, 136
Appalachian Trail (AT), 99, 117
Appalachian Trail (AT), hikes on
 in central Berkshires, 112–116, 159–163, 166–169
 in northern Berkshires, 13–15, 26–27, 34–35, 46–47, 82, 86, 95–99
 in southern Berkshires, 194–197, 205–209, 223–226, 239–240, 245–246, 264–268
Ashintully Gardens, 198
Ashley House, 263
Ashmere Lake, 121
ash trees, 164–165
Ashuwillticook Rail Trail, x–xi, 102–106

B

Bartholomew's Cobble Reservation, xii–xiii, 259–263
Bascom, John, 16
Bash Bish Falls, xii–xiii, 232–237
Bear Mountain (CT), xii–xiii, 264–268
Beartown State Forest, 205–209, 275
Beaver Pond Loop, x–xi, 138–143
beavers, 144
Becket, MA, hikes near, x–xi, xii–xiii, 159–163, 166–169, 199–203

Becket Arts Center, 203

Becket Quarry, xii–xiii, 199–203
Bellows Pipe Trail, viii–ix, 43–47
Benedict Pond Loop and Ledges, xii–xiii, 205–209
Berkshire Museum, 111
Berkshire Outfitters, 89, 277
Berkshire Scenic Railway Museum, 158
Berlin, NY, hikes near, viii–ix, 19–23
Berlin Mountain, viii–ix, 19–23
Berry Pond, x–xi, 107–111
Bicknell's thrush, 37
bird watching, recommended locations, 102–103, 231, 259, 261
The Bistro Box, 226
black bears, 94, 124
Blueberry Hill Farm, 248
blueberry picking, 248
Bob's Way, xii–xiii, 210–213
Bousquet Mountain Ski Area, 132, 134–135
Brace Mountain, xii–xiii, 270–274
Bryant, William Cullen, 182
Burbank Trail, x–xi, 145–148
Busby Trail, viii–ix, 54–58

C

cabins. See shelters and cabins
Campbell Falls, xii–xiii, 219–222
camping, 275–276. See also shelters and cabins
 in central Berkshires, 111, 116, 158, 163, 169
 Leave No Trace principles, xxii–xxiii

in northern Berkshires, 20, 27, 32, 53, 58, 66, 77
in southern Berkshires, 208–209, 236–237, 240, 242, 250–251, 266, 268
Canoe Meadows Wildlife Sanctuary, 116
central Berkshires
    easy hikes in, 102–106, 118–121, 138–143, 145–148
    moderate hikes in, 102–106, 122–126, 127–131, 132–135, 145–148, 149–152, 154–158, 159–163
    region description, 101
    strenuous hikes in, 122–126, 138–143, 154–158
charcoal making, 253
Charcoal Trail, x–xi, 149–152
Charlemont, MA, hikes near, viii–ix, 73–77
Cheshire, MA, hikes near, x–xi, 78–83, 90–93, 95–99, 102–106
Cheshire Cheese Press, 99
Cheshire Cobbles, x–xi, 95–99
children, recommended hikes for
    in central Berkshires, 102–106, 118–121, 132–135, 145–148, 149–152, 166–169
    in northern Berkshires, 3–7, 54–58, 67–72
    in southern Berkshires, 177–181, 183–187, 199–203, 205–209, 210–213, 219–222, 227–231, 232–237, 244–248, 254–258, 259–263
Civilian Conservation Corps (CCC), 48
Clam River Reserve, xii–xiii, 214–218
Clark Art Institute, 17
Clark Mountain, viii–ix, 73–77
Clarksburg, MA, hikes near, viii–ix, 13–17
Clarksburg State Park, 275
Clayton Park, 7
Copake Falls, NY, hikes near, xii–xiii, 232–237
Copake Iron Works, 237
cross-country skiing, recommended locations

in central Berkshires, 102–106, 107–111, 118–121, 127–131, 145–148, 149–152, 159–163, 166–169
in northern Berkshires, 3–7, 8–12, 61–66, 67–72, 73–77
in southern Berkshires, 172–176, 183–187, 188–193, 199–203, 205–209, 210–213, 214–218, 219–222, 227–231, 232–237, 244–248, 249–252
cycling, recommended rides
    in central Berkshires, 102–106

D

Dalton, MA, hikes near, x–xi, 95–99, 112–116, 118–121
Drew, Bernard A., 48
DuBois, W.E.B., 269
Dunbar Brook, viii–ix, 67–72
Dwight, Timothy, 30

E

East Mountain, viii–ix, xii–xiii, 13–17, 223–226
easy hikes
    in central Berkshires, 102–106, 118–121, 138–143, 145–148
    in northern Berkshires, 61–66, 90–93
    in southern Berkshires, 183–187, 199–203, 205–209, 210–213, 227–231, 232–237, 254–258
Egremont, MA, hikes near, xii–xiii, 227–231
emerald ash borer, 164–165
exotic plants, 153

F

Finerty Pond, x–xi, 159–163
Florida, MA, hikes near, viii–ix, 54–58, 67–72, 73–77
footwear and clothing, xx
Fort Massachusetts, 29

G

gear considerations, xix–xx
    gear stores and outfitters, 89, 277–278

George Darey Wildlife Management Area, 158
Gore Pond, 95–99
Gould Farm Roadside Store and Café, 209
Great Barrington, MA, hikes near, x–xi, xii–xiii, 177–181, 183–187, 205–209, 223–226
Green River, 42, 193
Greylock Range Traverse, viii–ix, 24–29
  old growth forests in, 38
Guilder Pond, xii–xiii, 244–248

H

Haley Farm Trail, viii–ix, 39–42
Hancock, MA, hikes near, x–xi, 107–111, 127–131
hardy kiwi, 153
hawks, 58
Hawthorne, Nathaniel, 30, 180, 182
highpointing, 274
High Road, 132–135, 136–137, 140, 147, 150
Hinsdale, MA, hikes near, x–xi, 118–121
Hoosac Range Trail, viii–ix, 49–53
Hoosac Tunnel, 52, 72
Hoosic River, 7
Hopkins Memorial Forest, viii–ix, 8–12
Hopper Trail, viii–ix, 32–37
Housatonic River, xii–xiii, 118–121, 183–187, 259–263

I

Ice Glen, x–xi, 172–176
Ice Gulch, xii–xiii, 223–226
insects, xxi
invasive exotics, 153
  ash borer, 164–165
iron manufacturing, 253

J

Jacob's Pillow Dance Festival, 163
Jones Nose, x–xi, 90–93
Jug End State Reservation and WMA, xii–xiii, 227–231

K

Kay Wood Shelter, 116
Kenneth Dubuque Memorial State Forest, 66
Kenver (winter sports store), 274
Kripalu Center for Yoga and Health, 148

L

Lake Bascom, 16
Lake Garfield, 213
Lanesborough, MA, hikes near, x–xi, 102–106, 107–111
Laura's Tower, x–xi, 172–176
Laurel Hill Association, 176
Leave No Trace principles, xxii–xxiii
Lee, MA, hikes near, x–xi, 154–158, 166–169
Lenox, MA, hikes near, x–xi, 132–135, 138–143, 145–148, 154–158
Lenox Mountain, x–xi, 138–143
  Burbank Trail, 145–148
Leonard, Tom, 226
Leverett, Robert, 38
Lime Kiln Farm Wildlife Sanctuary, xii–xiii, 254–258
locator map, iv
lookout towers, hikes to
  in northern Berkshires, 24–29, 32–37, 43–47, 84–89
  in southern Berkshires, 172–176, 264–268
Lulu Cascade, x–xi, 107–111

M

Mahanna Cobble, x–xi, 132–135
Massachusetts Museum of Contemporary Art (Mass MoCA), 47
Massachusetts War Veterans Memorial Tower, 87
Melville, Herman, 30, 180, 182
Millertown, NY, hikes near, xii–xiii, 270–274
Mill Pond, 231

moderate hikes
 in central Berkshires, 102–106, 122–126, 127–131, 132–135, 145–148, 149–152, 154–158, 159–163
 in northern Berkshires, 3–7, 13–17, 39–42, 49–53, 54–58, 61–66, 67–72, 84–89, 90–93, 95–99
 in southern Berkshires, 172–176, 177–181, 188–193, 199–203, 205–209, 214–218, 223–226, 232–237, 244–248, 249–252, 259–263, 270–274
Mohawk Trail State Forest, 73–76, 275
Mohhekennuck Club, 169
Mohican-Mohawk Recreational Trail, viii–ix, 49–53, 59–60
 over Clark and Todd Mountains, 73–77
Monroe, MA, hikes near, viii–ix, 67–72
Monroe State Forest, 67–71, 275
Monterey, MA, hikes near, xii–xiii, 205–209, 210–213
Monument Mountain Reservation, x–xi, 177–181
mosquitoes, xxi
The Mount (Wharton home), 152
mountain lions, 18
Mountain Meadow Preserve, viii–ix, 3–7
Mount Everett, xii–xiii, 244–248
Mount Frissell, xii–xiii, 270–274
Mount Greylock, viii–ix
 Bellows Pipe Trail, 43–47
 east side trail to summit, 84–89
 history, 30–31
 Hopper Trail to summit, 32–37
 old-growth forest on, 38
Mount Greylock State Reservation, 276
 Bellows Pipe Trail, 43–47
 East Side, viii–ix, 84–89
 Greylock Range Traverse, 24–29
 Hopper Trail, 32–36
 Jones Nose and Round Rock, x–xi, 90–93
 old growth in, 38
 Saddle Ball Mountain, 78–83
 Stony Ledge, 39–42
 visitor center, 93

Mount Hope Park, 42
Mount Race, xii–xiii, 238–243
Mount Washington, MA, hikes near, xii–xiii, 232–237, 238–243, 244–248, 249–252, 264–268, 270–274
Mount Washington State Forest, 235–236, 238–240, 249, 270–271, 276

N

Natural Bridge State Park, 276
Naumkeag, 176
New Ashford, MA, hikes near, viii–ix, x–xi, 78–83, 90–93
New Marlborough, MA, hikes near, xii–xiii, 219–222
Norfolk, CT, hikes near, xii–xiii, 219–222
North Adams, MA, hikes near, viii–ix, 24–29, 43–47, 49–53, 54–58
North Canaan, CT, hikes near, xii–xiii, 219–222
northern Berkshires
 easy hikes in, 61–66, 90–93
 moderate hikes in, 3–7, 13–17, 39–42, 49–53, 54–58, 61–66, 67–72, 84–89, 90–93, 95–99
 region description, 1–2
 strenuous hikes in, 8–12, 19–23, 24–29, 32–37, 39–42, 43–47, 67–72, 78–83, 84–89
Notchview, x–xi, 122–126

O

October Mountain State Forest, x–xi, 163, 276
 Finerty Pond, 159–163
 Schermerhorn Gorge, 154–158
 Upper Goose Pond, 166–169
old-growth forests, 38, 62–63, 67, 71, 76, 172
Old Mill Trail, x–xi, 118–121
Olivia's Overlook, 149, 152
outfitters, 277–278

282 INDEX

P

Palmer Brook Reserve, 187
Parker Brook Falls, viii–ix, 61–66
Parsons Marsh, 135
Petersburg, NY, hikes near, viii–ix, 8–12
Pine Cobble, viii–ix, 13–17
pitcher plants, 111
pitch pines, 177, 242
Pittsfield, MA, hikes near, x–xi, 107–111, 132–135
Pittsfield State Forest, x–xi, 107–111, 127–131, 276
Pleasant Valley Wildlife Sanctuary, x–xi, 138–143
poison ivy, xx
Pownal, VT, hikes near, viii–ix, 3–7, 8–12

Q

Quabbin Reservoir
    mountain lions and, 18

R

Race Brook Falls, xii–xiii, 238–243
Ragged Mountain, viii–ix, 43–47
Red Lion Inn, 176
Richmond, MA, hikes near, x–xi, 145–148, 149–152
Riverfront Trail (Housatonic River), xii–xiii, 183–187
Round Mountain, xii–xiii, 270–274
Rounds Rock, 90–93

S

Saddle Ball Mountain, viii–ix, 78–83
safety considerations, xix–xxi
Sages Ravine, xii–xiii, 264–268
salamanders, 71, 192, 204
Salisbury, CT, hikes near, xii–xiii, 264–268, 270–274
Sandisfield, MA, hikes near, xii–xiii, 210–213, 214–218
Sandisfield State Forest, 214–218
Santarella, 198
Savoy, MA, hikes near, viii–ix, 61–66, 73–77

Savoy Mountain State Forest, 53, 61–66, 276
Schenob Brook Area of Critical Environmental Concern (ACEC), 258
Schermerhorn Gorge Trail, x–xi, 154–158
Shaker Mountain, x–xi, 127–131
Shaker Museum and Library, 131
Shays' Rebellion Monument, 243
Sheep Hill, 23
Sheffield, MA, hikes near, xii–xiii, 223–226, 238–243, 254–258, 259–263
Sheffield Covered Bridge, 258
shelters and cabins
    in central Berkshires, 112–115, 125, 168–169
    in northern Berkshires, 34, 41, 46–47, 58, 66, 69, 71, 77, 88
    in southern Berkshires, 226, 247, 251–252
ski areas, 278–279
southern Berkshires
    easy hikes in, 183–187, 199–203, 205–209, 210–213, 227–231, 232–237, 254–258
    moderate hikes in, 172–176, 177–181, 188–193, 199–203, 205–209, 214–218, 223–226, 232–237, 244–248, 249–252, 259–263, 270–274
    region description, 171
    strenuous hikes in, 223–226, 238–243, 264–268, 270–274
Southfield Store, 222
South Taconic Trail, hikes along, 232, 249–252, 271–273
Spruce Hill, viii–ix, 49–53, 54–58
Stockbridge, MA, hikes near, x–xi, 149–152, 172–176
Stony Ledge, viii–ix, 39–42
strenuous hikes
    in central Berkshires, 122–126, 138–143, 154–158
    in northern Berkshires, 8–12, 19–23, 24–29, 32–37, 39–42, 43–47, 67–72, 78–83, 84–89

in southern Berkshires, 223–226, 238–243, 264–268, 270–274
Susan B. Anthony Birthplace Museum, 83
swimming, 159–163, 166–169, 205–208

T

Taconic Crest Trail, viii–ix, 8–12
Taconic State Park (NY), 232–237, 276
Taft Farms, 180
Tanglewood Music Festival, 143
Tannery Falls, viii–ix, 61–66
Thierot, N. Robert (Bob), 210, 213
Thoreau, Henry David, 30, 182
Thunderbolt Ski Trail, 47
ticks, xxi
Tilden Swamp, x–xi, 107–111
Todd Mountain, viii–ix, 73–77
Tom Ball Mountain, 193
trip planning, xix–xxi
Tropical Storm Irene, 66
Tyringham, MA, hikes near, x–xi, xii–xiii, 166–169, 194–197
Tyringham Cobble Reservation, xii–xiii, 194–197

U

universally accessible trails
    in central Berkshires, 102–106, 118–121, 138–143
    in northern Berkshires, 27
    in southern Berkshires, 172–176, 183–187
Upper Goose Pond, x–xi, 166–169

V

vernal pools, 204

W

Wahconah Falls State Park, 276
Warner Hill, x–xi, 112–116
Washington, MA, hikes near, x–xi, 154–158, 159–163

waterfalls, hikes featuring
    in central Berkshires, 107–111, 138–143, 154–158
    in northern Berkshires, 19–23, 24–29, 32–37, 61–66, 67–72, 84–89
    in southern Berkshires, 219–222, 232–237, 238–243, 264–268
West Mountain Wildlife Sanctuary, 58
West Stockbridge, MA, hikes near, x–xi, 149–152
West Stockbridge Mountain, x–xi, 149–152
Whale Rock, 187
Wharton, Edith, 152
Whitcomb Summit, 77
Whitney's Farm Market, 106
wildlife, 65
    bears, 94
    beavers, 144
    mountain lions, 18
    salamanders, 71, 192, 204
Williams, Ephraim, 29
Williams College Museum of Art, 12
Williamstown, MA, hikes near, viii–ix, 3–7, 8–12, 13–17, 19–23, 24–29, 32–37, 39–42, 78–83
Williamstown Historical Museum, 37
Windsor, MA, hikes near, x–xi, 122–126
Windsor Jambs, 126
Windsor State Forest, x–xi, 122–126
winter hiking, xxi. See also cross-country skiing, recommended locations

Y

Yokun Ridge, 136
Yokun Ridge South, 149–152

ABOUT THE AUTHORS

René Laubach retired in 2014 from Mass Audubon's Berkshire Wildlife Sanctuaries, which he directed for nearly 30 years. He is also co-author of AMC's Best Day Hikes in Connecticut, has written seven books on natural history, and has written for AMC Outdoors, Audubon, Sanctuary, and many other publications.

John S. Burk is an outdoor writer, photographer, and historian from central Massachusetts. He has authored or edited twenty regional books and guides, including AMC's *Massachusetts Trail Guide, New England National Scenic Trail Map and Guide*, and *AMC's Best Day Hikes Near Boston*. He has also contributed to *AMC Outdoors, Estuary, Northern Woodlands, Natural New England, Sanctuary, Uniquely Quabbin*, and other publications. John worked for ten years as an archivist and historical researcher at Harvard Forest. To see more of his work, visit johnburk.zenfolio.com.

ABOUT AMC IN WESTERN MASSACHUSETTS

AMC has a long-standing commitment to the forests, land, and rivers of western Massachusetts. With more than 3,400 members, AMC's Western Massachusetts Chapter is integral in conservation and trail maintenance efforts in the region. The chapter offers hundreds of activities, such as hiking, mountaineering, paddling, snowshoeing, and family outings.

AMC also manages properties in western Massachusetts. The Upper Goose Pond Cabin, on the Appalachian Trail and run exclusively for thru-hikers and section hikers, is owned by the National Park Service and managed by volunteers from AMC's Western Massachusetts Chapter. AMC's Noble View Outdoor Center in the Pioneer Valley accommodates groups of many sizes in cottages and campsites. The 360-acre property features 50-mile views over the Connecticut River valley and trails suitable for hiking, snowshoeing, and cross-country skiing.

Members maintain local trails—including the Appalachian Trail, Metacomet–Monadnock Trail and New England Trail—lead outdoor skills workshops, and promote stewardship of the region's natural resources. AMC also offers a Teen Volunteer Trail Crew program in the Berkshires. To view a list of AMC activities across the Northeast, visit activities.outdoors.org.

AMC BOOK UPDATES

AMC Books strives to keep our guidebooks as up-to-date as possible to help you plan safe and enjoyable adventures. If we learn after publishing a book that relevant trails have been relocated or route or contact information has changed, we will post the updated information online. Before you hit the trail, visit outdoors.org/resources/books-maps and click the "Book Updates" link at the bottom of the page.

While hiking, if you notice discrepancies with the trip descriptions or maps, or if you find any other errors in the book, please let us know by submitting them to amcbooks@outdoors.org or to Books Editor, c/o AMC, 10 City Square, Boston, MA 02129. We will verify all submissions and post key updates each month. AMC Books is dedicated to being a recognized leader in outdoor publishing. Thank you for your participation.

AMC Books

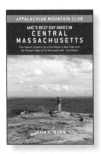

AMC's Best Day Hikes in Central Massachusetts, 2nd Edition
John S. Burk

West of Boston and east of the Berkshires, central Massachusetts is sometimes overlooked, but when you visit, you'll find beautiful and exciting hikes regardless of your experience and ability level. *AMC's Best Day Hikes in Central Massachusetts* features 50 of these hikes, ranging from historic Mohawk and Keystone Arches trails, Mount Grace State Forest, and beloved mountains such as Tully, Holyoke, and Tom.

$23.95 • 978-1-62842-167-5

Massachusetts Trail Guide, 11th Edition
Compiled and edited by John S. Burk

This new edition of the Appalachian Mountain Club's comprehensive and trusted trail guide provides all the information you will need to navigate more than 300 trails from the Berkshires to Cape Cod, with turn-by-turn trail descriptions and suggested hikes for all ability levels. A pull-out map features four of the state's most hiker-friendly public trail networks, while in-text maps display additional popular hiking trails across Massachusetts.

$24.95 • 978-1-62842-130-9

Quiet Water Massachusetts, Connecticut, and Rhode Island, 4th Edition
John Hayes and Alex J. Wilson

The first new edition of this guide in a decade has everything a recreational paddler could ask for in a regional guide. With an "At-a-Glance" quick trip planner, improved maps, handy icons that help readers instantly know an area's highlights, and more, paddlers of all skill levels and experience can discover 90 of the best flatwater lake and river trips in southern New England.

$26.95 • 978-1-62842-176-7

If You Can See The Dark
Timothy Mudie and Jenny Ward,
Illustrated by Mattie Rose Templeton

This first ever children's picture book from the Appalachian Mountain Club teaches children about the importance of dark skies—those devoid of artificial light—for animals, plants, and ourselves. Paired with stunning and evocative art, kids learn about dark skies in a way that will resonate with them and adults alike.

$19.95 • 978-1-62842-187-3

Find these and other AMC titles through ebook stores, booksellers, and outdoor retailers. Or order directly from AMC at **amcstore.outdoors.org** or call **800-262-4455.**